"I'll Take That One"

Dispelling the Myths
of Civilian Evacuation 1939-45

Martin L Parsons

BECKETT BK KARLSON

First Published 1998
by Beckett Karlson Ltd
The Studio
Denton
Peterborough
Cambs PE7 3SD

A catalogue record of this book is available from the British Library

ISBN 1 901 292 03 7

Copyright © 1998 Martin L. Parsons

Produced by
Beckett Karlson Ltd
The Studio
Denton
Peterborough
Cambs PE7 3SD

Design & Layout by Paul Holness
Map Illustrations by Peter McClure
Cover Design by Marc Lowen and Dean Hill

Printed in England by Page Bros. Norwich

In memory of my father
Donald L. Parsons (1923-1998)
who first encouraged my interest in history.

Dedication

This book is dedicated to all those involved in the Government Evacuation Scheme, both home and abroad, those who suffered and continue to be affected by the trauma of being removed from their home to an area of safety, the teachers who responded to the situation above and beyond the call of duty and finally, the hosts who took the evacuees, perfect strangers, into their homes.

The Title

It was very difficult to find a title for this book which summed up the experiences and memories of evacuees. Many came to mind and were dismissed as being inadequate or too flippant. However, when reading and listening to the written and oral accounts that ex-evacuees had sent me, it soon became apparent that the abiding memory of many of them was the 'cattle market' situation in various village, church and school halls in the reception areas in which they often found themselves unwittingly and unwillingly involved. As a result, the phrase 'I'll take that one!' became etched on the memory of many ex-evacuees.

It is fitting that the evacuees themselves provided the title for which I had been searching.

Picture Credits

Acknowledgements

I am indebted to the following:-

- All ex-evacuees who were prepared to trust me with their reminiscences and allow me to tell their story. The full list is in the Appendices.
- All other contributors who were not actually evacuees but who were heavily involved in the scheme.
- James Roffey, Chairman of the Evacuee Reunion Association, who not only introduced me to the Association but also provided a great deal of encouragement to get this book written.
- John Gould, who allowed me access to his own research into Camp Schools.
- The staff of the Berkshire, Buckinghamshire, Devon, Dorset, Hampshire, Flintshire, Shropshire and Wiltshire Record Offices for their co-operation and patience.
- The Staff of the Duchy of Cornwall Office, St. Mary's, Isles of Scilly.
- The Staff of the Isles of Scilly Council, St. Mary's, Isles of Scilly.
- The staff at the Dorset Reference Library for their co-operation in allowing me to use extended time on the micro-film readers.
- The staff of the Salvation Army Centre, Judd St., London for allowing me access to closed papers.
- Peter Farley-Rutter for supplying me with personal family papers pertaining to his father.
- John Rawlins, for allowing me access to his private papers and personal research pertaining to a group of small villages in North Oxfordshire.
- Helen Borthwick, for carrying out the onerous task of proof-reading the manuscript and for her constructive comments and suggestions.
- Geoff Rush for making objective suggestions about the manuscript from an independent, non-historical, point of view.
- Josephine, Hannah and Kimiko Parsons for acting as my unpaid research assistants.
- Dr. Julia Boorman who originally guided my research in this area over numerous cups of coffee.
- My publishers for seeing the merits of publishing this book.
- Peter McClure for bringing the topic to life with his maps.
- My wife Josephine and daughters Kimiko and Hannah who have lived with this project for nine years and without whose co-operation and enduring patience this book and related work would not have been possible.

Contents

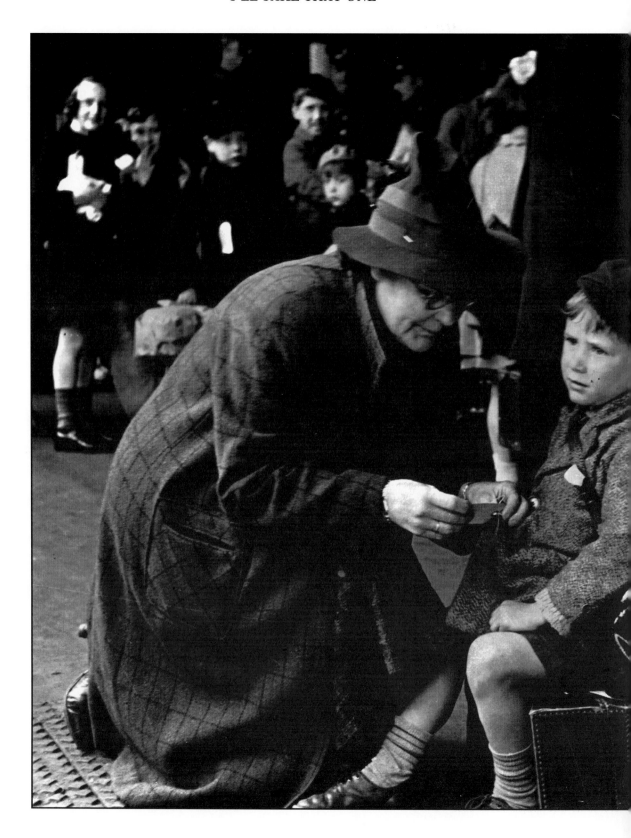

Evacuation

'The twentieth century is as much about cramming people into trains as about bombs though the atmosphere of our evacuation was extraordinarily light-hearted considering the adult fears that had made it come to pass. Certainly, some of us suffered full bladders and hunger, a little discomfort perhaps, but by and large it was viewed as a rather larky business altogether'.[1]

'All the time I was evacuated I used to tell myself that one day the war would be over and I could go back home. After the war we were living in a different part of London and I made my way back to where I used to live. The whole area had been completely obliterated during the first few days of the Blitz and I was quite unable to find the spot where my house once stood. This happened more than fifty years ago. I have lived in many other places. I now have a grown-up family of my own and I am a grandfather. I now have a lovely house, but somehow I'm still waiting to go home.' [2]

Preface

At 11a.m. on the morning of Thursday, 31st August 1939 the British Government issued an instruction long-awaited by those in the evacuation and reception areas primed to receive it. The message was very brief. Its words were simply 'Evacuate Forthwith'. Although the British Empire still encompassed the world the message was not sent to the Governor of some distant colony but, instead, directed to those who had been made responsible for the evacuation of hundreds of thousands of people, mostly children, from the major towns and cities of England. Places which were seen as being potential targets for intensive bombing by the enemy, as yet undeclared, of such ferocious intensity that it was expected to destroy vast areas and kill or seriously injure large numbers of personnel.

Throughout that Thursday and into the early hours of Friday morning people worked frantically to ensure that their carefully laid plans would be successful. Hundreds of train carriages were brought into marshalling yards around London and the other areas designated for evacuation. Fleets of buses were put on standby and even boats operating on the cross-channel ferry routes were recalled. Newspapers and radio stations were ordered to publish and broadcast official announcements that had already been issued to them, instructing parents to take their children who were to be evacuated with their schools to the designated assembly points. Early the next morning, Friday, 1st September placards were posted outside railway and Underground stations warning travellers that normal services would be suspended for a period of three days. Some major roads leading out of London were either closed or made one way only in order to ease the flow of evacuation traffic.

As early as 4 a.m. on the morning of 1st September some parents began to awaken their children to prepare for evacuation. This was at Dagenham where the evacuees were to board a fleet of paddle steamers and other vessels that had been moored on the River Thames near to Dagenham Dock. Within a few hours these children were to begin their long trek from their schools to the river front, although not all had to walk. Some were helped on their way by being carried in the fleets of local baker, laundry and other company vans to the gates of the Ford Motor Company works which lay within the confines of the dock. At dawn, the huge Ford plant was brought to a standstill as workers switched off their machines to help look after the children and, in some cases, carry them to waiting boats. Later, in line astern, these boats set off down river with their precious cargo heading for the east coast ports of Lowestoft, Felixstowe and Great Yarmouth. Within a year these same boats would be engaged in yet another evacuation, that of the British Expeditionary Force from the beaches of Dunkirk.

Later that same morning, but still early for those involved, Londoners and people in the other evacuation areas were brought face to face with the inevitable war as they saw long crocodiles of children, hundreds and hundreds of them, being led to the railway stations, each wearing a luggage label tied to their clothing or around their neck, carrying their gas-mask in its box across one shoulder and clutching small suitcases or haversacks, or even their few belongings stuffed in pillowcases or brown paper parcels. People cheered, waved and smiled and the children generally responded, but many were in tears and already feeling apprehensive. Others were puzzled. They had been told that they were going to the sea-side or into the country, that it would be just like going on holiday and that they would soon be home again. If that was true we wondered why so many of the women in the crowds were crying. Some parents snatched their children back at the last minute which only added to the puzzlement.

By mid-morning the great evacuation was under way as hundreds of special trains and fleets of buses headed out of the major towns. Neither the evacuees nor their parents knew what the destinations were, in fact parents would have to wait until much later in the day when notices were hung on the gates of school to find out where their children had been taken. It was not until the specially issued postcards arrived that they would know the names of foster parents and their addresses. In many cases these did not arrive until a few days later.

The great evacuation of September 1939 took three days to complete. It represented the biggest movement of people ever known in Britain. The Railway companies were stretched to their limits to cope with it. During the last morning of the exodus the Prime Minister, Neville Chamberlain, broadcast to the nation the news that Britain was at war with Germany and those evacuees who were old enough to understand realised that their absence from home would not after all be over so soon.

After the evacuees had left, a strange silence fell upon the residential areas of London and the other cities. The streets and playgrounds were empty of children. There were none of the usual games of hop-scotch or makeshift cricket being played and mothers had nobody to call in for tea or bedtime. Even the children who had not been evacuated were subdued as most of their friends had gone away. Nothing would be quite the same again for a number of years after the government had played the part of the Pied Piper. In the reception areas things were far from quiet as the local authorities, with the help of volunteers, struggled to cope with the influx of thousands of evacuees, most of them being children with their schools. Their task was made more difficult by the last minute changes that had occurred at the departure areas caused by the ever present worry that Germany might attack before the war had even been declared. There were fears that squadrons of Stukas from the German Luftwaffe would come screaming down from the skies to bomb and machine-gun the trains carrying evacuees, with the intention of creating mass panic and demands for peace at any price. Fortunately during those first few months the worst that was to happen were a few false alarms.

In spite of all the advance planning the actual arrival of the evacuees inevitably represented a major operation for the local authorities, many of them being small rural district councils with very limited resources. For many their population was immediately doubled or even trebled. Inevitably arrangements for the reception and billeting of the evacuees broke down, especially where hundreds of unaccompanied children arrived in areas where only mothers with young children and babies were expected. Others found themselves with very young children to care for when only teenagers had been expected.

At the east coast ports where the boats from Dagenham and the Medway towns discharged their thousands of unexpected children, cinemas, schools and halls of every description were pressed into service. Makeshift beds of straw were laid on the floors and teachers struggled to cook meals on open fires in makeshift camp kitchens. Three nights were spent in this way until the last of the children were billeted.

For most children all the excitement of what they had seen as a great adventure had evaporated before they had even arrived at their destinations. Many of the trains were made up of ancient carriages that had no corridors and therefore no toilet facilities. Journeys which should have been relatively short instead took many hours due to the congestion on the rail network and as a result many of the children arrived dirty, wet and very miserable.

It was this which caused the still widely believed myths about the evacuees to be formed. Myths which portray all the children as being from the inner city with behavioural problems and social attitudes to match. Some did come from such backgrounds but not the vast majority. Indeed, as Martin illustrates, many of them were to find the living conditions in their foster homes far inferior to what they were accustomed to at home. The popular image of the town-bred children finding themselves living in idyllic rural areas and cared for by kindly warm-hearted country folk was not, unfortunately, true in every case.

During the period known as the 'Phoney War' many of the evacuees drifted back to their homes, either because their parents could not stand the separation or were unable to resist the pleas of their homesick children. Sometimes the reason was simply because the child was being ill-treated or not being well cared for. However, the debacle at Dunkirk, the Battle of Britain and the Blitz brought about the need for further evacuations and many departed to the reception areas for a second time.

Some children were evacuees throughout the entire period of the war. They left their parents as youngsters but returned as self-assured, independent young adults. They spoke in the accents of their foster parents and had the attitudes of country people. Many, especially those evacuated overseas or for the whole of the war in British reception areas, were unable to re-settle to town life and became strangers to their own parents and siblings.

Many studies have been made of the great evacuation and numerous books written on the subject, but because the story has so many different facets no account can ever be considered complete. What has generally been overlooked is the long-term effects that evacuation had upon those who were involved. Many of these former evacuees try to avoid speaking or even thinking about this crucial part of their lives. Most cannot do so without finding long repressed emotions welling up inside them, emotions that have affected them throughout their adult lives and which will never go away.

In this book, using newly released material and oral evidence Martin has attempted to tell the true story of the greatest family and social upheaval ever known in modern Britain, an experience which altered not only the lives of those who were evacuees but also the attitudes and social structure of the nation.

James Roffey,
Founder and General Secretary of the Evacuees Reunion Association.
September 1998.

Introduction

'The House (of Commons) is mainly concerned with the evacuation of children. It seems that where children have been evacuated along with teachers everything has gone well. But, when the mothers have come there has been trouble. Many of the children are verminous and have disgusting habits. This horrifies the cottagers upon whom they are billeted. Moreover, the Mothers refuse to help, grumble dreadfully, and are pathetically homesick and bored'.[3]

The topic of evacuation appears in the syllabus of the National Curriculum at Key Stage 3 and GCSE World Affairs and it is particularly popular at Key Stage 2 as part of the study unit dealing with 'Britain from the 1930s'. Its popularity lies in the fact that many colleagues in the teaching profession believe that pupils in years 5 and 6 will be able to empathise with the children of the same age who were evacuated from British cities and other target areas in World War Two in order to lead a different life in the 'protected' and 'safe' areas of the countryside. However, by taking this line of reasoning they fall into the trap of only scratching the surface of a subject which, in essence, was not only complicated in its inception but had far-reaching social consequences which affected a significant percentage of the population both during the war and after it.

The vast majority of the population today cannot empathise with the sociological and psychological turmoil that many of the evacuees suffered and still suffer. Non-evacuees may have experienced homesickness at some time in their lives but where this has happened they have been aware that they would soon be returning home. It is too easy to forget that evacuees did not know when they would return home, if ever, and many of those who went abroad, some for seven years, often suffered from this common affliction and other traits of severe anxiety which was not talked about at the time and which many evacuees became experts in concealing, some until the present day.

How can the majority of us today be expected to empathise with situations such as this:-

Two girls, both strangers to each other and evacuated to Wales, were chosen by a lady who took them back to her house. They were sent around to the back door and told to strip off all their clothing. When they refused to do so the clothes were forcibly removed and torn off. They were then forced naked into the kitchen in front of the host's father and husband and pushed into a tin bath containing Dettol. After that, her husband cut off all their hair until they were bald, his excuse being that children from Liverpool brought lice, scabies and sores into the country areas. When they were taken to school the following day they met other children evacuated to the area and they were also totally bald.[4]

The shaving of heads was not uncommon. 'Dolly', an ex-evacuee aged 10 in 1939 recalled how her brother and step-brother, taken in by a different host than herself, turned up at school the following day with their heads completely shaved.[5]

These are not isolated examples. Many evacuees interviewed in the course of this research, some of whom wish to remain anonymous, mentioned sexual and physical abuse which has scarred them, in some cases physically, for life.

A letter written in November 1996 highlights the trauma some of them faced:-

> *'...we were taken in by two ghastly spinsters. They were a sadistic couple. We froze in winter as we were never given gloves, cardigans or wellington boots. When there was thick snow we got chilblains on our feet which cracked and burst and we had sores on our hands...to this day I put the heating on before I do anything else and I made sure that my children were never cold.....During the hot summers we were not allowed any water so we'd drink from the outside toilet. At one time I was so driven to despair that I attempted to cut my own throat. I was 10 years old and the knife was blunt....'* [6]

This one describes the heavy-handedness of some hosts to the point of cruelty.

> *'We got to the cottage with a bunch of flowers. Mrs Jackson was standing at the door. She took the flowers and threw them on the floor and danced on them.*
>
> *'Do you know what time it is?' It was 6 o'clock.*
>
> *'We were only picking flowers for you.' we said.*
>
> *Mr Jackson came in with a stick. 'Stand over there you two and face the wall.'*
>
> *We did, but we were shaking. We knew he was going to hit us. Wham, wham, wham on our legs. I screamed.*
>
> *Mary said, 'Don't hit me please, I will be good'.*
>
> *But he did and she screamed'.* [7]

In theory these situations should never have arisen. A Circular was sent out to Billeting Officers in the reception areas on the 27th August 1939 stating that one of their duties was to visit children in their billets and ensure that all was well.[8] In 1941, and again in 1942 and 1945, similar Circulars were sent to local authorities advising them that evacuated children should be visited not less than once a month. The later Circular in February 1945 was an urgent reminder to make sure all was well after there had been a case of cruelty in a foster home.[9] However, a lot could happen between visits and it is obvious from interviews that the experience of Mrs Hodgetts was not the only case of its kind. An interviewee and her sister representing their seven siblings at a recent Evacuee reunion stated that all nine had been evacuated and the eldest five had all been sexually abused while in their billets. One of the sisters was still having therapy which had first started in 1947![10]

There are numerous eye-witness accounts both for and against the evacuation scheme but sixty years later we must ask the question 'Are we being told the truth or are we still being fed only the opinions illustrated in the opening quotation?' Many of us are still being given access to written film and photographic examples of smiling happy children leaving their parents and going off to some unknown destination to live with strangers. Some photographs are edited to support this same impression. A classic example is on the front cover of Bob Holman's excellent book 'Evacuation. A Very British Revolution', where there is a picture from the Hulton Deutsch Collection showing six children who are all smiling through the window of a train carriage seemingly excited and happy about the prospect of going away. However, the rest of the photograph is shown on the back cover where there is a little boy who looks frightened and very unhappy. In many books this boy is cut out of the photograph completely.

Cover photograph from Bob Holman's "Evacuation. A Very British Revolution"

Few people are given access to material which explains why evacuation took place and, more significantly, the problems it caused. The aim of this book is to put Evacuation into perspective and illustrate the type of material at present missing from school text books and other media dealing with the topic.

There is a need to look beyond the type of jingoistic journalism that went on at the time, born out of propagandic expediency, which has influenced the images many people had, and still have, of the Government Evacuation Scheme. The following report from the Dorset Daily Echo dated Friday 1st September 1939, containing elements of truth, untruths and implied truth, is a prime example. This is not an isolated one. The same sentiments are re-echoed in other contemporary publications and film:-

GREATEST EVACUATION IN HISTORY HAS BEGUN

EXODUS OF THE BIBLE DWARFED: THREE MILLION PEOPLE ON THE MOVE

Britain today began its giant four day task of evacuating 3,000,000 children, mothers, blind, maimed. From the big cities of the land there began an exodus on a scale without precedent in human history.

Even the exodus of the Bible - the flight of the Israelites from Egypt - is dwarfed into insignificance by comparison, and there are many more people involved than in the French evacuation this week.

Nearly half of the three million are from Greater London, including the L.C.C. area. Today's contingent consisted exclusively of the school children.

In London, before dawn, teachers, marshals and officials were making their way to the schools to prepare for their big task.

Each child, their ages ranged from 3 to 13, carried a gas mask, food and change of clothing and bore three labels. [11]

None of the children knew their destination. 'I hope it is going to be the seaside,' said a boy of nine. 'I have brought my bathing costume along with me.'[12]

SMILING CHILDREN AT WATERLOO

The dexterity with which the children were shepherded through the arriving masses of morning workers at Waterloo Station was a perfect piece of organisation. Police, volunteer workers wearing armlets, and L.C.C. school officials saw that an avenue to their platform was kept entirely free.

They were a very cheerful crowd of youngsters, though a few had evidently shed some tears at the parting with their parents. At the station, however, their behaviour was what Mr. Herbert Morrison hoped it would be in his message to them yesterday.[13]

Parents shouted messages of farewell, little admonitions and gave other parental advice. Little tots smiled gleefully as they stepped out, getting hold of the hands of the elder children, boys whistled and exchanged jokes, while one boy, carrying a kit-bag over his shoulder in true military style, kept humming to himself as he marched earnestly and a little self-consciously with the rest. [14]

A PATHETIC SIGHT

While teachers, nurses and the special staff on duty kept as cheerful as they could be it was a pathetic sight. Here and there a little face was set hard in a big effort to be brave, the elders giving a good example in this. There were no tears. One little lad of five had a bucket and spade with him.

Some of the trains were bound for the west country as far distant as Taunton, while others were going to the Banbury district in the South Midlands.

Smooth and efficient working of the arrangements was reported at County Hall. It was stated that the evacuation was taking place prompt to schedule and no 'hitches' had been discovered.

It was not known whether the arrangements would be expedited in view of today's developments in the international situation. One official said that they thought the evacuation was being carried out almost as quickly as possible.

'GOING LIKE CLOCKWORK'

Miss Florence Horsborough, MP and under-secretary for Health, watched the entraining at London Bridge Station.

'Everything is going like clockwork.' said Miss Horsborough. 'I would like to pay a great tribute to the mothers for the part they played in making the scheme a success.'

Ambulance men and nurses on duty at stations had little to do. At one place their only call was from a little boy who wanted a glass of water.[15]

Endnotes

1   Ruth Inglis. Children's War. Fontana 1989. p3

2   Jim Bartley, former evacuee. Taped interview. November 1996

3   Harold Nicolson. The Harold Nicolson Diaries. Vol 2. 1939-45. 14th September 1939. Collins. 1967 p33

4   Lillian Evans. Yesterday's Children pub. Evans 1996. Extract published in The Evacuee November 1996.

5   Extract from a letter from 'Dolly' to her ex-host 1996.

6   Mrs Hodgetts. London (address withheld) Letter to the Author. November 1996

7   Lillian Evans 'Yesterdays Children'. 'The Scars' anonymous personal account. pub.Evans 1997

8   Ministry of Health Circular. No. 1857. 27th August 1939

9   Ministry of Health Circulars 2307 & 38/45. Cited in R.M.Titmuss Problems of Social Policy HMSO. 1950 p391

10   Interview with ex-evacuee sisters. 18th October 1996. Both expressed a wish to remain anonymous.

11   Parents sent their children to school everyday with a suitcase or bag packed, if possible, with items from a list provided by the authorities and enough food for the day. Margaret Harrod recalls that during the week leading up to evacuation they would walk around the playground of their school in pairs and then out the front gate to their mothers who would take them home to eat their sandwiches. (Letter to author. 1.3.97) Interesting to note that children from Portsmouth were not allowed to take suitcases. Children were not officially allowed to take hand-held toys such as teddy bears and dolls, although some managed to do so. However, this only applied to the government scheme. Those who were evacuated privately could take whatever toys etc. they could carry. They had the advantage, if advantage be the correct term, of having some 'comforter' and link with home. Rene Ringwood, née Alexander entitled her reminiscences 'And Dolly Came Too' because the doll given to her by her brothers was her constant companion for five years. (Letter to Author. 1st Feb.96)

12   No one knew the actual evacuation date or destination. Parents gathered at the school gates every day. Some evacuees have said that on the day they actually went their parents did not see them off because they thought it would be another practice. Others have said that one of their memories is of the parents who did witness the departure doing so in total silence. When they reached their destinations they sent postcards back home giving their new address and a message. In some schools in the days leading up to evacuation children practised what they were to write on these cards. James Roffey remembers having to copy from the blackboard.. 'I am being well looked after by nice people. I like it here. I am very happy.' (James Roffey. Correspondence June 1998)
Knowing that these cards and letters could be seen by hosts and people in authority, some children and parents devised a secret code which could be included in letters and cards to tell their parents that they were not happy. (Yesterdays Children. Lillian Evans)
It must have been very hard on the parents not knowing if their children would be home for dinner in the evening. The fathers too could not be sure that their children would be at home when they themselves returned from work.

13   See Appendix 6.

14   Many children had practised walking from their school to the nearest point of departure. Also some correspondents have said that they remember getting fed up with teachers who got them into pairs and then into a 'crocodile' to march around the playgound.

15   Dorset Daily Echo. 1st September 1939. (All Dorset newspapers relating to this period can be found in the Dorset Reference Library. Dorchester)

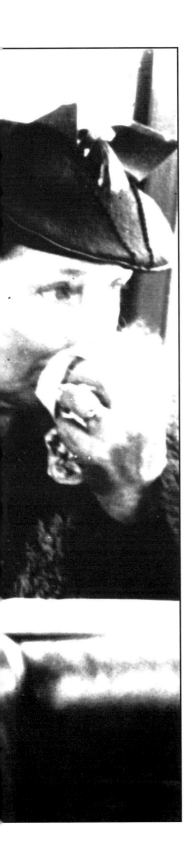

Evacuation in Britain and Europe

'To be torn up from the roots of home life, to be sent away from the family circle, in most instances for the first time in a child's life was a painful event.

This was no social experiment; it was a surgical rent only to be contemplated as a last resort.

....From the first day of September 1939 evacuation ceased to be a problem of administrative planning. It became instead a multitude of problems in human relationships'.[1]

Evacuation Planning in Europe

'With the sword drawn from its scabbard, but still held only at guard, Europe awaits a decision for peace and war' [2]

The evacuation scheme of 1939-45 was not the first civilian evacuation to be planned. At Wareham in Dorset, when the threat of a French invasion was at its greatest, a scheme was prepared for the removal to safety not only of population but also of livestock, food, vehicles and anything likely to be of use in a national emergency. Transport was commandeered, drovers were appointed to move cattle and sheep and overseers were given the task of seeing that arrangements were carried out. A document issued in Dorchester on 17th August 1803 by the Lord Lieutenant, laid down the procedure to be followed by a wider area, which was divided into districts and looked after by persons, who between 1939-45 would be identified as Wardens. A complete list of the inhabitants of each district was compiled as well as a register of livestock and an inventory of stores. The personnel list included qualifications and experience which could be useful during the emergency. Some were allocated to civil defence and others were given the role of preparing camps for evacuees! [3]

These arrangements were not restricted to the south coast. At the same time people in North Shields were issued with Evacuation permits and instructions:-

```
Ticket No.

You and your children belong to cart No.

Driver          Station No.

As soon therefore as the alarm is given pack up your blankets, and a
change of cloathes (sic) for yourself and children in the coverlid of
your bed and fix upon the Bundle this direction -

Number          Cart number        Driver Stations number
Of the Township of                 in the Parish of

Carry also what meal and meat and potatoes, not exceeding one Peck, you
may have in the house at the time; but on no account will any article
of Furniture, or heavy baggage, be allowed to be put into the carts.
One hour only will be allowed for preparation and then set out.[4]
```

The Evacuation scheme implemented in 1939, had been planned by an Evacuation sub-Committee of the Imperial Defence Committee as early as 16th February 1931 in order to prevent panic flight and create an orderly exodus from London in the event of war and designed, as Titmuss said, as 'A military expedient, a counter move to the enemy's objective of attacking and demoralising the civilian population'. [5]

However, it needs to be noted that these plans were based on assumptions of how any future war would be conducted and were therefore hypothetical plans based on limited research and conjecture.

On 10th November 1932, Stanley Baldwin, in a speech to the House of Commons, stated:-

'I will not pretend that we are not taking precautions in this country. We have done it. We have made our investigations much more quietly and hitherto without any publicity, but considering the years that are required to make our preparations, any government of this country in the present circumstances of the world would have been guilty of criminal negligence had they neglected to make their preparations'.[6]

Also on 28th November 1934 in a debate in the House of Commons, Churchill commented:-

'...Not less formidable than these material effects are the reactions which will be produced upon the mind of the civil population. We must expect that under pressure of continuous air attack upon London, at least 3,000,000 or 4,000,000 people will be driven out into the open country around the metropolis. This vast amount of human beings, numerically far larger than any armies which have been fed and moved in war, without shelter and without food, without sanitation and without special provision for the maintenance of order would confront the government of the day with an administrative problem of the first magnitude, and would certainly absorb the energies of our small army and our territorial force. Problems of this kind have never been faced before, and although there is no need to exaggerate them, neither, on the other hand, is there any need to shrink from facing the immense, unprecedented difficulties which they involve'.[7]

In fact the first evacuation scheme initiated in September 1939 turned out to be a mass exodus before the event!

The planning and implementation of the evacuation programme was the responsibility of the Sub-Committee for Evacuation of the Imperial Defence Committee, known as the Anderson Committee and established after continued interest by MPs in the need for explanation about any evacuation scheme. The Air Raid Precaution Bill of November 1937 had made no mention of evacuation, although after pressure from some MPs for the inclusion of a clause dealing with the matter, an amendment was tabled to make local authorities responsible for dealing with questions of evacuation. This was resisted by the Home Secretary who said:-

'The Committee for Imperial Defence is actively engaged upon this problem. We already have certain plans in existence. We intend to make them more comprehensive and we shall have them ready for the emergency...we have the question of evacuation firmly in our minds'.[8]

By the time the Bill had reached the committee stages the Home Secretary had made a concession and introduced a new clause which made it the duty of all local authorities to provide information to the Government for the purpose of assisting the preparation of any evacuation scheme. However, he maintained that the Government should remain as the co-ordinating body.

This policy was reinforced in the Board of Education Circular 1461 issued in January 1938. It stated that:-

```
'...in areas which were so exposed to danger that it would be decided
to close schools during the whole period in which raids might be
expected, the ideal solution would be evacuation and the difficulties
of such a scheme should not prevent its consideration'.[9]
```

Local Authorities were advised to contact the Home Office for help in preparing schemes. However, it soon became clear that this lack of direction in shifting responsibility to Local Authorities was creating a great deal of confusion and a later Circular, No.701262/8, issued by the Home Office on 28th March 1938, instructed Local Authorities not to prepare any plans at all until told to do so by the Home Secretary.[10]

It later became clear after the problems incurred during the mini-evacuation which took place during the Munich Crisis in September 1938, that it was vital that the Government still remained in overall charge while working closely with Local Authorities.[11]

The same circular stated that 'Authorities will recognise that no single or comprehensive plan for evacuation is practicable. If the necessity arose for evacuation on any large scale, it would be carried out in co-operation between the Government and the Local Authorities. The matter is under examination by the department who will be able, at a later date, to arrange for the subject to be considered in co-operation with the authorities who may be concerned. In the meantime authorities need not take action on this matter in respect of their schemes unless and until specific directions have been issued by the Secretary of State'.

On 12th May 1938 the Government refused to initiate a billeting survey stating that the problem of evacuation was being studied. Later in the same month, in defiance of Government advice and having received a number of requests to act, including the example below from the Marylebone Labour Party, the London County Council approved the principle of evacuating school children:-

```
                                      St. Marylebone Labour Party
                                                  Office: 41,
                                                  Daventry St.,
                                                  London NW1

                                      27th May 1938.
```

The Home Secretary.
Whitehall,
SW1.

Dear Sir,

I have to inform you that the following resolution was passed
unanimously at last night's meeting of the General Committee of this
party:-

'That, pending the development of a comprehensive scheme of Air Raid
protection for the entire civilian population of London, plans be made
by the LCC immediately, so that, upon the first threat of war, the
whole school population under the control of the teachers can be
transferred at short notice to safer emergency quarters in the Home
Counties; such plans to be put to the test before the emergency occurs
by means of actual temporary transfers'.

I shall be obliged if you will lay this resolution before the Committee
which has just been set up by the Government to consider the question
of evacuating civilians in the event of air raids. I have, of course,
sent a copy of the Resolution to the LCC.

Yours faithfully,

G.E.M.De Ste.Croix. Secretary.[12]

The Anderson Committee, when established, met in Committee Room 13 of the House of Commons on Friday 27th May 1938 under the Chairmanship of Sir John Anderson. Its terms of reference were:-

'To examine the problem of the transfer of persons from areas which might be exposed to continuous air attack and to recommend plans for the purpose'.[13]

Among its responsibilities was to divide the country into three categories: evacuation, reception and neutral. According to Titmuss over 200 Local Authorities in England and Wales designated as reception areas asked for their classification to be changed to neutral and a further 60 Authorities, above those already listed, wanted to be classified as evacuation areas.[14] This was not completed until January 1939 by which time the Government had decided to transfer all responsibility for the implementation of any evacuation scheme to the Health Departments. They had taken over officially on 14th November 1938 and Sir John Anderson was given a new role of co-ordinating the whole question of Civil Defence. No authority on the evacuation list argued with the Ministry of Health's decision and no authority asked to be a reception area.[15]

The Anderson Committee made sure that priority was immediately given to London, and elements of specific detailed planning were also prioritised:-

a. To what extent there were vital activities which must be kept going.

b Conditions under which public order could be controlled.

c Transport.

d. Necessity to feed and house those evacuated so Government departments concerned i.e. Food, Health, the Board of Trade etc. could be consulted.

The Committee felt that it might be necessary to work out two schemes, one for an orderly evacuation and the other for a sudden emergency. Under the former, known as plan 2, 13 million people were in designated Evacuation areas, 14 million in Neutral areas and 18 million in reception areas. The Committee also suggested that they should investigate how the French proposed to evacuate Paris should the need arise.

(In July 1934 Baldwin had informed the House of Commons that '...so far as I know every country in Europe has carried its work a great deal further than we have carried ours'.)[16]

By January 1939, a report to the Home Defence sub-Committee of the Committee of Imperial Defence on 'The State of Readiness of the Civil Defence' concluded that 'Evacuation plans are, at present, very backward'.[17] Although this was true in relation to the French planning, the British scheme was in fact in advance of Germany's which was not as well prepared.

The French had in fact organised their evacuation as early as 1931, as a document dated the 17th December 1937, and headed ARP Intelligence Branch indicates. The extreme vulnerability of Paris from air attack had been recognised in the early 30s so in February 1931 Marshal Petain had been appointed as Inspector General of Aerial Defence for France. He established a plan for the evacuation of the city which was based on the premise that 1 million citizens would leave voluntarily. The information about evacuation was to be contained in a leaflet of which 1.5 million were to be distributed throughout Paris.

The French Scheme was to take 2 forms:-

A. LONG RANGE: Those persons who did not have public or private duties to fulfil or whose presence in the city was not essential, were to be removed to areas as far away as possible from the vulnerable centre. Their departure was to be implemented at the first threat of war and they were to remain in their reception areas throughout the duration of hostilities. It was estimated that two days' mobilisation would be enough to remove 200,000 citizens from the area. The actual numbers were to be decided by the Mayor of each district.

In the reception areas, approximately 150 kilometres to the South-West of Paris, the billeting arrangements were to be organised by the Prefects of the Departments involved. Each person to be permanently evacuated was to be issued with a card to act as a rail ticket. On it would be marked the name of the billeting area, entraining and detraining stations, the day and time of departure and the number of trains.

Arrangements were to be made for coaches to transport the evacuees from the train stations to their billets.

B. SHORT RANGE: This evacuation was to be either permanent or on a daily basis. However, it was not to be implemented during an air-raid warning. This daily evacuation was primarily concerned with the officials, shopkeepers, tradesmen and other workers who had to work in a vulnerable area during the day but who could leave at night to join their families in a safer place outside the city. It was estimated that this would affect 250,000 Parisians.[18] In the event children were evacuated from Paris on 30th August 1939, the same day that 'stand-by' orders for evacuation were issued in London.

It is interesting to note that it was reported in January 1940 that France was way ahead of Britain in terms of home front organisation. Colonel Baldwin-Webb the Conservative MP for Wrekin, Shropshire returned from a fact-finding tour of France where he found there was virtually no blackout, no evacuation and no rationing. He questioned whether Britain was justified in applying stringent controls thought necessary for safety.[19]

The Germans also considered evacuation.[20] Their plans were not investigated by the Anderson Committee as being relevant but in fact Germany and Britain had similar priorities when considering initial planning.[21]

The official German policy was to avoid evacuation at the outbreak of hostilities but instead to implement a gradual dispersion of the population away from the towns and cities. The German argument against evacuation at the commencement of hostilities was that it was likely to result in panic and thereby obstruct vital communication networks.

The German High Command also felt that the effect of any air attack on civilians might be overestimated and that during the first week or two after war had started the situation might be clearer.

As early as 1935-6 a series of articles appeared in 'Gasschutz & Luftschutz,' ('Gas Protection and Air Protection') the official magazine of the Reich Air Protection League, discussing the difficulties of evacuation. In October 1936 Colonel Teacher, an official at the air protection department of the German Air Ministry, maintained in this publication that the practicality of evacuation would depend on three considerations:-

a. The number of people to be moved.

b. The time the movement was to take place.

c. The means of transport involved in the movement.

Teacher went on to suggest that the first consideration was impossible to forecast because those in the military would have left home, the German ARP would absorb the others as anyone over the age of 15 was required for ARP duties, and anyone under the age of 10 had to stay with their parents wherever they were, even in vulnerable areas.

Government officials and businessmen would remain, as well as the old and infirm who would be unable to travel. Prisoners should be evacuated, not for any humanitarian reason but because of the danger they would cause if the prisons were bombed and they escaped.

He recommended that some people should be allowed to find their own accommodation. However, although departure should not be hindered, the people would have to satisfy the police that they had made arrangements for the care of their homes. They would also need to obtain written permission from the police in order to move. It was felt that too much voluntary evacuation would develop into panic flight.[22]

By 1942 this official line had changed and indicated a climb-down on the part of the High Command which had promised that no bombers would ever get through to attack German cities. Controlled evacuation began from those areas which were considered to be in most danger from Allied attacks and Baldur von Shirach was given the responsibility for implementing the scheme that had first been put forward as a possibility in 1940. Hitler gave his approval for 'erwiterte Kinderlandverschickung' (expanded sending of the children into the country) which was a means of treating the process as an extension of the rural vacations scheme rather than evacuation. By November 1942 a total of 1,198,377 people had been transported by 1,654 trains and 78 ships on the Rhine and Weser rivers.[23] A total of 335,409 of these were youths aged between 10-14 who were in camps for the Hitler Youth and 862,968 were mothers and children who were being cared for by the Nazi Welfare Agency. These 'evacuees' were issued with 127,000 tubes of toothpaste, 7,500 first aid kits, 9,900 musical instruments, 140,000 suits for boys, 130,000 suits for girls and 110,000 pairs of wooden shoes.[24]

No British evacuees were given such official help with clothes and basic necessities, although a series of Ministry of Health circulars which arrived in the reception areas only six days before evacuation took place, gave permission to those authorities responsible for evacuating persons from their areas to buy boots, clothing and knapsacks up to the value of £1 for every 200 children on the strict understanding that no publicity was given to such help.[25] However, unlike their German counterpart, the planning of the Anderson Committee was to be more far reaching both in practical details and social upheaval.

Endnotes

1   Titmuss. op. cit.

2   The Sydney Morning Herald. Editorial 1st September 1939.

3   C.F.Carr. Talk to Bournemouth Rotary Club. 17th October. 1939

4   Dorset Daily Echo. 2nd May 1940

5   Titmuss. Op.cit p23

6   House of Commons Debates. 10th Nov.1932 Vol 270 col 633 cited Titmuss op cit p23

7   M. Gilbert Winston S. Churchill Vol V 1922-39 Heinemann 1976 p573

8   House of Commons Debates. 25th November 1937. vol 329 col 1447. cited Titmuss. op cit. p26

9   Exeter Blitz. Box 5. Devon Record Office. Exeter

10   ibid.

11   Titmuss. Op.cit. p27 Footnote

12   Exeter Blitz. Box 5. Devon Record Office

13   PRO HO45/17636

14   Titmuss. op cit. p32

15   ibid.p33

16   House of Commons Debates. 30th July 1934. vol.1292 cols. 2335-6 cited Titmuss op.cit.p33

17   Titmuss op.cit.p33

18   Exeter Blitz. Box 16 Group O 188. Devon Record Office

19   Reported in Dorset Daily Echo 12 January.1940

20   Exeter Blitz. Box 16. Devon Record Office

21   PRO HO45/17636

22   PRO HO45/17636

23   Earl R.Beck. Under the Bombs. The German Home Front. 1942-45. University Press of Kentucky. p24

24   Earl R. Beck. op cit. p25

25   Ministry of Health Circular. GES 13. 25th August. 1939. cited Titmuss. op cit. p92

The British Experience

'You must have been a very naughty boy. My Mum and Dad would never send me away to live with strangers'.[1]

At the second meeting of the Anderson Committee W. Eady, Under-Secretary of State at the Home Office, reported that the question of evacuation had been studied over a number of years. According to his figures, 63% of London's population were in essential industries, 35% were classified as being 'not sure' and 2% were classed as non-essential. This was considered by the Committee members to be a very superficial interpretation of the details available.

Basically at this stage, 30th May 1938, the Committee had to consider two important details:-

- Which were the danger zones in London?

- Which were the essential industries that had to continue?

The Committee agreed that the Metropolitan Police District, Potter's Bar to Epsom, could not be regarded as highly vulnerable. So Greater London was divided into three distinct areas:-

a. Evacuation, if possible, from an area encompassing Hammersmith to Dagenham and Holloway to Dulwich.

b. A wider area of restricted movement.

c. An outer ring receiving hospital patients.

In order to make this feasible the Committee needed precise information from employers as to the number of men they could do without. They hoped to bring the number needing to be evacuated down to 4,500,000.

The main concerns underlying this plan were as follows:-

a. There was an expectation that a number of people would lose their nerve and stream out of London. Therefore the plans were designed to facilitate this exodus which, to some extent, the Committee felt would take place in any event and therefore ought to be regulated and controlled.

b. It was important that some men who were essential to vital industries would not be lost to the national effort but would be able to continue to work in the safer zones.

c. There would be the need to move between 3 and 4 million people from the city within 72 hours. This would rely heavily on the efficiency and co-operation of the Railway network.

d. There was a need for the Government to implement this plan as soon as tension began.[2]

The third meeting of the Committee concentrated on the evacuation of children. Although they, and representatives from the LCC Education Committee, felt that responsibility for this lay with the Government, they did agree that school staff already had great experience of moving large numbers of pupils. Examples such as 100,000 going to the Crystal Palace in 1911, 70,000 for the Silver Jubilee celebrations and 37,000 to the Coronation in 1937, were cited as positive evidence. In order for the scheme to be effective it was felt necessary for the Committee to liaise closely with the teachers and their professional bodies. The National Union of Teachers had already been approached in January 1938 when Circular 12461 'ARP in Schools' was being considered, so there was a degree of co-operation already established.

On 4th June 1938, the National Union of Teachers executive passed a resolution stating:-

> *'That the executive of the NUT, while not subscribing to any suggestion that war is inevitable, is prepared to co-operate with the Government and Local Authorities in making plans for the safety of school children as effective as possible and to recommend its members in the local areas to consider the desirability of co-operating on a voluntary basis'.*

The NUT realised that the general scheme of evacuation was bound to be preceded by decisions or policies made by the Government for which teachers would have no responsibility, but they regarded themselves as duty-bound to co-operate with the Government. This of course raised the question of the evacuation of teachers. On a number of occasions Sir Percy Harris asked the members of the NUT present if they felt that teachers would leave their own families. If not, he questioned whether it could be organised so that teachers with family commitments were not employed in the scheme. As it turned out, most teachers from the evacuated areas, with families or not, were involved in the evacuation.

From this point on, teacher representatives were heavily involved in the discussions relating to evacuation. Sir Fred Mander, General Secretary of the NUT, said that it would be impossible to launch a scheme of compulsory evacuation of school children because it was not practical to override parental responsibility. Mrs Parker, President of the NUT, thought that the first reaction of parents would be to refuse, but if properly explained to them they would agree. J. Brown, Chairman of the ARP Committee suggested that any scheme had to be 'elastic', allowing parents, previously against evacuation, to change their minds and send their children with the others.

Anderson argued that parents would be inclined to ask a lot of questions about any evacuation scheme. Therefore they must assume that adequate attention would be given to the welfare of their children.

Teachers were strongly in favour of billeting children in private houses rather than in camps, hostels or boarding accommodation. Billeting was represented as a dispersal and therefore, in theory, it was possible to put some responsibility upon the host and thereby taking some of the daily responsibility away from the teachers. Under the scheme foster-parents and other hosts were to be given the authority to act in loco parentis. Government Evacuation Scheme. Memo Ev.4 from the Ministry of Health 1939. Clause 72 stated:-

'In circumstances in which evacuation would take place, householders in
the receiving areas could be relied upon to do everything possible to
lighten the lot of the children and mothers compelled suddenly to leave
their homes and families and finding themselves in strange
surroundings. So far as unaccompanied school children are concerned,
the householder will be in loco parentis, and should have no great
difficulty in controlling the children and preserving reasonable
discipline. The children will be accompanied by their teachers, who
will know them and will be able to assist in their control'.[3]

In the event, some hosts proved to be very effective in taking full responsibility, but teachers in many areas found themselves coping with virtually the 24 hour supervision of charges who were, in some cases, to be spread over hundreds of square miles.

However, even for those hosts who took their role of foster parents seriously, it was not always possible for them to control 'difficult' children and some were not prepared to impose any discipline because of the possible consequences from the child's family and the authorities.

The issue became a serious one and in May 1941 the Rural District Councils Association forced questions about it in Parliament [4] and on 12th July 1941 the Chief Billeting Officer in the Dorchester area of Dorset wrote the following letter to the Clerk of the County Council expressing concern and offering suggestions:-

12 July 1941

From: Dorchester RDC.

Ref. Government Evacuation Scheme. Difficult Children

1. Cases arise from time to time of children of both sexes who are
unruly and with whom the average householder is unable and willing to
deal.

2. It can be understood that where stern measures are indicated, any
householder applying them may be proceeded against by parents and
guardians in the courts and that is a risk most people will not
willingly incur.

3. The only possible solution is for these children to be placed in
Institutions, under competent supervision, where they can be brought
under proper discipline until in the opinion of the person in charge,
they can be safely sent back to private billets.

4. The Southampton Authority already run such a home for boys only,
evacuated from their area, at Wiverley Park in Lyndhurst. It is always
full and additional accommodation is needed. So far as is known, no
provision is made for London children or for girls of any evacuated
area.

5. I am unable to give figures for the total number of school children billeted in the County, but in this area the figures are Boys 317 and Girls 279.

6. I suggest provision should be made for 1% of the total number in the County in assessing the size of the accommodation required.

7. I therefore recommend:-

a. The County Council be asked to set up two such homes in the County, one for each sex, in suitable houses not in towns, the co-operation of the Evacuation Authorities being asked in provision of higher staff.

b. The administration of each Home to be in the hands of the Local Authority in whose area it is situated.

c. Administer to the Homes through the Director of Education of the County Council and all applications for the admission of a child be backed by the Head School Teachers of the Parish in which the child is billeted.

Signed W.de. M. Egerton. Chief Billeting Officer.[5]

Transportation

'After what seemed like hours of stopping and starting we arrived at our final destination. We had expected green fields and trees. What we got was Luton!' [6]

On the 16th June 1938 the Committee tackled the very difficult problem of transportation. They needed to plan how to evacuate an estimated several million adults and 750,000 children from the Metropolitan Police district. In the event 827,000 Primary-school children, 524,000 young children and mothers, and 12,000 expectant women were the ones eligible. Also evacuated were 103,000 teachers and helpers, a pupil-teacher ratio of 8:1.[7] The unpaid helpers were women who had been appointed by the evacuation authorities to accompany the children to their destination where they were usually billeted by the host authority. During the first evacuation of 1939 around 40,000 had taken part but some of them were totally unsuitable and by the middle of 1941 32,000 had been dismissed reducing the pupil-helper ratio to 100-1.[8]

The Committee realised that any plan had to be simple, flexible and allow for immediate adjustment to meet conditions which had not been foreseen. They also recognised that the proportion of inhabitants being evacuated would differ from area to area because of the density of population and their vulnerability.

Frank Pick, the Vice-Chairman of London Passenger Transport, had indicated that the LPT was responsible for an area of 25 miles radius from the centre of London which was in fact 10 miles more than the Metropolitan District. He suggested that the eastern area of the Zone should be considered to be the highest priority especially the Southwark area, south of the Thames, which was very densely populated. The western area had less population and in his opinion there was no risk to the north. His definition of a congested area was one of more than 150 people per acre where bombs would cause great havoc.

Pick pointed out to the Committee that all motor coaches had been earmarked for ambulance work and therefore would not be available for evacuation. However, although 50% of the city's 6,000 buses had been assigned to carry on the normal service in the area, 250 had been assigned to work with the Police, which meant that the remaining 2,750 buses could be used to move a limited amount of the population. Although the final figure would very much depend on the amount of permissible luggage, it was estimated that a total of 110,000 people could be taken by bus. This meant that, allowing for a three hour return journey to railway stations, 330,000 could be moved per day and this could be increased to 500,000 per day if the number of buses withheld from the scheme was reduced to below 50%. Many of the Committee had felt that the purpose of the buses would be to transport evacuees to mainline stations but Pick had been adamant that it would be far more prudent to take them out of the city to entrain at smaller stations such as Harrow.[9]

The question of use of the underground system was also discussed at some length as the carrying capacity of the buses was well below that of the tube. The decision had been taken for the District

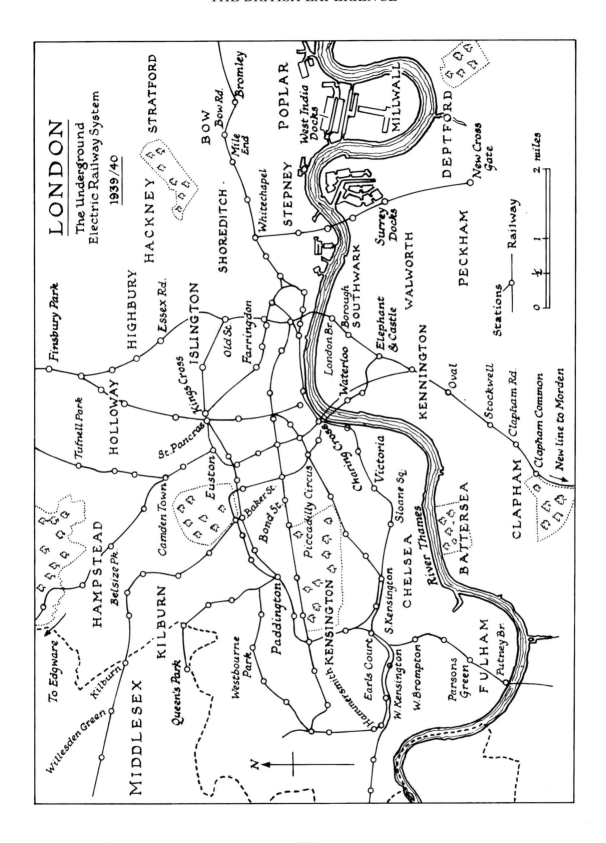

LONDON

The Underground
Electric Railway System

1939/40

Line to transport evacuees to join the Great Western Railway at Ealing Broadway and the Southern Line at Wimbledon. The Bakerloo Line would link with the mainline at Willesden, the Metropolitan Line at Harrow. However, it was decided that the Piccadilly Line would be of limited use because there were no useful connections after Finsbury Park and that the Morden Line was not to be used because it had no mainline connection at all. However, the Tube system did have a greater passenger capacity and it was estimated that 100,000 people per hour could be moved if 2 trains were full. But there were drawbacks.[10]

The two serious disadvantages of the Tube were the ventilation system which would have given no protection at all in the event of a gas attack, and the risk of flooding from both water and sewage, especially if evacuation was taking place during a raid. The latter was a particularly serious risk at Bond St. where the Fleet sewer passed over Farringdon St. If this was damaged in any way the District, Metropolitan and Central lines would all be flooded. Any bomb damage near the Embankment would also create serious disruption at Charing Cross Station where three mainline railways converged. Even as early as June 1938 a serious debate was taking place within the Anderson Committee as to the actual use of the whole underground transport system. The question of whether or not it should be used as shelters, closed down altogether for safety reasons or kept going, was discussed at length but no decision was made. It was not until 1940 that Londoners made the decision to use the Tubes as shelter themselves.[11] Angus Calder refers to this move as:-

'...an heroic assertion of popular rights against a legacy of inept bureaucracy and Tory rule'. [12]

Ultimately 80 stations became shelters for 177,000 people.

The actual transportation of so many evacuees was seen as having massive inherent problems. However, the Transport Board worked out a scheme which, under Bank-holiday conditions, would evacuate 100,000 persons per hour by underground, 500,000 per day by bus, or 330-350,000 under normal conditions. Their target was 1,000,000 per day for the first two days and then 500,000 thereafter.[13] These numbers were far in excess of the numbers which could easily be coped with by the mainline stations, therefore, the companies concerned were asked to investigate how they could overcome this potentially chaotic situation. The movement of vast numbers of people also created the problem of how it would be possible to differentiate between genuine evacuees and those who were just entering the underground system for shelter. Although there would not be enough Police on hand the Committee decided not to use the Army to keep control and so, like the question of the tube shelters, the problem remained unresolved.

All the Committee proposals on transportation were sent to the major railway companies and on the 21st June 1938 the Committee invited Sir Ralph Wedgewood, Chief General-Manager of the L.N.E.R., Mr G. S. Szlumper, General-Manager of Southern Rail and Mr V. M. Barrington-Ward, Chairman of the Railway Companies Technical ARP Committee to give their response to the original proposals.

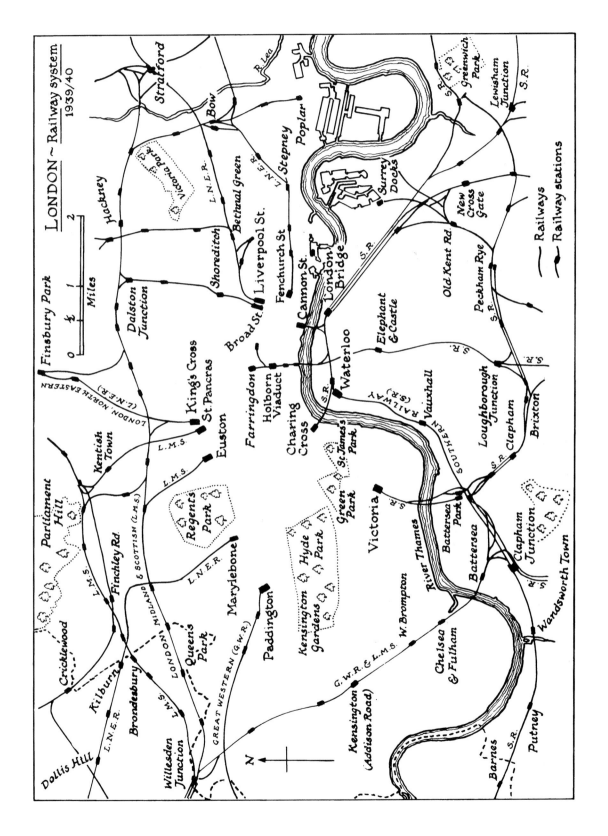

LONDON ~ Railway system 1939/40

The Committee needed some reassurance on the actual carrying capacity of the trains. They had envisaged a scheme which did not involve long journeys but short ones taking refugees to a belt of indeterminate width around London, where, it was contemplated, the population could be detrained at suitable points within the belt. This was not seen as a problem by the companies. In fact some years before, the Southern Rail had been asked to plan an evacuation scheme to take refugees up to 50 miles from the capital from the main-line stations and these plans were still available.

The railway companies calculated that they could move 3,600,000 persons in 72 hours if they just ran a skeleton regular service. This was a much higher estimate than the one sent to the Ministry of Transport when the companies said that 60,000 could be moved to a 20-25 mile radius per hour if a skeleton service was used or 115,000 per hour if all trains were utilised.[14]

The companies reassured the Committee that the same capacity could be carried even if main-line stations were damaged. They suggested that suburban stations such as Queen's Park or Finsbury Park could be used instead. Carriage sidings would be readily available at most sub-stations and it would be easier to work 'through' platforms than entrain people at passenger bays.

As well as the question of numbers of evacuees the Committee also had to decide upon safety factors, especially those concerning the timing of the evacuation. For instance, was entraining to go on during a raid? Would railway workers be disinclined to work through a raid? What about the transfer of passengers from the tube to the trains?

In consultation with the rail companies it was decided that trains actually running during a raid should continue their journey but other activities in the station area would stop, thus allowing station workers and others to take shelter. The biggest problem would be the transfer of evacuees from the tubes. Quite naturally they would be unwilling to come to the surface and it was estimated that a tube train which would normally take 5 minutes to empty might be delayed considerably longer, thus causing problems both in the stations and in the tunnels where trains would be backing up. Therefore, it was suggested that instead of transferring passengers, an alternative would be to take the tubes to the termini. At least in this way the passengers would be taken out of the city and the evacuees could be distributed by the local buses from these points. In the event many evacuees were transported from their home areas using a combination of transport networks and systems.

Virtually all archive film depicting the actual movement of evacuees from London such as 'Westward Ho!', made during the second evacuation in 1940, shows them being transported by bus and overground suburban trains to main railway termini and this does seem to be the most common form of transportation used. However, only a small percentage actually left from the termini, going instead from stations with through platforms as favoured by the Anderson Committee. Most of the children travelling westwards on the Great Western Railway left from Ealing Broadway. Not only did it have a through platform, required to make the entraining and departure of evacuees quicker, but it also had very good links with the Underground system. In the

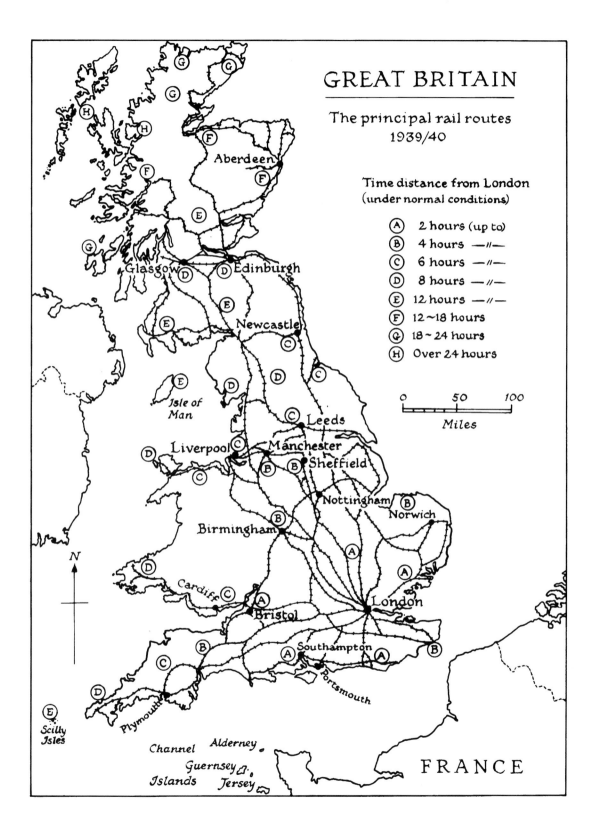

GREAT BRITAIN

The principal rail routes
1939/40

Time distance from London
(under normal conditions)

(A) 2 hours (up to)
(B) 4 hours —//—
(C) 6 hours —//—
(D) 8 hours —//—
(E) 12 hours —//—
(F) 12~18 hours
(G) 18~24 hours
(H) Over 24 hours

0   50   100
Miles

first four days of September 1939, 164 trains carrying evacuees ran from three stations, Ealing, Acton and Paddington. The first train, numbered 101, left Ealing at 8.30am on 1st September and went to Maidenhead arriving at 9.00am. Others of course went further distances. The trains, made up of twelve carriages and capable of carrying 800 people per journey, were marshalled at Acton and Old Oak Common.[15]

Original estimates suggested that 850 children could leave Paddington per day, 3,200 from Acton and 46,500 from Ealing. In the event these numbers proved to be inflated.[16] On the first day 58 Great Western Railway trains, rather than 64, ran carrying a total of 44,032 evacuees, reducing by the fourth and final day to 28 trains carrying 17,796 evacuees.[17]

London County Council staff assisted G.W.R personnel in organising the children and adults at the stations. Tickets had already been issued at the schools where the children had assembled, Yellow tickets to children with teachers and Pink tickets to children accompanied by their mothers.[18] They had been told to arrive 15 minutes before the departure of the train. The 166 page timetable for evacuation had been printed in early August but because there was still the Government concern that evacuation might cause panic a note on the front cover of the timetable warned:-

> 'The Evacuation Train arrangements shewn in this Notice must not be circulated to more members of staff than is necessary for the smooth working of the Programme and information must not be circulated to the General Public'.[19]

As well as the London evacuation, on the 1st and 2nd of September the G.W.R moved 22,739 evacuees from the Birmingham area in 64 trains. These travelled to South Wales and Gloucester. The company also moved 35,606 evacuees from Liverpool and Birkenhead.[20]

Of course other railway companies were involved. James Roffey recalls travelling from Queens Road Station to Pulborough on the Southern Railway. This embarkation point created its own problems. The station had always been a make-shift place. The railway line itself was high on an embankment and to reach the platform children had to climb up a very steep flight of wooden steps with their bags and cases. Gas-masks were also a problem as the sharp cornered boxes banged against knees and the string cut into the owners' necks.

A serious situation almost occurred when a girl tripped over on the stairs causing many others to fall with her. When the train eventually came into the platform made up of old fashioned carriages with a door to every compartment a melee ensued. Everyone surged forward, brother and sisters and friends struggled to keep together and everyone wanted a window seat.[21] A scene far removed from the orderly entraining shown in the propaganda films such as 'Westward Ho!' made in 1940.

Some evacuees have stated that they travelled by an alternative method of transportation not mentioned at all in the Anderson Committee minutes. They did not use trains, buses or the tube but were taken directly to their reception areas by boat from the Ford Motor Company jetties at

Dagenham. Paddle steamers such as the 'Golden Eagle' owned by the General Steam Navigation Company, normally seen on cross-channel routes, had been brought in to pick up evacuees at Dagenham and take them to the east coast ports of Felixstowe, Lowestoft and Great Yarmouth. These steamers were given a destroyer escort.[22]

Unfortunately, in the event, they were not expected and many evacuees spent a few nights sleeping on the floors of schools and church halls in straw filled sacks, before billets could be found.[23] In total 16,984 children had registered for evacuation in this manner but not all turned up. Other boats used in the scheme included The Royal Eagle, The Crested Eagle, The Royal Sovereign, The Royal Daffodil, Queen Charlotte, The Medway Queen and The City of Rochester.[24] The Medway Queen still exists, although in a poor state, and an appeal has been launched to save her. She has had quite a history.

Having evacuated children from Dagenham on 1st September 1939 she took children from Gravesend on 3rd September and was then taken to Deptford to be fitted out as mine-sweeper and became part of the Royal Navy. In 1940 she earned the title 'Heroine of Dunkirk' having made seven journeys across the Channel to Dunkirk and brought back an estimated 7,000 soldiers. [25]

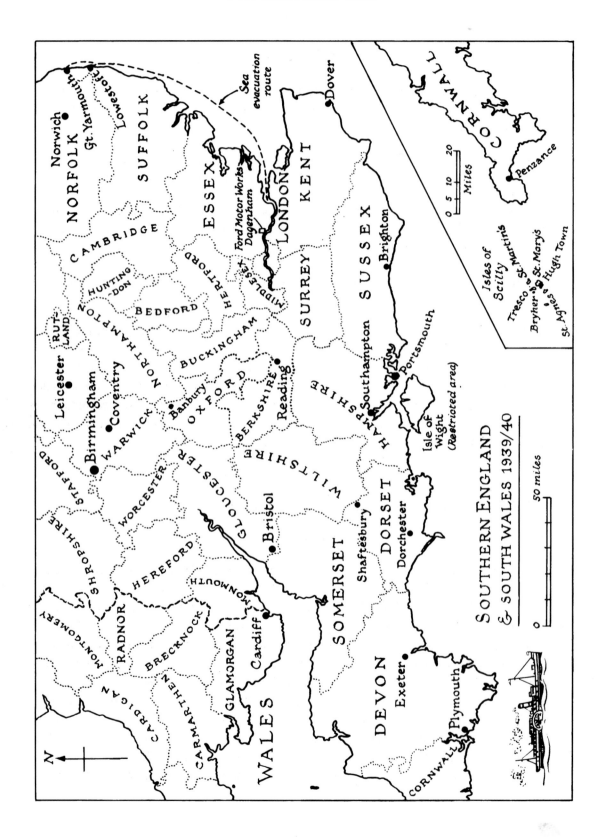

SOUTHERN ENGLAND & SOUTH WALES 1939/40

Billets

' ...the general public hardly realises how arduous and how important a service is being rendered by this great army of volunteers. The finding of a billet is only the beginning. The real work starts later'.[26]

Having sorted out the transport problems the Anderson Committee was then faced with the problem of how to decide on reception areas and how many billets would be required.

On the 23rd June 1938, J. C.Wrigley, Director of Housing and Town Planning at the Ministry of Health, attended the meeting to give advice on evacuation accommodation and the provision of water supplies in the reception areas.[27]

His own information came from two sources, both of which were incomplete for the purpose intended.

One was the 1931 Census, which gave the numbers of persons living per room, and the numbers of houses erected by local authorities and private companies. There were no statistics on the rates of occupation of these new houses but it was assumed that it was not higher than the country's average of 4 persons per house. He also used the Ministry of Health Paper EC7 on accommodation in Buckinghamshire as a sample area. Wrigley explained that houses erected by local authorities were usually of the non-parlour type and might be assumed to have 4.5 persons resident in them. Private enterprise houses could be analysed by rateable value:-

- Below £12 per annum they would be similar to authority housing.

- £12-£25 per annum could be seen as Lower Middle Class.

- £25+ per annum would be the largest houses.

It was necessary at this stage to have some standard on which calculations of how many could be billeted were made. The Committee adopted the standard of overcrowding contained in the Housing Act of 1935 and the Consolidating Act of 1936. However, this represented a very low standard and so could only be regarded by the committee as a starting point for dealing with overcrowding. It was felt by some that if the recommendations outlined in the Act were adopted in time of war as a standard of billeting, they would produce a social situation of which Britain had no experience. In 1938 the average percentage of houses in the country below the required standard of the 1936 Act was 1%. Using the calculations based on this information it was reckoned that a Lower Middle Class house, comprising 2 reception rooms and 4 bedrooms and with an average residency of 4 persons, could take in an extra 10-12 people as evacuees. If children were involved the figure could be higher because those under 12 months did not figure in the equation and those under 10 counted as 0.5.[28] These figures were amended drastically and the billeting standard used on all accommodation surveys in England and Wales during the war was one person per habitable room.[29]

Wrigley supplied figures for other counties and a preliminary survey suggested that 1,000,000 evacuees could be accommodated in Berkshire, East and West Sussex and Buckinghamshire, but the Committee still doubted whether the provisions of the Act were too low and therefore problems would be created if billeting was carried out to its limits. Special consideration was given to the question of coastal towns which had spare capacity outside the holiday season but no special arrangements were made.

Wrigley was questioned about the increased need for water and the problem of sewage treatment in those areas expecting to receive evacuees. It was calculated that the doubling of the population in the Home Counties would create a 33% increase in water consumption and this increase could be dealt with adequately within a 50 mile radius of London except in a few rural districts. Those areas with a particular need were able to be helped by a £1,000,000 grant for the provision of piped water and the subsequent sewage and drainage disposal.

People living in small reception areas with a great deal of local knowledge informed their local councils of any specific problems relating to water supply and disposal. The following letter was sent to the Clerk of the Dorset County Council on 17th February 1939 and is an indication of some of the localised problems faced by the evacuation planners.

```
Ashmore Rectory.
Salisbury.
Wilts.                                          17 Feb. 1939

Dear Sir,

Billeting and Water

A visit from the ARP visitor yesterday reminds me to recall to your
notice the irregularity of the water supply here. For at least 7 years
to my knowledge, there have been breakdowns in the water supply,
insufficient for necessary requirements, on average twice a year, of
periods varying from a few days to several weeks.

We have always been assured that it will not happen again but it always
has. The next breakdown is due about Easter if the weather is warm and
dry.

Such a lack of water would be much more serious still if Ashmore were
filled to capacity with persons evacuated from dangerous areas.

Keeping this in mind you will I daresay either arrange that Ashmore is
only moderately used for evacuated persons or that a special watch on
the hydrostat, especially washers, be maintained by a competent person,
or both. A reservoir is, I understand, not to be finished...'[30]
```

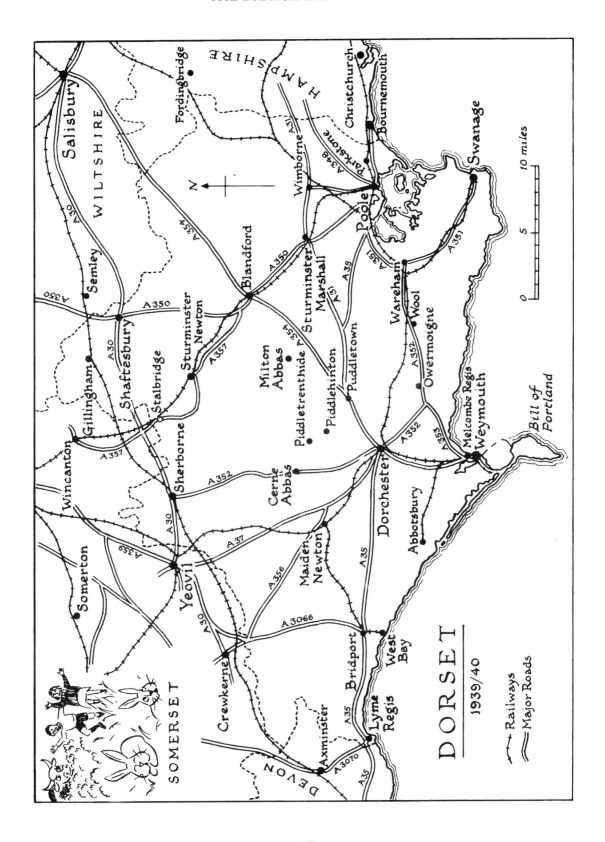

DORSET
1939/40

↗ Railways
〜 Major Roads

On 15th March 1939 a confidential letter was sent from the Clerk of the Dorset County Council to the Sherborne Reception area in North Dorset indicating the expected numbers of evacuees which could be supported in the area based on the amount of water available in the villages. The Rural District Council was asked to inform the Clerk if the numbers suggested had to be reduced in line with the availability of water.

The villages in Dorset designated as reception area were also divided into three categories. Those which could take evacuees immediately, Category 'A', those which would be considered a second line of billeting should the need arise 'B', and those which could only be used after work had been carried out on the water supply 'C'. When all the details had been collected the following list of the possible numbers of evacuees per village was drawn up:-

Parish	Persons Ordinarily Resident	Children	Helpers	Others	Total	Relatives	Poss. Military Billet	Exc. Empty Houses
C. Ashmore	151	20	11	8	39	18	-	208
C. Bourton	596	72	55	49	176	80	300	1,152
B. Buckhorn Weston	309	44	39	53	136	10	-	355
A. Cann	334	29	52	66	147	32	-	513
A. Compton	165	22	17	16	55	46	-	266
A. East Orchard	93	15	9	12	36	43	-	172
B. East Stour	324	35	23	29	87	37	-	448
A. Fontmell	428	31	66	38	135	78	-	641
B. Gillingham	2,950	420	234	256	910	377	3,000	7,237
A. Iwerne Minster	417	73	33	34	140	66	-	623
C. Kingston Magna	2,553	48	10	18	76	33	-	362
A. Margaret Marsh	38	4	4	10	18	3	-	59
A. Melbury Abbas	262	22	18	19	59	34	-	355
C. Metcombe	572	82	63	61	206	227	-	1,005
C. Stilton	135	14	8	14	36	18	-	189
A. Stour Provost	378	48	46	46	140	64	-	582
C. Sutton Waldron	127	30	12	10	52	21	-	200
A. Todber	99	11	4	2	17	12	-	128
A. West Orchard	60	11	4	8	23	11	-	94
C. West Stour	108	11	16	37	64	15	-	187
Total	7,797	1,042	724	786	2,552	1,225	3,300	1,4876

'Visitors' in Shaftesbury, Dorset collecting information for the Government survey in January 1939 had been asked to note down the Water Supply and Sanitary arrangements available in individual houses under the following codes:-

WATER SUPPLY
W.W. Where the water was obtained from a well.

P.W.C Where the water was obtained from piped water supply belonging to the council.
P.W.P Where the water was obtained from piped water supply privately owned.

SANITARY ACCOMMODATION
E.C. Where the sanitary accommodation was an earth closet.
W.C. Where the sanitary accommodation was a water closet.[31]

The water supply was also an important issue during the second evacuation in 1940. On 30th October 1940 the Town Clerk of Chipping Norton, Oxfordshire wrote to the County Clerk, F.G. Scott describing the difficulties experienced in the town with regard to the general water supply. The only answer he received was:-

> '...the County council were very well aware of the serious strain being put on all public services as a result of evacuation and trusted that some solution to the problems might be found before the winter'.[32]

As early as 1938 social problems relating to evacuation were on the agenda and, in the light of what was to transpire, discussions were very cursory and measures were ineffective. Wrigley believed that there would be different problems inherent in housing adults and children. In his view, bearing in mind 'normal' domestic arrangements, the latter could easily be fitted in, albeit at some inconvenience to the householder, but adults were a different matter. He envisaged family members being divided up among a number of reception households thus creating problems of transport, communication and mutual family support, and he was also concerned about men being taken from their work in London and having nothing to do in the reception areas. This was not to become a problem as these men, not called up for military service, tended to stay in the target areas to continue their jobs. Later, in 1940, special arrangements were to be made in some areas for those men with wives and children resident in the reception zones to visit their families for a weekend or longer periods; few men were actually evacuated.

Wrigley had in fact initiated a housing survey during September 1938 at the time of the Munich Crisis. On the 16th September he sent out a very urgent and confidential circular No. 1742 to the Clerks of all housing authorities in England and Wales asking them to provide him with the information about the amount of accommodation available in the country. For this purpose he defined such accommodation as 'in excess of a standard per house of 1 person per habitable room, a child for this purpose being treated as a whole unit'.[33] He gave the Clerks very little guidance beyond stipulating that the return must include all houses and that they would be able to use the material gathered during an Overcrowding Survey carried out under the Housing Act of 1935. Where this information was not available the Clerks were to make an estimate. He realised that the information would not necessarily be totally accurate but the purpose of the return was to provide a broad picture of accommodation in specific districts. Clerks in rural areas were to provide the information parish by parish. In other areas the total could be given as a single figure. The Clerks were given only three days to collect and collate the information and send their replies to the Clerk of the relevant County Council. By necessity this was an emergency and an interim measure dictated by external events. The information gathered would have been of limited value.

By far the most extensive domestic survey was carried out in January 1939 with the object of ascertaining not only a comprehensive picture of the amount of accommodation available for evacuation purposes, as it was reckoned that at least 90% of places would need to be provided in private houses, but also the numbers of householders who would be willing to take in evacuees. The survey, conducted by 100,000 interviewers, covered 5 million houses. Details of how it was to be conducted and the responsibilities of those collecting the information were sent to Local Authorities in early January 1939 by the Ministry of Health via a series of Circulars[34] and Memos and the general public had been informed of the survey and the reasons for it in a radio broadcast given by Walter Elliot on 6th January 1939.[35] The information in both the broadcast and the official documentation was carefully worded because of the element of secrecy inherent in the scheme but at the same time encouraging people to participate in the collection of data without creating any panic. The survey was to take account not only of the amount of accommodation but of its suitability, and of the circumstances of individual householders.

The Government asked the local authorities to concentrate primarily on finding accommodation suitable for children, whether school children who came in school units accompanied by their teachers, or younger children who came with their mothers or other adults.

The purpose of the survey was to collect detailed information relating to three specific areas of concern:-

a. The amount of surplus accommodation on the standard of one person per habitable room;

b. The amount of surplus to be found in houses which were suitable for the reception of evacuees;

c. The amount to be found in houses where the householder was willing to receive unaccompanied children or teachers.

The survey would also provide an opportunity to ascertain and consider the amount and suitability of supplementary provision which could be made in other ways. Members of the Welsh Nationalist Party complained strongly that Wales should not have been involved in the scheme at all on cultural and social grounds. On 13th January 1939. J. E. Jones, the Organising Secretary of the W.N.P. said in an article to the North Wales Chronicle:-

> *'The indiscriminate transfer of English people into Wales will place the Welsh Language and even the very existence of the Welsh nation, in jeopardy. The national welfare of the Welsh people should be a matter of first consideration by the authorities who are planning evacuation into the countryside. We, as Nationalists, demand that there should be no transfer of population into Wales that would endanger Welsh nationality. If England cannot make its emergency plans without imperilling the life of our little nation let England renounce war and grant us self-government'.[36]*

This viewpoint was held by the Welsh National Party throughout the war but was a minority one as the total membership could be numbered in hundreds. They issued a Memorandum in February 1939 expressing further concerns.[37]

The survey itself was a massive undertaking and Memo.Ev.1 outlined the need for the careful selection of volunteer interviewers who would take on the role with administrative efficiency.

These volunteers, called 'Visitors', while not being allowed to enter houses for the purpose of obtaining information would have to satisfy themselves that the home was suitable for children and that their presence would be willingly acceptable. It was suggested that the work of the volunteers would be made easier if the Local Authorities were to send a printed letter signed by the Chairman of the Council or the Mayor to all householders appealing for their co-operation with the collection of the data. The content of such a letter was to be left to the discretion of the Council.[38] Other suggestions of gaining the goodwill of the people included the use of the local clergy, women's organisations and other local societies to add their positive comments about the need for such a survey and their co-operation with it.

The Local Authorities were asked to appoint a responsible officer to oversee the conduct of the survey. The Council were then to appoint sufficient volunteer 'Visitors' to cover the whole district. The Minister of Health outlined the criteria for choosing such Visitors. Special regard was to be paid to their capacity for dealing in a kindly, tactful and confidential way with the householders, many of whom they would know socially or as neighbours. It was suggested that many people in local government employment such as health visitors, teachers, school attendance officers etc. would be ideally suited for such a role.[39] According to the Government Memo Ev2. Part IV. their task was to:-

```
'...enlist goodwill in time of peace forming a register of assistance
which every humane person would hasten to offer if war came.....The
compilation of the register of accommodation is therefore in the
interest of the householders, as it is only in this way that
difficulties and misfits can be avoided'.
```

How these words would come back to haunt those who sent children to very poor and sometimes dangerous billets!

In the Amlwch Urban District of Wales concern was expressed by the local Medical Officer about the appointment of lady Visitors.

'...my main object is to prevent you from too hurriedly appointing lady visitors who, while they may be admirable, say as members of a nursing committee on account of social prestige, may not only be quite incapable of summing up the possibilities of a household from billeting point of view, but partly in a small community like this, may be regarded as unwelcome intruders into the privacy of their neighbours, especially if their qualifications are inadequate'.[40]

After initial training each Visitor was to be provided with a form of authorisation and a record book for the purpose of making a report. These record books were printed by the Ministry and distributed to local authorities in order to save time and provide some semblance of continuity.

The Visitors function was to ascertain:-

a. The number of habitable rooms in each dwelling.

b. The number of persons ordinarily resident in the house and, by deduction from the number of habitable rooms, the number of persons who could be accommodated.

c. Where there was a surplus, whether the home conditions would be suitable for unaccompanied children.

d. Where the premises were deemed suitable, whether the householder was prepared in the event of an emergency to receive and care for unaccompanied children up to the maximum on the basis of the Government scheme. Where the householder was unwilling, or willing to take fewer numbers, the facts and reasons were to be noted.[41] The Visitors were to point out to householders that although the acceptance of children should be voluntary they might be required to take other persons.[42] There were of course those persons who although willing to take in evacuees were incapable of doing so. These would include:-

   • The aged and infirm living on their own who were barely able to look after themselves.

   • Houses where there was a confirmed invalid.

   • Persons living alone whose employment required them to be absent all day.

In such cases the Visitors were asked to explore the possibility of the householder taking in children if they were accompanied by an adult or some arrangement could be made for the child outside school hours.

Where householders were willing to receive evacuees but were unable to do so because of lack of appropriate beds and bedding the Visitors were asked to indicate this information on the form.[43]

The Visitors were also asked to report where householders had already made private arrangements to house relatives or others in the event of any emergency. The Government were concerned that 'private evacuation' did not get out of hand and that enough billets would be available for the official scheme.

The Visitors were given some interesting instructions on how to deal with farms in rural areas. In wartime the Government planned to increase home production. Therefore, under the Evacuation Scheme it wanted to ensure that there was enough flexibility to allow for the housing of additional labour on the farms but not to the extent that this impeded the farmer's normal activities. They were also to consider the degree of isolation especially where a farm, or other dwelling, was a distance of more than 2 miles away from a suitable school.[44]

Although these concerns were laudable, in practice many children were billeted on isolated hill and moorland farms in Wales and the West country and many teachers had problems keeping in contact with their charges.

The Local Authorities were asked to provide information about empty houses in their locality, especially large ones, which could house a substantial number of evacuees. Other suitable buildings were also to be listed. The exceptions included local schools, for obvious reasons, but school houses were to be treated as private houses and could be considered when housing any accompanying teachers and helpers. However, when the scheme was implemented many teachers were forgotten about and had to find their own accommodation.

The Government laid down detailed guidelines as to how the information was to be collected and recorded. As soon as returns came in from Visitors the officer in charge of the survey had to examine the book and tabulate the information on a form issued by the Ministry. He had to make a provisional entry as to the numbers of transferred persons to be accommodated in each house and identify in specific columns the numbers of unaccompanied children, accompanied children with mothers, helpers, teachers and others, including those who had made private arrangements. With the latter he was also asked to work out how much space for extra evacuees was available in the house when these numbers were taken into consideration. He was also given the task of deciding whether reasons given by householders for not having evacuees were valid and could therefore justify exemption. If he thought that exemption was unjustified he had to note the number of persons, other than unaccompanied children, who could be housed.

It is obvious that those householders who came into this category were not going to be too happy about having evacuees forced upon them. Inadvertently, by adopting this policy, the Local Officer, under instruction from the Government , was creating a situation where problems and ill-feeling would be inevitable within some billets from the very start of the scheme.

Considering the amount of work which had to be co-ordinated both at regional and local level and then carried out 'in the field', the time scale for the return of the forms was very tight. A summary of the Survey was to be sent to the Ministry of Health by the 28th February 1939 and a copy sent to the Clerk of the County Council by the same date.

Details of the progress of the operation within each Parish were kept centrally and a close check was made on the distribution and receipt of relevant information so that all parishes kept to the time allowed. The following is an extract from the progress document kept by the Clerk to the Dorset County Council. (RO represents Registration Office).[45]

Parish	Sent to RO	Return from RO	DO.OC Noted	Form B Noted	Sent to Visitor	Return From Visitor	Sent to RO Decision	Return with Decision	Passed for Reg	Registered
ASHMORE	21.1.39	21.1.39	NIL	27.1.39	1.2.39	20.2.39	20.2.39	21.2.39	21.2.39	24.2.39
BOURTON	23.1.39	4.2.39	9.2.39	9.2.39	9.2.39	16.2.39	16.2.39	18.2.39	21.2.39	24.2.39

The Visitors books and the completed register of the survey were to be kept in a suitable place. These were then to be distributed to those operating the Evacuation scheme should the need arise. The final summary, sent to the Ministry on Form E4, contained all the relevant information collected from all parishes and villages in the designated areas. The following is an extract from the final submission from Shaftesbury in Dorset.

Government Evacuation Scheme. Form E4
Ministry of Health Circular 1759
(Grand) Summary of Accommodation
County: Dorset Rural District of Shaftesbury
(In rural districts a separate return is required for each parish and a summary of the district as a whole.)

	Total No. habitable rooms	Total No. addit. persons who could be accom.	Provisional Declaration of LAs as to Nos. To be Accom					Additional Bedding Req. Mattresses		Blankets	
			Unacc. Child	Teachers	Others	Private	Total	D	S	D	S
Private Houses	11687	4387	1037	718	776	1076	3607	121	285	435	1020
Hotels /Boarding Houses	177	133	3	4	2	140	149	-	-	-	-
Empty Houses, Camps & Hostels	-	10	-	2	8	10	-	4	2	12	6
TOTAL	11864	4530	1040	724	786	1216	3766	125	287	435	1026
ASHMORE Private Houses Total	234	92	20	11	8	8	57	-	1	-	3
BOURTON Private Houses Total	900	332	70	55	49	80	256	6	7	33	63

Etc.....Etc. [46]

It is important to note that the figures in the columns headed Mattresses and Blankets were supposed to provide an indication of the shortfall of these articles within the reception areas. This was especially important when the villages were small and yet were required to accept significant numbers of evacuees. It was well known in the reception areas that in the country parishes farm labourers, often on low wages, did not keep a large stock of extra bedding. However, in practice the use made of these figures did not work out in the way everyone expected. In response to the form, the Ministry of Health had arranged to send 2,000 blankets and 800 mattresses to the Dorchester Rural District Council for dispersal as required. However, by the 31st August 1939 only 150 blankets had arrived and no mattresses. The Chief Billeting Officer sent a telegram to the LCC and the Ministry of Health suggesting that, under the circumstances, evacuees should each take their own blanket with them into the reception areas. He simply received a reply stating that this was not possible. There were also problems with basic furniture. Again many farm labourers were not able to purchase the extras needed to house evacuees. When this was pointed out at a Council meeting the Billeting Officer replied that there was nothing in the Government's billeting notices that allowed the local areas to purchase extra furniture and charge the expense to the scheme. All they could do was point out the problems and send a letter of protest, which he duly did.[47]

Considering the haste in collecting material mistakes were inevitable and on the 13th March 1939 the Minister of Health sent the following memo to all Local Authorities.[48]

```
'Not all Local Authorities completed forms E4 correctly. The column
'Others' was meant to be the number of persons, other than
unaccompanied children, who the Local Authority considered householders
might reasonably be required to receive after allowing for such factors
as extreme age or infirmity. Although most Local Authorities did,
others have only entered the numbers the householders volunteered to
receive'.
```

The Local Authorities were therefore asked to confirm their final numbers with the Ministry in London.

When all the returns were collated and analysed, the results showed that on a basis on one person per habitable room, there was enough space for 6,050,000 people.[49] However, not all this space could be used, for various reasons such as requisition by Government departments, empty houses already earmarked for use by companies leaving London, lack of water supplies and sewage disposal and proximity to target areas and military installations. Some Authorities expressed their concerns even before the Census had taken place as this entry in the Didcot Parish Council Minutes of 19th January 1939 indicates.

'In relation to the order that a census should be made to ascertain how many places would be available for evacuees within this Parish.

The Council still maintains that this area is not suitable for the people evacuated from other areas owing to the undoubted extra number of people such as extra depot workers, railway workers and military who would have to be accommodated in Didcot and, in the circumstances, this Council does not consider any good can be done if this census is taken'.[50]

The 'still' refers to a minute quoted in the Didcot Advertiser on 21st October 1938 when the Council had explained its reasons for not having evacuees.

'In the opinion of this Council it is undesirable that Didcot should be used for the billeting of children from other areas owing to the proximity of government stores and the railway junction'.[51]

The problem of who was entitled to accommodation was not one which went away easily. Even after the Evacuation scheme had been fully implemented some reception areas which were deemed to be in the front line of evacuee billeting were still having to compete with other agencies for billeting places. On 5th November 1940 the Dorchester Rural District Council discussed this question of billeting at some length. It had been intimated by the Ministry of Health that all suitable empty properties in their area could be requisitioned and now empty furnished houses could also be used for evacuees. The Chief Billeting Officer, Admiral Egerton, informed the Council that a Co-ordinating Officer was to be appointed to liaise between all parties competing for the same accommodation and maintain an overview of the situation. However, it was thought that although this would be useful for the Ministry, it would not help the Billeting Officer in the villages. [52]

Taking all the various reasons for not having evacuees into consideration the final billeting figure was reduced to 4,800,000.[53] This still remains a remarkable figure and shows a generally favourable response from householders to the Government's request for billets.

One very interesting feature to come out of this 1939 survey was that 18% of the available billeting accommodation in England and Wales, amounting to 1,100,000 rooms, had already been reserved by private evacuees.....seven months before war was declared! In Scotland the figure was 21% probably due to the number of people making temporary arrangements in Scotland.[54] Of the accommodation available in Hotels and Boarding Houses, amounting to 207,000 rooms, 8% had been privately reserved by February 1939.[55]

A number of 'domestic' places reserved were in the western and south-western counties of England but the most significant percentages were in Buckinghamshire, where although 116,245 places were available 27% were reserved by unofficial evacuees, West Sussex (26%), Berkshire, Oxfordshire and Herefordshire (25%), East Sussex (24%) and Dorset and Westmoreland (23%). Generally speaking the private reservations were highest in those counties with the largest proportion of large houses.[56] The importance of the flight to the West at the outbreak of war can be seen in the figures from Devon where private evacuees out-numbered official evacuees by 700%.

According to Titmuss it was not until he himself had produced his official analysis on evacuation figures in 1943 that the Government realised that although 1.5 million people had been evacuated under the official scheme, nearly 2 million had made private arrangements. [57] Householders who took in private evacuees were only entitled to billeting allowances if it could be proved that the children's parents were unable to pay an adequate payment direct to the householder.

Titmuss's accommodation analysis was based on his study of the movement of population between mid-summer 1939 and 29th September 1939 when National Registration was introduced. This registration excluded all service personnel and those crews on ships or actually berthed in ports and totalled 2.2% of the total population in the UK.

Six of the larger evacuated areas were used by Titmuss and the loss of population, including both official and private evacuation during the period was:-

Greater London 1,444,000

Liverpool, Bootle and County Boroughs 86,500

Birmingham, Smethwick and County Boroughs 50,000

Manchester, Salford and County Boroughs 123,700

Leeds County Borough 33,000

Sheffield County Borough 13,200

Total **1,750,400**

Titmuss based his findings on the fact that by 29th September it had been estimated that 22% of evacuees had returned home. Calculations were then made of the number of official evacuees still away from home. The difference between these figures and those indicating the loss of population represented the number of private evacuees who had not returned by 29th September.

Although the Government was concerned about these private reservations they could do very little about it beyond appealing to people not to take up this accommodation until the Government scheme had been fully implemented. Unless people went to stay with relatives it was generally the more well-off members of the community who could afford to take themselves into the country for an indeterminate amount of time.

> *'I spent the day at Tadworth, near Epsom Downs, with Pamela Foster who has evacuated her children there'.* [58]

Newspapers contained advertisements from hotels in safer areas where some people stayed for the duration of the war. One actress stopping at a luxury hotel in North Wales in 1940 found it contained:-

> *'...women whose sole occupation seemed to be backgammon, a lot of drinking and a little knitting for the troops'.* [59]

But by 1941 even journalists on the Times were becoming a little sarcastic when describing these hotel guests:-

> *'The hotels are filled with well-to-do refugees, who too often have fled from nothing. They sit and read and knit and eat and drink, and get no nearer the war than the news they read in the newspapers...'* [60]

Owners of Hotels, Boarding Houses and anyone else providing accommodation for payment had to inform the police. The following notice appeared in newspapers on the 1st September 1939.

POLICE NOTICE
ALIENS ORDER

NOTICE IS HEREBY GIVEN that under the Aliens Order, 1920, as now amended, ALL PERSONS PROVIDING LODGING OR SLEEPING ACCOMMODATION FOR REWARD shall cause a Registration Form AR-E to be completed by all persons, except members of H.M. Forces in UNIFORM, using their premises for lodging and sleeping accommodation.

Any hotel, boarding house, lodging house, apartment-house keeper etc. wishing to obtain further information on the subject is requested to apply to the nearest police station and an initial supply of the form AR-E will be given free.[61]

Some owners of the larger estates and houses took in 'paying guests' to help the upkeep:-

'In order to keep Uppark going, which with its silver plate, its large rooms and its periodical repairs is no light task, they (Meg Fetherstonhaugh and Admiral Sir Herbert Meade-Fetherstonhaugh) have taken in some paying guests for the duration of the war...The PGs (sic) included Lady Mary Glyn, daughter of the 8th Duke of Argyle and widow of the Bishop of Peterborough,...There was also A.Cecil, nephew of the Prime Minister Salisbury, Mr. Charles Mead, whose interests centred on hunting and shooting. Lastly there was Audrey Paget, daughter of Lord Queenborough'.[62]

The Final Anderson Committee Recommendations

'Each of the children, apart from their pathetic bundles, had a large carrier bag and in that there were iron rations. They included a tin of bully beef and a tin of pears. We were in the carriage for four and a half hours during which time the kids ate their pears and were sick'. [63]

On the 26th July 1938 the Anderson Committee report was completed and the Home Secretary presented the main principles to Parliament:-

a. That, except in so far as it may be necessary for military or other special reasons to require persons to leave some limited area, evacuation should be compulsory.

b. That, for the purpose of supporting the national war effort and supplying essential civilian needs, production in the large industrial towns must be maintained, but it is desirable to provide organised facilities for the evacuation of substantial numbers of people from certain industrial areas.

c. That arrangements for the reception of persons who become refugees should be mainly on the basis of accommodation in private houses under powers of compulsory billeting. These arrangements will require very detailed preparation in order to avoid unnecessary hardship either to the refugees or to the persons who receive them.

d. That the initial cost of evacuation arrangements should be borne by the Government, but that refugees who can afford to contribute towards the cost of their maintenance should be expected to do so.

e. That, to meet the needs of the parents who wish to send their children away, but cannot make their own arrangements, special arrangements should be made for school-children to move out in groups from their schools in the charge of their teachers'. [64]

Despite reaching this report stage very quickly, the Committee for Imperial Defence did not even consider the report until 15th September thus wasting almost two months of precious time. Sir Samuel Hoare, while agreeing that a detailed evacuation plan should be drawn up suggested that 'in existing conditions it was not desirable to publish the Anderson report'.[65] It was eventually released on 27th October 1938.

This release was ten months before the outbreak of war and one wonders why the general plans and views were not amended during that time to take into account the more social and human side of the evacuation scheme. It is very apparent that little, if any, notice was taken of the views and opinions of parents and indeed the children and other evacuee groups who were to take part in the process, basically because of the desire to keep the planning and implementation 'secret'. There was a certain dehumanising element inherent in the organisation. These recommendations came from a bureaucratic procedure which ostensibly ignored the feelings of the individuals concerned both in the designated reception and evacuated areas, relied on the unquestioning co-operation of teachers without whom the scheme would have collapsed before it was instigated, and thought fit to create a billeting scheme which required no expert supervision and monitoring from outside agencies both before and during the whole evacuation process. The latter responsibility was very much left to the teachers.

It is interesting to note that throughout its deliberations the Anderson Committee made no reference to or sought the advice from members of the community who had actually been involved in an evacuation scheme in Cambridge. Had the committee investigated this in more detail they may have gained some very useful pointers for dealing with the evacuation of children. In 1936 a group of 3,826 Basque children, refugees from the Spanish Civil War, had arrived in England. Twenty-nine of these were housed in a hostel and then billeted in private houses around the Cambridge area. This scheme provides an interesting comparison in many ways, not least the way in which local people raised money to support the hostel in Pampisford Vicarage, and the general supportive attitude they had towards their charges, at least in the beginning, a trait which is not so evident in the Government Scheme from 1939. Members of the local community got together to decorate the Vicarage before the arrival of the children. Jessie Stewart makes reference in her article 'Recuerdos' in the Cambridge Daily News in 1938 to the work done by the Secretaries in the Hostel and the fact that:-

> '...they had the support of a large committee including representatives of Societies, Clubs, Laboratories, Syndicates, Schools and Villages which had 'adopted', i.e. made themselves responsible for, the weekly payments for individual children'.

Although this type of benevolence would not have been possible on the large scale of the Government scheme there were other community led events which could have been replicated. Within the area businesses provided funds and there were entertainments which included 'sports, recreation and asking the children away for holidays, and fund raising events such as fetes, and house to house collections.

However, the group were not to escape the anti-evacuee campaigns that future migrants were to suffer in 1939. The national press criticised the presence of the children and although this was countered by letters from those involved with the Basques, it did have the unfortunate result of putting landlords off having evacuees in their houses, with excuses such as 'the property will deteriorate', 'the neighbourhood will object' being common.[66] Something to be witnessed again in 1939!

Endnotes

1   Comment made to James Roffey by a 10 year old pupil in a London school in September 1996.

2   PRO HO45/17636

3   Ministry of Health. Government Evacuation Scheme. Memo Ev.4 1939.Clause 72

4   Official Circular. May 1941. p137 col.2

5   Dorset County Council. Correspondence File.

6   B.Wicks. No Time to Wave Goodbye. Bloomsbury 1988. Reminiscence of Walter Leeds p 49

7   Titmuss op.cit. p103

8   ibid. p391

9   PRO HO45/17636

10   PRO HO45/17636

11   R.Calder. Carry on London. pub. Cape. p91

12   Angus Calder. The Myth of the Blitz. Cape. 1991. p47

13   PRO HO45/17636

14   PRO HO45/17636. See Appendix 5.

15   Tim Bryan. Great Western Railway at War. pub. Patrick Stephens Ltd. 1995. p13

16   ibid. pp10-11

17   ibid. p16

18   ibid. p13

19   Great Western Railway. Circular. London Evacuation Scheme No.2. Also Altered working of through passenger trains. August 1939. cited GWR. op cit.p11

20   GWR at War. op.cit. p16

21   James Roffey. Letter to Author. June 1998

22   J.Rawlins. Private papers.

23   'The Evacuee' Journal of the Evacuee Reunion Association. June 1996

24   ibid. December 1996

25   ibid. January 1997. Other ships were involved in both the evacuation of children from London via the Thames and soldiers from Dunkirk. The 'Royal Daffodil' brought 1600 Frenchmen from Dunkirk but was put out of action when a bomb went through three of her decks. The 'Queen of the Channel' brought 600 from the beaches but was hit the following day by a bomb which broke her back. The 'Royal Sovereign' collected 6,856 men over a period of a few days. The 'Crested Eagle' was hit by a bomb at the Dunkirk mole while tranferring 700 men from the 'Fenella' which had also just been hit. The 'Crested Eagle' caught fire and was abandoned on the beach. (the Evacuee. Feb.1997)

26   Ernest Brown. Minister of Health in a pamphlet called 'Government Evacuation Scheme'. (no date). Devon Record Office. Exeter.

27   PRO HO45/17636

28   ibid.

29   Titmuss. op. cit. p394

30   Dorset County Council. Correspondence File. County Record Office. Dorchester.

31   Letter to nominated 'Visitors' 20th January 1939. From J. Stace Macey. Clerk to Shaftesbury RDC.

32   Chipping Norton. Doc. 106. Oxfordshire Record Office.

33   Circular No. 1742

34   Circular No. 1759

35   For full text see Appendix 4.

36   North Wales Chronicle. p13. Cited in North Wales. A Case Study of a Reception Area under the Government Evacuation Scheme. 1939-45. Gillian Wallis. unpub thesis. p63 Flintshire Record Office

37   For full text see Appendix 18.

38   For a copy of the letter sent to the residents in Shaftesbury, Dorset. see Appendix 7.

39   Ministry of Health Circular 1759. 21st January 1939. para. 11

40   North Wales Chronicle. 10th February 1939. cited Wallis op.cit. p19

41   Paragraph 7. Ev. 1

42   Paragraph 8. Ev.1

43   Memo. Ev. 2 Paragraph 13.

44   Memo. Ev.2 Paragraph 11d. January 1939

45   Dorset County Council Minutes.

46   File E3 Shaftesbury RDC. Evacuation of Refugees. General File. 16th September 1939 to 16th March 1939. Dorset Record Office.

47   Dorset County Chronicle and Swanage Times. 7th September 1939.

48   Ministry of Health Memo. ref. 99043/101

49   PRO HO45/17636

50   Didcot Parish Council Minutes. 19th January 1939.

51   Didcot Parish Council Minute quoted in Didcot Advertiser, 21st October 1938.

52   Dorset County Chronicle and Swanage Times. 7th November 1940

53   Titmuss. op. cit. p37

54   ibid. p37 and p102

55   ibid. p38

56   ibid. p38 plus. Wartime Bucks. 1939-1945. Buckinghamshire Record Office. 1995

57   Titmuss. op. cit. p102

58   John Colville. Fringes of Power. Downing Street Diaries. 1939-55.. Hodder and Stoughton 1985. 28th January 1940. p75

59   Norah Bearing. A Friendly Hearth. pub. Cape 1946 p11. cited A. Calder. The People's War. Panther 1971. p42

60   The Times. 10th January 1941

61   Dorset County Chronicle and Swanage Times. 1st September 1939.

62   Colville. op.cit. Thursday 15th February. 1940. p86

63   Ben Wicks. No Time to Wave Goodbye. Bloomsbury. 1990. Reminiscence of a teacher.

64   House of Commons Debate. 28th July 1938. Vol. 338. col. 3283. cited Titmuss. op.cit.p28

65   ibid. p30

66   Jessie Stewart. 'Recuerdos'. Cambridge Daily News. p23. The original intention had been to repatriate the Basque children when the situation in Spain improved. However, the alternative was adoption in English homes and this was the course the Committee took because of lack of food and employment in Spain at this time made it a better option. Therefore the 29 children in the Cambridge area left the Hostel and stayed with foster parents in various parts of the country.

The Local Experience

'It was a problem for me to move from a working class school into an upper class one...In Battersea there was no awareness that there was something on the other side of the fence because all the London children were the same. I had to have elocution lessons when I went to Bromley because I was South London...'ain't ya'and all that'.[1]

The Local Experience

In the months leading up to the war Councils at County, District and Rural level were planning what to do in their areas. As an example the official memorandum relating to the billeting of children was submitted to the Dorchester Rural District Council. It stated that there would be no evacuation rehearsal and that the railway company would make the entire arrangements for the transport of evacuees from London to the local detraining stations, in this case Dorchester. The Council's responsibility would be to undertake the reception and it was expected that 'children would be marched as quickly as possible to a central place where sanitation, first aid facilities and rough sleeping accommodation, in case trains were delayed, would be available. From here they would be dispersed to outlying villages. The Ministry of Transport would provide sufficient vehicles to transport the children to a central 'de-bussing' station in each village. The Rural District Council would take charge of the children at each of these points.[2]

During the week immediately before the Evacuation scheme was implemented, hosts in some of the designated reception areas were given an indication of their responsibilities and the amount of money they would receive as well as how they could claim it. In Weymouth a loud speaker van was organised to tour the streets telling hosts of the time their charges were arriving and also any other important details they should know![3] They were expected to 'control and care for evacuees as if they were their own children and should any difficulty arise they were to inform the Billeting Officer'.[4] The payment of 10/6 per week for the first child and 8/6 for the subsequent children was to cover 'full board and all the care that would be given to a child in their own home'.[5] The payments were not meant to cover the cost of clothes or medical expenses, which hosts were under no obligation to meet. Payments were to be made weekly , in advance, at the local Post Office on a form issued by the Billeting Officer. Although as the following advertisement suggests not all payments were made at the Post Office.

BILLETING PAY DAYS

Payments to persons who have received evacuated children and mothers in the Wareham and Purbeck area are made as follows:-

Wareham. 17, West St.	Wednesdays. 9 - 1 and 2 - 5
Winfrith. Village Hall.	Tuesdays. 9 - 12.30
West Lulworth. Conservative Rooms.	Tuesdays. 2 - 5
Bere Regis. Women's Institute.	Wednesdays. 2 - 5
Morden. Village Hall.	Wednesdays. 9.30 - 12.30
Corfe Castle. Room at Mrs Thomas's, West St.	Mondays. 9.30 - 12.30
Steeple. Blackmanston Farm.	Mondays. 2 - 4.'[6]

A teacher evacuated with his school from Liverpool described how some hosts took on the extra financial burden of providing evacuees with extra clothes and shoes despite not having to do so.

'The billeting money they, the foster parents, drew from the Post Office each week would barely cover the cost of a child's board and lodging. It has never been generally known what personal sacrifices were made by the humble cottagers. They willingly accepted responsibility for an evacuee, provided it with food and a bed and then saved every spare penny to buy it something new to wear for Chapel on Sunday. In Wales I have soon learnt that one must go to Chapel suitably attired. This was one reason, maybe the main reason, why the villagers wanted their evacuees to look respectable on one day, at least, during the week'.[7]

They were also asked to look out for those children suffering from home-sickness and to report cases when they were particularly concerned. Although hosts were informed that the children would arrive with rations to last them for 48 hours they were advised to buy and store an additional week's requirements of staple foods.[8]

When all the plans had been made and the necessary advice given, 'Pied Piper' the code name given to the implementation of the September evacuation, became active.[9]

By Friday 1st September 1939 all the transport arrangements required to move an estimated 4 million evacuees from vulnerable areas were in place.

On the same day thousands of hospital patients were moved to safer areas or sent home to make space for hospital beds; 2,200 doctors and 15,000 nurses were posted to casualty hospitals. Private vehicles, coaches and trucks were sent as auxiliary ambulances to various areas of the country and thirty civilian casualty trains were sent to specific locations.[10]

The day before the London Passenger Transport Board announced:-

'From about 9 a.m. tomorrow until 6 the scheme for evacuating school children and others under Government direction will begin.

Both rail and road services for ordinary passengers will be severely curtailed between these hours for the next three to four days....

As necessary stations will be closed altogether to traffic other than official evacuation traffic.

It is felt that the public will co-operate so that the organisation may run smoothly. They are advised that they should travel only if compelled.

From approximately 7 o'clock tonight London Transport Green Line coach services will be curtailed or withdrawn'.[11]

All advertised L.M.S railway excursions were cancelled throughout the weekend!! [12]

Some newspaper headlines described the extent of the organisation and planning in biblical terms:-

GREATEST EVACUATION IN HISTORY HAS BEGUN

EXODUS OF THE BIBLE DWARFED; THREE MILLION PEOPLE ON THE MOVE

EVEN THE EXODUS OF THE BIBLE...THE FLIGHT OF THE ISRAELITES FROM EGYPT....IS DWARFED INTO INSIGNIFICANCE [13]

By mid-September 1939 the plans made specifically for London were adapted and extended beyond the Capital to other areas regarded as potential targets. By the end of September a total of 1,500,000 people were officially evacuated, 35% of those eligible from the LCC, 66% of those from Merseyside, 33% from Portsmouth and Southampton and 20% from Coventry.

These variations may be explained by the amount and intensity of poverty or hardship within particular evacuated areas. Parents with few material possessions and perhaps ill-educated may have been more easily persuaded by local government officials, or were simply more compliant and followed instructions issued by the local Authorities to evacuate. They might also have been persuaded by the fact that the Government implied that they would look after all their needs if they left home. It was also unlikely that families in poor areas were able to make their own arrangements to travel to safety and the figures seen here are an indication of only those in the scheme who could not evacuate themselves. It is also worth remembering that some of those eligible did not want to go. It is unfortunate that the figures for this group of people are not available. If they were, they would provide an interesting indication of the acceptance of the scheme by the general population at whom it was aimed.

To be absolutely successful the scheme demanded a high degree of parental confidence in the efficiency of Government arrangements. Asking parents to send children away for an indefinite period, to an unknown destination and to the care of strangers was not a decision that would be taken lightly. It also meant that the local preparations in the reception areas had to be equally efficient and required a great deal of co-operation between the agencies involved.

Travis Crosby has suggested that the authorities in areas such as Manchester, where the planning was carried out very effectively, created a confidence which led to an overall success rate of 70% of those eligible for evacuation, whereas areas inadequately prepared, fraught with bureaucratic red-tape or remote from the people were less successful.[14] Other areas were simply handicapped by lack of time.

There were also other factors which dissuaded families from sending their children away. Some older children were needed at home to look after younger siblings while the mother was out at work. Some were ill and could not travel. Some were caught up in a certain amount of family fatalism:-

> *'If one of us is going to die, it would be better if we all died together'.* [15]

This fatalism is often referred to by evacuees when interviewed. Joan Faulkner, now of Englefield Green, Surrey, stated that:-

> *'My mother, in her wisdom, decided that if we were going to die then we should die together as a family. That meant all the aunts and cousins as well'.* [16]

But this fatalism was not confined to the beginning of the war and in some cases later decisions to remove evacuees because of the bombing created a conflict of interests between family and evacuee. Lyn Mendlson recalls that while living in Weston-Super-Mare in 1941 the town was bombed on many occasions and her parents decided to take her back to London 'to die together'. However, she did not want to go. She lived with a kind family, loved the sea and walking along the causeway to Anchor Head. The train line to Paddington went along the bottom of the garden and she remembers leaning out of the window waving and sobbing and taking the last look at a garden which she had been allowed to cultivate. This desire to stay made her feel very guilty at the time. (Even now when she regularly visits Weston she always looks out of the train window at the garden.) [17]

The evacuation plans did not apply to the cities of Bristol, Nottingham, South Wales or Plymouth. These were designated by the Government as 'Neutral Evacuation Areas' and it was difficult to get children out of these areas unless the parents had the money to do so.[18] The Welsh Nationalist Party, in a memorandum issued in February 1939, protested against the classification for South Wales stating that the increased industrial activities in the seaport towns and dense industrial districts would make the area an important military objective in a time of war. They also stated that children should be evacuated from these areas with first rights to be moved to the Welsh rural areas.[19] The Nottingham City Council also strongly objected to this classification but nothing is available to indicate the views of Plymouth, even though there had been a definite change in policy. On 22nd December 1938 a confidential report which had been sent to the Lord Privy Seal by a Ministry of Health Committee containing a list of 'Areas from which evacuation is desirable' included Plymouth, and local areas such as Stonehouse and Devonport. A map also clearly indicated the city as an area of evacuation. But within ten days there had been a dramatic change in policy and Plymouth found itself classified as a neutral area, not listed for either evacuation or reception. This change was to have serious unforeseen consequences on Plymouth.[20] Had the original designation stood the area around Plymouth would have avoided the influx of evacuees from other parts of the country. As it was, the area became saturated with evacuees. Again there was the additional problem of those who could afford to do so evacuating themselves to the area and taking up accommodation initially reserved for official evacuees. This problem was replicated all over the country where private evacuees took over the accommodation designated for the official scheme and it put a great deal of pressure on the local planning and support services. One reason for this 'privatisation' was that some hosts thought that the private evacuees were a better sort of person and were therefore willing to take them in preference to the official evacuees.

Education

'Not the least of the problems placed on the shoulders of the education authorities is the provision of accommodation for children in rural areas. In one case there is a complete school divided among four villages, while in another only half the school came to the Dorset area and the other half went to Somerset'. [21]

Many rural areas 'did their bit' and accepted their fair share of official evacuees. However, by doing so they put the local administrative infrastructure under some considerable pressure, especially with regard to education. The local community of Purley (on-Thames) became a reception area for two distinct groups of people, those who had been officially evacuated and those who owned plots of land along the bank of the river and came to live there for the duration of the war. The former group of 50 children and accompanying mothers came from Islington and Holloway and were found billets within the community. The latter group brought with them a further 100 children of school age. Together this number of evacuee children put considerable pressure on the school, so much so that a second teacher had to be appointed to cope with the pressure. Some of these pupils left during the 'phoney war' period but when the bombing of London began in 1940 the Rural District Council of Bradfield was asked to accommodate 700 children of whom 20 went to Purley. [22]

The entries in the school log book of Bradfield Primary School, situated in a small rural village in Berkshire, which usually had a constant 110 pupils on the school roll, provide a fair indication of the difficulties faced by Headteachers:-

Oct.4th 1939. On instructions from the LEA the children evacuated from the LCC were admitted to school this morning. 57 children were admitted bringing the number on roll up to 206. There is insufficient seating for all the children and some are sitting three to a dual desk.

This had been the second group of evacuees to arrive at the school. The first children had been privately evacuated.

Nov. 1st 1939. Received from the LCC 25 tables and 50 chairs for the use of the evacuees'.

Dec. 1st 1939. Several of the evacuated children have returned to London.

June 17th 1940. Admitted 11 further evacuated children, mostly from the Page Green school in Tottenham. Mrs Murpitt, a teacher, accompanied them and commenced duties in the school.

Oct. 11th 1940. 184 children have been admitted since September 22nd 1939 of whom 82 have left. These consisted mainly of evacuated children'. [23]

At least this village had sufficient, albeit cramped, accommodation. The lack of communication between central and local government resulted in a great deal of confusion as regards reception areas with suitable education facilities for evacuees. It is also apparent that some Local Education

Authorities were not entirely blameless and a lack of local knowledge did not help the situation. For example the West Sussex authority allocated 50 evacuated children to the village of Nutborne which had school facilities for only the 20 children already taught there by one teacher. 140 children were sent to Thakeham which also had a resident school population of only 20, and 90 were allocated to Coldwaltham which had a tiny two room school with a staff of two who taught everyone between the ages of 5-14![24] These teachers would have been overwhelmed had not two staff come with the evacuees. There were also difficulties in some parts of North Wales where children from Liverpool were sent to schools which had their lessons in Welsh.[25]

Despite the fears of the WNP that situations such as this would harm Welsh nationalism many Liverpool children learnt Welsh very quickly and some even competed successfully in local Eisteddfods.[26] When the second group of evacuees arrived in Caernarfon in 1940 they were even called derogatory names in Welsh by those who had been evacuated in September 1939! [27]

The problems inherent in dealing with this ever changing migrant child population in village schools were so serious that in 1940 the Ministry of Information made a ten-minute propaganda film called 'The Village School' [28] which illustrated some of the problems that teachers, and indeed school buildings, faced during the time of evacuation. It was released in 1941. However, as in similar films portraying a positive message, the producer was intent on showing that, despite the vagaries of the war and the pressures put on the local community and the school, everything was working out well, everybody was coping and any problem could be easily overcome. This was not always the case and there are many examples of the system breaking down under pressure of numbers and conflict of personalities where school communities of sometimes totally different social experiential backgrounds, were trying to co-exist.

The film was in fact pure propaganda and the content had been arranged to suit the needs of the producers who had obviously been given the brief to put across as many positive aspects of the school as possible in nine minutes. In the school log book of the Ashley Green Church of England Primary School where the film was made, there are three significant entries which prove that the film was actually made in the school holidays and the content matter of the film had been pre-planned.

> *July 5th 1940. End of Summer term.*

> *July 29th 1940. For the Ministry of Information and by kind permission of the Board of Education, the Strand Film Company of London this morning began to make a film of the work done in this school. Various and considerable changes had to be made to the school time-table.*

> *August 9th 1940. The children's part of the film is now completed and the school is closed for a fortnights holiday.[29]*

The school was closed on the 16th June 1941 so that the pupils could see the finished film. However, although this film was made for propaganda purposes, it has to be said that the teacher in the film, Mrs James, Headteacher of the Ashley Green C.of E. School in Buckinghamshire, who was depicted as overcoming all the problems she was confronted with, both educationally and socially, was not entirely a figment of the film maker's imagination. Mrs James ran a two-roomed village school and research into the school registers for the years 1939-45 reveals that she received evacuees from 29 different schools. Although some of them stayed only for a few days they nonetheless put a great deal of pressure onto Mrs James' workload and her management of the school. She did all the teaching herself with the exception of one other helper who came into the school to work with the infants.[30]

Other teachers fought tirelessly in order to provide any semblance of education for their charges. Bill Granger recalled that having been evacuated from Walthamstowe with his school he started off using a wooden shed at the bottom of someone's garden, before being appointed Headteacher of the local village school while the incumbent was on extended leave. Like Mrs James, Bill divided the school into three groups, seniors, juniors and infants, but unlike Mrs James he was only afforded the luxury of one classroom where all groups had to be taught at the same time.[31]

These were similar problems with school buildings and accommodation throughout the war. In June Mr G.T. Giles, President of the National Union of Teachers visited Dorset as part of a fact finding tour. He is quoted as saying that:-

> '...he had learnt more about conditions within the teaching service than he had learnt for years.....However work was done in schools by only two teachers with children of varying ages was beyond his understanding and yet good work was being done'.

He went on to say that during his trip he had visited about 40 schools in the county. He had seen some of the new senior council schools, which he admired, but of the remainder, the school buildings, except for a few 'were now only fit for the scrap heap'.... He had seen schools with no water laid on and water closets were a rarity. Many of the outsides of the buildings were presentable but the insides were never designed for schools as we should know them today.

> 'Here is picturesque poverty. Dorset has the children and the teachers but money is not being spent on the buildings'. [32]

It was not only schools evacuated to Dorset which faced these problems. The following account from a teacher describes the problems he faced when wishing to move into larger accommodation. He and his school had been evacuated to a small village in Berkshire where, the existing village school buildings, although cramped, had been adequate. When extra families arrived it was necessary to move to bigger premises and he sought the permission of the local Rector to move into the semi-derelict, wooden, church hall at the opposite end of the village to the school. It was not until the spring of 1940 that the evacuees were able to move and one afternoon the older boys carried the desks along the main street followed by the juniors carrying books and chairs. Over the weekend the pupils cut down the hedges, tidied the paths, put up temporary notice boards and hung pictures and maps on the wall to make them a little more presentable. On the Monday the teacher

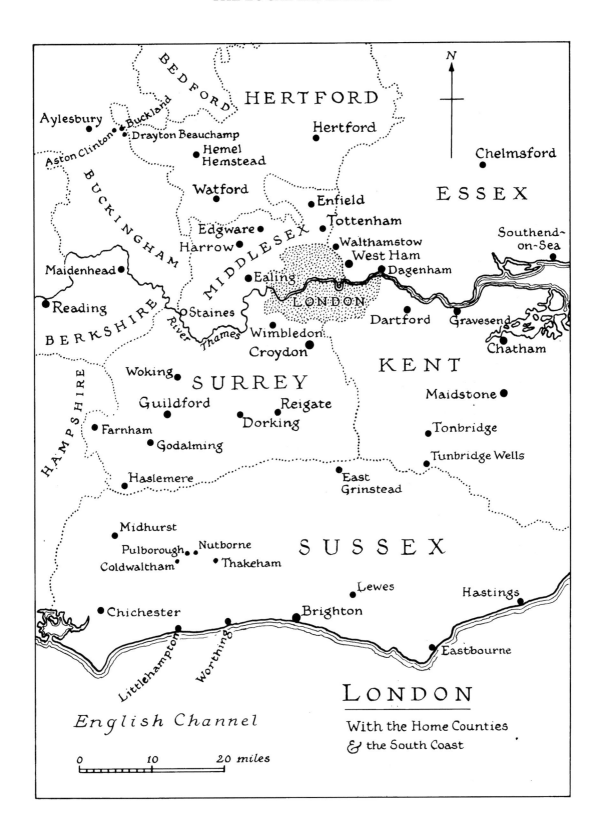

LONDON

With the Home Counties
& the South Coast

sat the class according to size....smallest at the front, largest at the back. The rest is worth describing in his own words:-

> *"I gave the order to stand, with the idea of marking the occasion of the move with a little ceremony.*
>
> *'Well school,' I began, ' here we are in our new home...'*
>
> *Suddenly the floor began gently to subside and rows of children sank before my eyes like little ships going down. A few books slid off desks and one or two children sat down, standing up quickly again as though they had done something wrong; the smaller ones clung to their desks and everyone stood a little lopsidedly, but they were calm and left it to the stupidest senior to state the obvious.*
>
> *'Please sir,' he said, ' the floor's guv away.'*
>
> *So we all went home."* [33]

Other evacuees tell of similar situations. For example, the Peckham Central Girls School, which had strict rules about the wearing of uniforms, turned up for their first day of schooling in the old Corn Exchange in Pulborough to find that everything was covered in dust, the floor was rotting and there was little furniture suitable for a temporary school. It was not long before the impeccable uniforms became dusty and dirty as the girls were expected to sort out the furniture and clean up the building.[34]

Many evacuated schools were simply imposed on existing classes and classrooms in the reception areas and even LEAs complained that they received no information directly from the Boards of Education either as to the numbers of teachers and pupils expected or the particular schools where they were coming from. This lack of information led to some evacuated schools and existing classes being 'farmed out' to other establishments in order to find space in which to work.

Entries from school log books in Berkshire, such as these...

> *'Feb.26th ...classes in the Junior Department are still receiving instructions in the afternoon sessions at Park Institute (a local church hall), Anderson Baptist Chapel and the Primitive Methodist Chapel'.*
>
> *'March 4th...The remaining London schools:- All Saints, St. Peter's Vauxhall, St. Joseph's RC and Lawn Lane Infants, Vauxhall are to be accommodated at St. Bartholomew's and Anderson Baptist Hall'.* [35]

are commonplace in many school log books of the period.

In some areas there was a certain amount of resentment that evacuees had taken over local facilities. In Pulborough the recently built village hall, the centre of all village activities, was turned into a school. The necessary equipment was sent to the area from Peckham and the rooms changed their purpose. The projection room became the typing class, the room beneath the stage was used for current affairs and had pictures of German and British aircraft plus propaganda posters stuck to the walls. The main hall was used by eight different classes. Trestle tables were formed into a square with a blackboard and easel placed in the middle and lessons on different subjects were delivered in adjacent 'squares' which made it very difficult for children to concentrate.[36]

Some evacuees were not afforded the luxury of remaining in one building. Sylvia Rose (née Eden) recalls that as a member of the Walworth Central Girls School evacuated to Sturminster Newton in Dorset she had her lessons all over the town:-

> *'Our schooling was exactly the same as in London but we had to walk to different parts of the town for our lessons. We used to go to the Senior School for our cookery lessons where there was a domestic science room. Other lessons were in the school room of the Wesleyan Chapel....and the Bridge Chapel room. Games lessons were on the recreation ground and there were other lessons in the Royal British Legion Comrades Hut. This is also where we had our communal dinners'.* [37]

It was after some negotiation that the school was eventually housed under the one roof at the Tithe Barn.

Even some London schools which had previously been evacuated in 1939 to their own premises found they were imposed upon by newly evacuated schools without notice. The following extract comes from the school log book of the Commercial Street London County Council School which had been evacuated to Aston Clinton .... then Anthony Hall .... then to very small premises in Buckland:-

> *'25th September 1940. Miss B.M.K. Knight of Hillbrook Demonstration Infants School, came this afternoon with 14 London school children to join our school. I was given no official notice of this event. They had been evacuated on the 21st September to Drayton Beauchamp and then to us. They come chiefly from Battersea and Tooting. This brings the total number on roll to 38'.* [38]

In one instance the pressure on accommodation was so great that there was obviously nowhere for the children to go at all and their classroom during the day became their sleeping quarters at night as his comment from the minutes of the Didcot Parish Council indicates:-

> *'It is unfair for classrooms to be used as classrooms during the daytime and as a common lodging house at nightfall....I am anxious that the school should not cease to be used as a school but, if no accommodation can be found then it was their duty to insist the school should be closed as a school'.* [39]

This problem of dispersal was not restricted to those evacuated to urban areas. Some schools found themselves billeted in a number of small villages covering many miles. The pupils of one school evacuated to Norfolk were spread over an area of 400 square miles.[40]

In some areas the pressure on buildings and existing classes resulted in the removal of the evacuee children to other premises. In his paper entitled 'The Shipton Saga' John Rawlins highlights a situation which stands as an example of how things could break down. Using evidence from log books and personal diaries one can trace the problems which this particular school, the Upton Cross Junior from West Ham, faced during the first few months of the war. The party of 63 children arrived in early September with two teachers and five assistants and started their lessons in the local Shipton School on the 13th using a double shift system 9.00 -1.00 for the local children and 1.30 - 4.00 for the West Ham pupils. Within two days alternative accommodation had been found at the YMCA Red Triangle Hut which meant that the school buildings could be used for written work and the hut for any oral work.

On the 18th September the Headmaster had secured the use of the local Beaconsfield Hall for the children of Upton Cross in order to cut down on transfers between other buildings. Within ten days the Head of the local school had received a letter from the County accusing him of refusing to allow the Upton Cross children to use his school. The answer to which was quite simply that this had not been the case and the new arrangements were much more convenient. The local school Inspector asked whether or not it would be possible to pool accommodation and on 2nd October it was decided that the School and Hut would be used alternatively, morning and afternoon, with opposite arrangements every week. On the 4th October the schools were told that the Beaconsfield Hall had been taken over by the LEA because the lighting and ventilation in the Red Triangle Hut was considered to be poor. The situation became even more confusing when on 23rd October the Headteacher received a letter from the LEA stating that the Red Triangle Hut and Beaconsfield Hall had been commandeered by the military, the former for canteen purposes,[41] and all the children now had to be accommodated in the existing school buildings. This resulted in a great deal of reorganisation in terms of pupils, personnel and equipment. This situation continued until January 1940 when an entry in the log-book states simply:-

> *'The Upton Cross children assembled here this morning in order to be conveyed to Launton Village school near Bicester. They took all their registers of attendance with them and each was supplied with pencils and stationery......The reason given for the move was the unsuitable and unsanitary conditions pertaining to this old building....'* [42]

This whole saga raises some important questions. Firstly, if the reason for moving the children from the school was because of unsuitable and unsanitary conditions why was this decision made in January 1940 and not before. And, more importantly, why were the local children expected to put up with these conditions. Presumably they had had to suffer them long before the arrival of the Upton Cross pupils and they had to continue to do so. According to the log-book it was not until April 1941 that there was an inspection to investigate the re-siting of new 'offices' and these were not built until fourteen months later. It is odd that the evacuee children were removed for this reason when other village schools in the area had bucket toilets and one, Idbury, had no piped water at all until 1944.

Secondly, why was the Red Triangle Hut considered suitable for canteen purposes but not for education? Some children were being taught in a Church room in nearby Milton without any toilet facilities at all and worse lighting and ventilation than the YMCA.

Thirdly, log-book entries for Launton school would suggest that there were no problems at this school. Could this whole scenario simply have been a clash of personalities between the resident and visiting head teachers and the unsanitary conditions was simply a viable excuse?

Situations such as these were not uncommon and resulted in a breakdown in school organisation and communications which caused a great deal of confusion when school children who were to return home in the official scheme of 1945 could not be located.[43]

Some school administrators and Headteachers, having made the effort to find out about their host areas for planning reasons, were even given incorrect information:-

```
Whitehorse Manor School
Senior Boys School
Thornton Heath
Surrey.

June 11th 1940

Dear Sir,

I am the leader of a party of evacuees from Croydon (N1 and N2) which
should entrain here for Exeter next Tuesday and arrive somewhere in the
neighbourhood of 6 o'clock. I fully appreciate how busy you are
preparing for our invasion but it would help me considerably if you
could find time to send me a post card just to intimate to me the
nature of the district we are likely to reside in for the next part of
our earthly pilgrimage. If you simply write on the enclosed card
'urban' , 'semi-urban', 'rural' or 'coastal' the information will be
most helpful in planning the necessary limited clothing each child must
bring.

Yours faithfully

Sam. J. Cook.
```

Although the school was evacuated to the city centre the answer sent back was rural! [44]

Other evacuated schools had to find their own accommodation which in itself created problems. The trials and tribulations of one such teacher can be found in the diaries of Eric Gadd who was a teacher in Southampton. The diary entries highlight the problems he faced when attempting to establish a part-time school for evacuees.

'June 30th 1940

During the past month I have been conducting a private war with the County Education Officer on a matter which I regard as of vital importance, the grave risks which are being run by the children attending the Gore Road Junior School there. I have put forward these points:-

1. The building is an ex-army hut, a relic of the last war. Having been in use continuously for about twenty years, it is in a dilapidated condition.

2. It is constructed entirely of wood, with the exception of the roof; the walls are of thin matchboarding and weatherboard of a combined thickness of about one inch and in no way reinforced.

3. The lighting system is of gas.

4. The roof is low, solid and heavy.

5. The building is less than 400 yards from the main Southern railway line.

Leaving aside the effect of a direct hit, this building would be vulnerable even to the effect of a bomb dropped anywhere within half a mile, while an incendiary could have unthinkable results'. [45]

Despite his protestations Gadd was only able to convince the authorities to build air-raid shelters in the corner of the playground.

Gadd was to have problems later with his evacuees as well as the local authorities as his diary entry for the 3rd January 1941, concerning some newly arrived evacuees, indicates:-

'Within a few hours of their arrival a number of the younger members of the party broke into the fowlhouse and killed the fowls, which were consumed by some of the Furzie Close (address of the hostel) guests. The police were called in.

- Contrary to instructions their people light fires in the wards and cook what they fancy there.

- Most of the men come in drunk each night. At Christmas the doctor was called in to deal with a number of boys of 12 and 13 who had been sick. He pronounced them drunk'. [46]

Some schools were not even afforded air-raid protection. In May 1940 the Board of Education sent out a circular which advised that not all schools in rural areas need be provided with shelters in the same way as urban schools. Instead the pupils were to be instructed in how to take shelter within the school if bombs were falling in the area. They were to practise lying on the floor and keeping away from windows and they were to be told that under no circumstances should they leave the school buildings and go into the open !! [47]

The safety of some schools was even affected by the personal decisions of local figures. In 1940 the Rector of Purley-on-Thames rigorously opposed the suggestion made by local ratepayers, that a shelter should be provided for the pupils of the Primary school. He claimed that because the village had been declared a reception area it was obviously considered safe from attack and a shelter would be a waste of money. He went on to say that he had called in experts to inspect the arrangements made at the school and they were found to be satisfactory. On the 16th July 1940 the Parish Council agreed with the Rector but did supply five stirrup pumps [48] and in April 1941 the County Council agreed to spend £307 on a shelter in nearby Pangbourne to accommodate 110 people. [49]

The Rector was not alone in his belief that schools did not need shelters. At the Berkshire County Council Meeting on 29th September 1939 the General purposes Sub-Committee reported:-

'Para. 1 subsection a. As a general principle, children should be kept under cover in school buildings during an air raid. In each school therefore a room, or rooms, should be set apart in which, when an air-raid warning has been given, children should be congregated under the supervision of their teachers. The rooms selected for the purpose should be those in which the walls are of substantial thickness and where the amount of window space is relatively small. In such rooms, all windows should be protected by half inch wire mesh netting and, if the walls are not of sufficient thickness, they should be strengthened to a height of about 3 feet 6 inches with suitable material.

Subsection b. In accordance with the general policy outlined in the preceding paragraph it was not considered expedient to provide outside trenches or shelters but, in certain schools additional protective measures might be necessary in view of the large amount of window space which exists and also because of the light type of construction which is to be found in some schools'.[50]

The same policy was apparent in Dorset. On 7th September 1939 the Weymouth Town Council agreed that in the event of an air raid those children who lived nearby could go home. But protection in the form of trenches and revetments would be provided for those who could not get home! This decision was based on parents' wishes. The Town Clerk stated that 799 held the view that children should be kept at school, 963 wanted them sent home immediately and 1,400 wanted them to remain in school until collected.[51] Also at a meeting of Dorset's Education Committee in July 1940, the Chairman, Councillor Le Berton, stated that a number of petitions had been received asking for covered trenches to be provided for schools in rural areas. But in his opinion he felt that such people were under a misapprehension. He suggested that there was not the same amount of danger in remote villages as in areas which were defended by anti-aircraft guns where there was also a danger of falling shrapnel. He thought it not practical to provide cement coverings in all rural districts because the material could not be obtained and he had been told, and agreed, that there was no danger in rural areas from shrapnel. He went on to say that the whole scheme would cost £40,000 and he did not think that the ARP committee would think it necessary or desirable. This committee followed the instructions detailed in the Circular; in the event of a bomb dropping in the vicinity the children were to lie under their desks.[52]

Provision for expenditure on items such as sandbags and wire netting for schools was made in the Berkshire Education Committee accounts of 1939:-

'Item 4. Air Raid Precautions: The Committee recommend that the undermentioned expenditure be approved for the protection of schools on the lines indicated previously.

```
Elementary Schools: Sandbagging, Wire Netting etc. and obscuration of
lights. £1500

Maintained and Aided Schools for wire netting and obscuration of
lights. £650'.⁵³
```

Expenditure, rather than safety seemed to be the prime concern of some councils. Complaints were made at the Dorchester Town Council meeting on the 13th February 1940 that there were no air-raid shelters in the town and that something should be done about it. An Alderman, Mr Rossiter, asked that as there was nowhere that the town's children or evacuees could go in the event of a raid was it possible to bring pressure on the County Council to provide them. The answer, from the Town Clerk:-

'...It is not part of the County Council measures. This sort of thing costs money'.[54]

A search through school log books for village schools in North Wales suggests that air-raid shelters were not provided until September 1940, by which time the area had received numerous air raid warnings. The lack of shelters at this time created problems for some of the teachers. On 17th November 1939 the Headteacher of St. Matthew's Infants School Buckley, North Wales had to send children home during a potential raid:-

'An air raid warning was given this morning about 11.15. As we have no shelters and deployment into wet fields is not conducive to good health, I dispersed them to their homes. The school was evacuated in a very short time. Some of the children live 20 minutes walk away. Long distance children are a problem in this respect and something must be done to cater for them'.

This action did initiate some response:-

'Monday 20th September. There have been several complaints over Friday's dispersal of the children. A manager's meeting is to be held tonight'.

There is no further indication of when, or if, shelters were provided.[55]

Education Reform

'Any day now the senior boys will take in hand a piece of national work, the cultivation of a large piece of waste ground offered to them by Major Stilwell. After clearing the site it will be trenched in readiness for the growing of root crops. All boys will have to take a turn at gardening'.[56]

Some educationalists believed that evacuation broke the traditional methods of educational practices and prepared the way for change. Those teachers who were absorbed in the scheme were seen by some of their contemporaries as leading the movement for educational reform.[57] There was a firm belief that city children could be introduced to new first hand pedagogic experiences such as real nature study and first hand history and geography. In November 1939 the Board of Education commented:-

'Evacuation gave schools a chance for personal initiatives and resourcefulness by challenging them to jettison unreal teaching to look outside at real things rather than at apparatus indoors'.[58]

Brian Simon, in his book 'Education and the Social Order 1940-41', suggests that:-

'Primary School teachers, thrown on their own resources in the chaos of evacuation, learnt how much younger children could gain from work with improvised apparatus, pioneering group and informal methods of working and forays into the countryside'.[59]

However, such new methodology presupposed that the teachers could, and would, take advantage of the new experiences on offer. Many were married women, some elderly, and some were retired school masters. Of the total number of teachers in primary and secondary schools in England and Wales in January 1946, 9,458 were aged over 60, and 33,159 were married women.[60] These had been recalled to the profession, some after many years away from the classroom, to fill the places of between 20,000-22,000 teachers who had been called up into the armed forces,[61] and one would suggest that neither group would necessarily have made the development of new methodologies their highest priority. Certainly not during the first wave of evacuation. On 27th November 1939, the Director of Education in Anglesey wrote:-

'...the educational needs of the evacuated children had certainly not been the first concern of either the Evacuation or Billeting Authorities, or indeed the Government departments concerned. For not only were large schools evacuated into rural districts and the pupils scattered over a wide area, but also the billeting arrangements had been more concerned with family units than with school units'.[62]

Investigation into school log books in the reception areas, yields very little evidence of any new curriculum initiatives beyond references to 'Nature Study Trail', 'Nature Talks' and 'Nature Walks' which seemed to be put on at the end of the afternoon and were often cancelled because of bad weather. There are numerous entries in the log books which describe this practice. However, a report in the Dorset Daily Echo on 13th October 1939, did describe the efforts of Mr. G.W. Greening, the Headmaster of the Evershot village school who used 'Agricultural studies' as a basis for what would now be called cross-curricular studies.[63] The Caernarvonshire Education Authorities did initiate new courses for evacuated teachers on 'Nature Study' (7th November 1941) and 'The Historical Background of Caernarvonshire' (February 1942) to help them get the most from their surroundings.[64]

However, although curriculum content initiatives were not necessarily a high priority there had to be a change in actual teaching methodologies and it is perhaps this experience which led to a great deal more child-centred learning taking place in post-war classrooms. Having to teach a large number of children of various ages and abilities, some of whom were there for only a short time, in cramped conditions with few resources meant that teachers had to draw upon new ideas and methods to cope with the situation. In some areas such an environment gave rise to learning programmes and schemes of work suited to individual pupils. By implementing such schemes, even on a limited basis, one could argue that some basic curriculum changes were forced upon some teachers.

The following Inspection report from the Ely Market Street School, September 1944 illustrates how such initiatives came about.

Report by H.M.I. Mr. S.N.Godfrey

Owing to the limitations and inconvenience of the premise the children attending this school are denied much of the movement and activity that are essential to development. The inadequate provision for washing and the limitations of the office accommodation simply deprive them of the opportunities for social training which should form part of their education. The conditions of heating, lighting and ventilation are unsatisfactory for some of the classes. The inadequate accommodation necessitates promotion of children to the Junior School every 6 months instead of annually and gives rise to considerable difficulty in the Junior and Senior Schools. By the careful planning of work along individual lines and the keeping of detailed records, the headteacher and her staff have tried to ensure a continuous course for each child. Much of the work done however needs to be reviewed in the light of modern teaching practice....'[65]

These changes took place in 1944 when the situation on the Home Front was relatively stable and the pastoral side of the teachers role was perhaps less of a priority and more time could be spent on developing the school curriculum. It is useful to compare this with the experience of Win Elliott and Sylvia Lewis as evacuated teachers in 1939. It is obvious from the description of their experience teaching in a small school in the village of Leiston that curriculum initiatives were low down in their priorities.

'At Leiston school, for one session each day, we had the use of one small room which we and our evacuees shared with a Dagenham headmistress. We had no apparatus, no guidance as to what to do or teach.....we gradually acquired a small collection of reading books, paper, pencils and crayons etc. No high-faluting syllabus, or structured curriculum, but the children learned to read and write and calculate with enjoyment.....The rest of the school day we had to play in the park, or walk the children around the lanes and go to the woods'.[66]

One teacher, keen to do something new with her pupils, inadvertently created an invasion scare when she organised a Treasure Hunt for her class in the local area. They had been given strict instructions to destroy all the clues but one was found by a villager. It simply said 'Go forward 500 yards to a gatepost near the cottage. Look for Oxo tin and follow instructions inside'. The locals thought it was the work of Fifth Columnists![67]

Neither did the November 1939 document take into account the other duties which were now put on teachers in the reception areas as well as those who had been evacuated with their schools. There is a lot of evidence to illustrate the new role of the teacher from the designated target areas involved in the evacuation process, but little is said about those in the reception areas who carried out duties which were more of a social service rather than educational nature.

Some teachers, having taken on the role of the proposed billeting officer in July 1939, took their duties very seriously and one in particular, Mr M.T. Perks, the Headteacher of The Grammar School, Gillingham, Dorset, organised a full Evacuation rehearsal in meticulous detail using pupils and staff from his own school, in order that all people involved in the reception area could evaluate and amend procedures they were to use when called upon to do so officially. He was keen to ensure the Clerk of the Shaftesbury Council that:-

'I propose on Monday to treat the children as if they were strangers for the purpose of rehearsal and shall treat the member of my staff in charge of the bus as the evacuated Head Teacher, I shall not acquaint him with the suggested routine as arranged'.[68]

It is worth quoting his schedule in full because it is one of the few examples of how local plans were implemented and similar procedures would have been replicated in some form or other in many of the reception areas. Note, than even in this document, Mr Perks was keen to imply that Evacuation was not a foregone conclusion.

```
In the event of Evacuation taking place.

PROCEDURE provisionally fixed for Semley Station.
(For trains containing evacuees for Shaftesbury Borough, Shaftesbury
RDC areas.)
Evacuees will be either
(a) Unaccompanied children. i.e. School Parties in charge of teachers.
(b) Mothers and children under school age.
```

The procedure in most details will be similar for (a) and (b) but *
indicates alternative arrangements according to the nature of the
party.

EVACUEES on ARRIVAL

Detrain on platform.

Lead off over bridge across road into Room allotted for Assembling
guided by Marshals.

(The First Aid Room will not be on the station, but possibly some First
Aid personnel might be on the platform in case of any evacuees needing
immediate attention or assistance in getting to the Assembly Room.)

ENTER Assembly Room. Evacuees are arranged by Marshals in rows and told
to sit down.

NB. Walk up to far end of the room first.

Rows parallel to long side of room and fill right hand side of the room
first (i.e. side furthest from the Ration Room.)

Leave space between rows.

One gangway in middle of row.

Doorways clear.

Enclosure, near door left-hand side at top of room, clear.

When all are in Assembling Room [Marshal reports to R.O. (Reception
Officer) Whistle blows and R.O. gives short explanation of what is
going to happen, e.g. First Aid facilities etc.]

R.O. requests Head Teacher or Leader (leaders) of party to accompany
him to R.O's. office to exchange necessary information. Deputy R.O.
takes charge in the room.

* In a (b) party, if there is no leader, list or roll of party is
required for the R.O's. office.

Deputy R.O. asks all who wish to visit the lavatory to stand up.

Those requiring this are escorted out in batches by Marshals, and by
teachers in an (a) party.

If all boys, or all girls, or Mothers and children, use the United
Dairies Lavatories.

If Mixed School   Girls; United Dairies lavatories

                        Boys; Lavatory on Semley Station platform.

Children are returned to their original places as far as possible and
they sit down.

R.O. has now made billeting allocations as between RDC and others and
returns with Head teachers or Leader to Assembly Room.

Check that no one is left in lavatories or outside. Marshal to report.

R.O. Instructs.

(i) Half will now go to Shaftesbury direct where they will receive
Rations and Milk. Remainder will receive Milk or Water in room and
Rations.

(ii) Shaftesbury section to prepare to leave.

Stand Up and make sure they have all Baggage, Gas Masks etc.

(Detail either certain classes on information of Head Teacher or if a
(b) party those occupying part of the room. Count roughly by Marshal
and Deputy R.O.)

Milk distribution now begins among the remainder.

R.O. Calculates such as to be sent to debussing point.

```
R.O. to Leader of the Party, 'Send into enclosure e.g. 45 children and
5 teachers or helpers'.
Leader of the party, who will know their names, details this number
from those nearest the 'enclosure'.
R.O. sends warning message to be telephoned to Billeting Officers.
*R.O. to Deputy R.O. and Marshals, 'Send in e.g. 20 mothers and 30
children'.
Evacuees enter enclosure.
Deputy R.O. or Marshal counts them and checks. Have all got Baggage
complete?
* If (b) party, check also that no incomplete family is included in
'enclosure'.
After check, R.O. gives Deputy R.O. the order to transport Officer and
Driver. Deputy R.O. takes party through Ration Room where they will
receive rations,... except first of Shaftesbury section when Deputy
R.O. will instruct the Ration Officials 'No rations' and go out and
load on the bus.
Deputy R.O. hands orders to the transport officer and returns to report
to R.O. 'Bus Loaded'.
```

On the 24th July Mr. Perks sent a detailed evaluation to the Clerk of the Council outlining the events of the day with some suggestions as to how the initial reception could have been more effective.

```
Dear Mr. Stace-Masey,

The 'refugees' arrived 16.35 hrs. and were allocated to billets and the
Billeting forms completed by 17.10. They were not dispatched to billets
which would have taken at least another hour.

It was found that 3 helpers, in addition to the 2 Billeting Officers,
were necessary to deal with the clerical work and the handing over to
the local transport drivers and foot guides.

The instructions and forms issued worked quite satisfactorily. The
words 'Billeting Orders' should be struck out in Form Ev. JSM/9.

Billeting Officers would like to have a list of local car transport
they can draw on, also information available about extra blankets and
bedding.

At Semley I think Mr Perks will find it difficult to deal with the
whole 500 in the one room and some 'waiting accommodation' is
necessary.

With regard to my suggestion to form a committee in each Parish I now
think it will be sufficient to inform the Senior Billeting Officers
that, as a result of the test, it has been found advisable to have
additional help when billeting and to suggest that the Billeting
Officers concerned, together with the 'helpers', should constitute a
```

```
small permanent Committee who would also deal with the after care and
'supervision' as decided in the penultimate paragraph of your draft.

This will avoid any overlapping which might occur if we ask someone who
is not appointed as Billeting Officer to form a Committee'.[69]
```

Even after 'practices' and meticulous local planning there were still problems and, in some ways, Mr. Perks was quite correct in assuming that the smooth running of any evacuation scheme was not a foregone conclusion. For example, after the results of the accommodation census were made known to local councils the billeting officer in the parish of Bradfield, West Berkshire, was told to expect 300 evacuees in two consignments on the 3rd and 4th of September 1939. Three weeks before these dates he was sent more details about the party which would consist of 270 children and 30 teachers and helpers. Blankets and mattresses were to be made available. The billeting officer and his helpers then re-canvassed the whole parish to make sure that this division of expected personnel could be housed. They were to arrive at the nearest train station, Theale, at 5.30pm where they were to be taken by bus to the local men's club room for distribution to the billets. The local representative of the WVS had set up a committee to distribute the blankets and mattresses and to help with the administration and distribution of the evacuees throughout the parish.

By 1st September neither blankets nor mattresses had arrived, although everything else was now ready. The billeting officer had every household's voucher already filled in with details about the numbers of children and the money due, only the names of the children remained to be added. It was planned that all 300 persons would be at their billets within an hour of arriving. This being the case they decided not to provide refreshments other than water, which had to be fetched from a nearby farm, and that the existing toilet facilities in the club would be sufficient. Everyone was in a state of readiness.

On the evening of Saturday 2nd September a telegram arrived stating that the evacuees would not now arrive until the Monday.

On Monday, at 11 am, another telegram arrived which simply stated 'expect children this afternoon'. At 3pm a third telegram was received with the message... 'arrangements cancelled'. The billeting officer told all the helpers to go home until he contacted them again. At 5.30pm on the same day a fourth telegram came... 'children arriving at 6 pm'. The billeting officer's daughter was then sent on her bicycle around the parish searching for her father who had gone back to work. By 6.30 he had been found and the WVS reception committee had been reassembled. At 7.30 the buses arrived and deposited 35 school children and 220 mothers and infants. Totally unexpected! All the billeting arrangements that had been made had to be reorganised.[70]

An eye-witness account from the time describes in some detail the problems that this unexpected group created and one can sense the frustration of those in the evacuation 'front line' who had done their best to organise suitable accommodation from the information they had been supplied with for a group of people they were simply told to expect.

> *"The evacuees straggle into the clubroom laden with babies, toddlers, parcels and gas masks. The overcrowding, confusion, noise and squalor is unbelievable. Some cannot speak English, many have lost their parcels or their toddlers. Ventilation is inadequate because of the darkened windows. We sort out the unaccompanied children first and without undue delay despatch them to their new homes.*
>
> *Now for these mothers. Next billet has room for mother and one child. 'You mother and young baby, come this way please'.*
>
> *'Oh, I can't go without my friend here. I'd rather spend the night where I am'.*
>
> *'Well you there with the little girl then'.*
>
> *'Oh those other five belong to me'.*
>
> *Hasty search through the books for accommodation for six.*
>
> *So it goes slowly on. The first carloads begin to come back with such messages as 'Mrs Hodge says she can't possibly take the mother and four children because her sister has just arrived from Manchester with six', or 'Mrs Brown wouldn't let us in because she said she had asked for two little girls and would not take in a Polish family instead'.*
>
> *Meanwhile the countryside has grown dark. The mothers and babies in the hut are tireder and less reasonable than ever. An Irishwoman stands up and declaims in eloquent but unprintable language against all of us and all our race and all our ancestors. Some eight or nine women refuse to part from each other and we agree to bed them down for the night in the clubroom. Our transport driver reports that the householders have gone to bed and billets can be found for no more. We bed up the residue as comfortably as we can in the hut on sacks of straw and retire to our respective homes for the night".* [71]

When one reads an account such as this, one realises where some of the inherent dissatisfaction with the scheme and the anti-evacuee propaganda emanates from. This seeming lack of organisation was not the fault of either the evacuees or the reception authorities but both sides tended to level the blame at each other in terms of intransigence and lack of sympathy for the situation everybody found themselves in.

In many of the other designated reception areas most teachers had returned early from their school holidays and 'were holding themselves in readiness to carry out any instructions which may have been given to them and also to assist locally in the reception and billeting of evacuated children'. [72]

Mavis Cordery, then a newly qualified teacher in the Caversham Senior School in Harley Rd., Reading, recalled in an interview that:-

'Staff in school reported to the billeting officer in our own school to be allocated.[73] Prospective hosts had been told to arrive at the school at a specific time. It was our job to check these people and their assessments and to help calm them down as some were extremely nervous at the prospect of meeting and then housing children from London. There were rumours that the evacuees were coming from the dock and 'slummy' (sic) areas of London and there were all sorts of stories circulating about poor personal hygiene, revolting eating habits, dreadful social habits and low morals. By the time the bus turned up with the children hours later, most people were a bit jumpy to say the least!' Other staff had spent their holiday participating in courses on first aid and anti-gas measures'.[74]

Although there may have been little curriculum change what the war did bring about was a shift in the relationship between the teacher and pupil. There was a significant move towards a more pastoral role which was to become a significant part of a teacher's job after the war and has been ever since. One major reason for this was that both teacher and pupil were experiencing the evacuation process together and as a result had a common bond.[75]

Some teachers were dealing with social problems way above the call of duty. The following entry in the log book of the 'Boys Evacuated School', Aston Clinton, Buckinghamshire, is significant in two respects. First, it shows that some of the problems dealt with in loco parentis were very serious. Second, some of the fears parents have today regarding child safety were just as apparent in the 1940s. It is often overlooked that crime still existed despite the war.

'11th December 1939. Joseph Mack d.o.b. 5.12.31
London Address. 111 Nathaniel Buildings. Flower and Dean Street.
Billeting Address. 6 Buckland Wharf, Aylesbury.

I have today received official information from the Aston Clinton Police officer, in relation to the indecent assault of Joseph Mack, aged 8 years, on Saturday afternoon 18th November 1939 at 3pm in a wood beside the main road in Aston Clinton. The matter came to Police notice about 14 days after the event and within two days an Aylesbury man named ****** was arrested in Aston Clinton and has since been identified by the children concerned.

The papers concerning the matter have been placed in the hands of the Director of Public Prosecutions. A copy of the above entry is being sent to the LCC Divisional Officer, No. 6 District and to the Community Secretary at 37, Stepney Green. E1.

Children have been repeatedly warned about walking about singly in lonely places at anytime, though of course no details of what to fear have been given'.[76]

Another example was reported in the Dorset County Chronicle and Swanage Times on the 23rd October 1941:-

A 34 year old man from Swanage was gaoled for '12 months imprisonment in the Second Division' for indecently assaulting three evacuees in his care. His claims of using them as 'human hot water bottles' were not accepted by the jury.[77]

Teachers were also responsible for those pupils who, for any reason, decided to run away and this pastoral work put an additional strain onto an already overworked profession. As today, the Headteacher concerned in this incident was keen to write down all the actions that took place so that no accusation of negligence could be levelled at him.

22nd January 1940. It was reported to the Headteacher by Mrs Webb at 5.30pm tonight, that a pupil of Commercial Street LCC Junior, Mixed and Infants School, one Bernard Saunders aged 11, billeted at 36, London Rd., Aston Clinton, had left his billet between 9 and 10am after a quarrel with another child billeted at the same address.

Action Taken:

(a) Head. visited Mrs McWhal the foster parent.

(b) Head. visited Mr Delamonte, Headteacher's assistant, to whom absence was reported by Aaron Saunders, during registration.

23rd January. Head. 'stood by' all night and kept in contact with the Police. No news received from any source since yesterday morning. Head. phoned Chief Dispersal Officer D.O.6 reference the case. Was asked to wait until 2pm for any news. In the event waited until 4pm and then phoned CDO.

Mr Butcher, CDO, then informed the parents who told him that the child had arrived home on the previous day. The CDO wired the Headteacher to this effect'.[78] *The boy returned to school on the 29th January.*[79]

There is no indication of what the headteacher thought about the outcome, but the whole incident does raise a series of questions:- Why did the hosts take so long to report the boy missing? How did he manage to return to London unchallenged? Why did the parents not report that he had returned home? They could have given little thought to the emotional state of the teachers involved, especially the Headteacher. Had it not been for the action taken by Aaron Saunders in reporting it to his teacher Mrs Webb, the whole incident could have gone entirely unreported.

In spite of their efforts, teacher help was not well received in all areas. The Billeting Officer in Exeter wrote to the Town Clerk in November 1940:-

Ref. Rumbold Case.

I would like to point out that the responsibility for billeting evacuated children in suitable billets rests with the billeting officer and NOT with the teachers. While at the same time fully agreeing that any assistance that can be given by the teachers in arranging necessary transfers is very welcome and of great assistance, I am also bound to add that from my own personal knowledge many quite unnecessary transfers have been suggested by teachers, which, if they had been acted upon by the billeting officer would have caused unsettlement in both children and householders, who are entitled to consideration as well as evacuated children'.[80]

Another example comes from the Director of West Sussex Education. On the 23rd September 1939, three weeks after the London schools had been evacuated to his area, he held a conference which was attended by seventeen liaison officers, two Government inspectors and three LCC inspectors. The Headteachers from the evacuated schools were not invited or represented. He is quoted as saying:-

> *'Whilst they are teaching in West Sussex, all London County Council teachers are to be regarded as being on the staff of West Sussex Education Authority, whose decision would be final in any matters affecting staff. Any cases of 'friction' caused by 'difficult' teachers should be reported to the Director who will consult the LCC on the matter'. No mention was made of local teachers being considered 'difficult'.* [81]

Discrimination of evacuee teachers was not always the norm. In some areas such as Buckinghamshire, Headteachers from evacuated schools were invited to attend regular meetings of the Local Education office to discuss general and specific issues relating to evacuation. [82]

Despite all their help and concern for the billeting of their pupils there is evidence to suggest that in some areas teachers were responsible for finding their own accommodation after all the children had been housed. The suggestion made in January 1939 that empty school houses could be used for evacuated teachers was not taken up and in many instances teachers found themselves homeless. Three arrived at Aldeburgh on 1st September 1939 and had housed all the children by 10pm. They then found no billets had been allocated to them. The billeting officer duly employed the Town Crier who went through the town shouting out 'Anyone take in a teacher!' By 11.30 they were given lodgings. [83]

A Headteacher and his wife described three attempts to find a billet when they were first evacuated. The first time they were somewhat disconcerted when, trying to find a billet on a Sunday, they were met by an irate gentleman who came to the door and fiercely announced...'I am a Christian, and I am not going to take in Evacuees on a Sunday' ...and he didn't.

The second attempt was at a very large house standing in its own grounds. They were ushered in by the butler... but half an hour later they were on their way again. They had been given a room and were quietly unpacking when a voice shouted...'What's all the noise up there?' The butler reappeared to tell them that 'Madame requires quiet at all times'. They decided to leave.

Their third attempt was in a farm cottage where the Head. remained, but his wife returned home. The cottage had no bathroom and everybody had to wash in the sink. [84]

Teachers billeted in some aristocratic houses were not highly thought of:-

> *'Mr. P. asked Mrs W. the housekeeper, if she had a cloth to put on the teachers' table. When the Lady of the house was approached the Gentleman replied, 'Surely a bloody newspaper is good enough for them!'* [85]

Some 'digs' were found on a very ad hoc basis. After five hours of walking around in the rain finding billets for the children a teacher quoted in her diary for Mass-Observation:-

> *'I was fortunate in securing a billet that night with people who passed us in their car when we were leaving the distribution depot .....These kind people followed us around in their car and relieved the kiddies of their belongings whilst waiting to be fixed up with a billet . It seemed incredible to me that no arrangements had been made for teachers and we had to depend on people's kindness of heart to supply us with accommodation for the night'.*[86]

One teacher describes her plight vividly:-

> *'Two of us were dumped at 6.30pm at an ancient cottage; its condition and contents shouted of extreme poverty.....We were greeted by our hostess who told us that, the house being near a river and mouldy all through, she had done her best to ensure well-aired beds by keeping them in the garden all day, it had been raining since 11am!*
>
> *The railway lay nearby but she knew that we should soon get used to waking up at 5am when the milk train thundered by.*
>
> *We sat on the bed in the 'sitting room', spreading a mackintosh first, to have some rations, our hostess meanwhile entertaining us. It appeared that she was disappointed at receiving only two teachers; she had hoped for a third, as there was another spare bedroom, 'Too cold to sleep in' and therefore used for storing apples; but it 'would have been so nice to put a teacher in there'.*
>
> *A bottle of milk was placed on the table. Later, considerably later, a cup and saucer followed. But... 'Don't use that cup till I get a cloth and wipe it out. I'm not much of a housewife and nothing in this house is over clean'.*
>
> *Next, a cat was brought in, with the comment... 'I'm sorry to say this animal has been distributing fleas all over the place, and the worst of it is my eyes are so bad. Of course when they jump on me, I can catch them...like that, suddenly slapping her shin. Lest the beds should need nocturnal slapping, however, she produced a tin of 'Flit'.*
>
> *The curtain fell on our first billet. At 7pm we flitted'.*[87]

In districts where the number of evacuees under the Government scheme was substantial such as in Berkshire where there were 89 schools involved, and where there were teachers to take charge of these children, the Head teachers of the reception schools were asked to get in touch with their evacuated colleagues and arrange for the reopening of schools on a double-shift system.[88] The following timetable was drawn up by staff at the Aston Clinton evacuated School just a few days after their arrival in Buckinghamshire. They were to have the afternoon shift. It is interesting to note that despite their new countryside environment there is little evidence here of the pedagogic enlightenment suggested by educationalists at the time.

1.00 - 1.05	Registration
1.05 - 1.35	Scripture or Religious Instruction*
1.35 - 2.15	Arithmetic
2.15 - 2.45	Geography or History or English
2.45 - 3.00	Recreation
3.00 - 3.30	English or History or Geography
3.30 - 4.00	Physical Training
4.00 - 4.30	English or Nature Study or Art

The host school had a very similar morning timetable from 9.00 - 12.30.

* There were many Jewish children in this party of evacuees, Party 941, so later in the term permission was sought from the Governors to provide Hebrew lessons during the day instead of Scripture.[89] It also meant that some of their school holidays were different to account for the Feast of the Weeks and Feast of the Passover. This was acceptable in London but caused some administrative problems in the reception areas. The teacher concerned with this party was very annoyed at the short notice she was given in September 1940 to move the holiday from October 3rd, authorised by Buckinghamshire's LEA to the 30th September. Despite seeking permission earlier in the month she was not given permission until Saturday 28th September which meant she had to notify all the children and foster parents by visiting their billets and cancelling the weekly milk.[90]

Day to day organisation was also affected by other religious denominations. The log-book for the Idbury and Fifield C of E school in Oxfordshire indicates that on a number of occasions Roman Catholic children did not attend assembly and the children from St. Anthony's School, Forest Gate were not allowed to attend. This is another example of an administrative oversight which begs the question.... why evacuate a Roman Catholic school to a small Church of England village school.[91] For one particular evacuee being a Roman Catholic had an advantage. He was the only one at the village school in Shipton and exempt from attending morning assembly. Therefore he had a lie-in every morning and did not have to attend school until 9.40am![92] One particular Council, Cricklade and Wootten Bassett RDC wrote to the Ministry of Health in March 1940 expressing serious concern about the wisdom of sending Roman Catholic children to mainly Protestant areas or to Protestant families with the comment that 'Roman Catholic children and Protestant householders do not harmonise'![93]

This difference in religion created serious problems in North Wales where many children from Catholic backgrounds were billeted with Calvinistic Methodists. Many local people objected to

Priests and teachers from Catholic schools trying to impose restrictions on how they treated their evacuees and a great deal of correspondence was sent to local councils in an attempt to rectify the situation. This disharmony was particularly difficult to overcome in some areas where the authorities had been forced to initiate compulsory billeting. The Evacuation Officer in the Aled Rural District reported:-

> *'The Billeting Officers generally, whilst disliking the task, are prepared to carry out these duties and to use compulsory powers, providing that Protestant children are the only ones sent to the district. They all explain that householders will not, under any circumstances, receive Catholic children into their homes again, and the Billeting Officers have threatened to resign rather than use these compulsory powers as their sympathies are all with the householders. They all emphasise that this attitude is not the result of religious bigotry, but because of the interference and religious intolerance of the Catholic priests and teachers accompanying the children'.*[94]

In some areas Protestant hosts were chastised by Catholic priests if their charges did not attend mass. This in itself created problems as there were few Catholic churches and in some cases they were many miles away. If hosts complied with the Priest's requests this often meant them foregoing their own Chapel attendance on a Sunday. In April 1940 the Clerk of the Nant Conway RDC reported:-

> *'...during the last evacuation, children were made to walk as much as eight miles to attend Mass on Sunday mornings and I consider this a hardship on the younger children to have to do this in all weathers'.*[95]

One priest in Liverpool went so far as instructing the parents in his parish whose children had been evacuated to North Wales to bring them home alleging that:-

> *'...any physical danger they might incur in Liverpool was trifling when compared with the spiritual danger they ran by remaining'.*[96]

Sometimes attempts were made to transfer evacuees on religious grounds but in November 1939 the Clerk to Denbighshire County Council wrote to Evan Evans, Evacuation Officer for Wales stating:-

> *'I am tired of these attempts to move children simply because they belong to one particular faith and intend to take as firm a stand as I can against any further nonsense of this kind. I hope I can have your support'.*[97]

During the second evacuation in 1940 slightly more care was taken to place Roman Catholics in areas where facilities were available for them. But, in truth the situation should not have arisen during the first scheme. On 2nd May 1939 a representative from Liverpool Council, H.W. Lowe, addressed a conference at Caernarfon where he told the evacuating authorities in the reception areas to expect 30% Catholics in the total of 24,000 evacuees allocated to the area.[98]

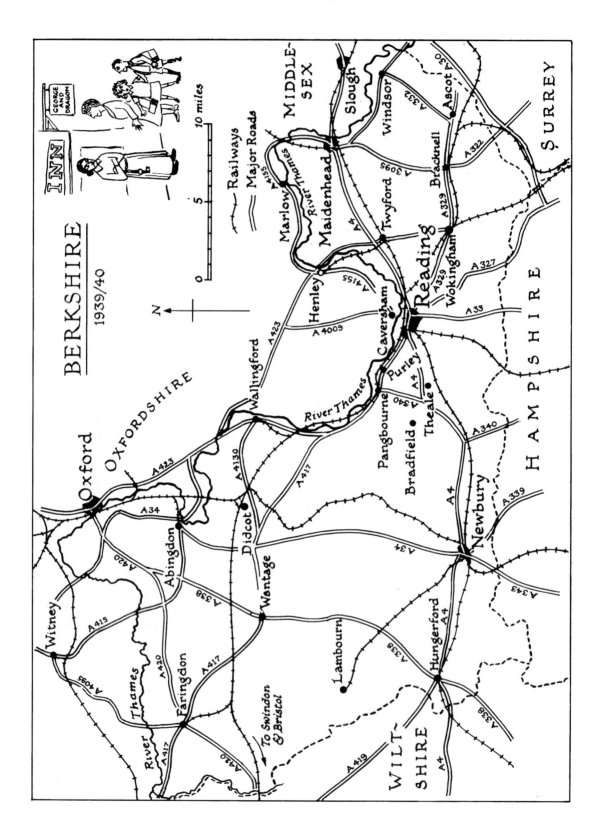

BERKSHIRE
1939/40

Railways
Major Roads

0   5   10 miles

In Dorset the two shift system had been introduced at the very beginning of the war but by the end of October pupils had been absorbed into the existing system and less than 20 Dorset schools were providing full time education.[99] In Berkshire the shift system resulted in local children attending school from 8.30am to 12.30pm while the schools from Greater London were given the afternoon period from 1.00pm to 4.30pm. This plan was to start on the 12th September, after schools had reopened after the delayed summer break. Later, the time of 1.00 was changed to 1.30 to allow for mid-day meal arrangements in the children's billets. The only other time changes were made during the winter when afternoon school finished earlier at 3.30, or when staff with particular expertise were recalled to London to help out in schools there, or joined the Armed Forces, thus reducing the number of staff in the evacuated schools.

There were difficulties in operating a 'double-shift' system. A resident teacher in Wales working this system wrote in a log book on 19th February 1940:-

> *'Working the afternoon shift this week. The children arrive in school tired out after playing all morning and in no frame of mind for schoolwork'.*[100]

The following account from Mavis Cordery provides an interesting insight into the problems such school sharing could create:-

> *'...some children were billeted in the Lower Caversham area. Most of these were from the Rays Central Boys School. We were told that the Headteacher, Mr Fabian, his six staff and the boys, were to share our school. There were too many to absorb into the school and they wanted to stay as one unit, so we had to work out a sharing system. Basically, we had the school premises for the morning and they had the afternoon. This did not mean that we had half-day schooling. We were told that we had to fit in wherever we could and run informal club sessions if normal teaching was impossible. The first week I remember one afternoon having to occupy more than 60 girls under the shelter of the bicycle sheds....we also got round the problem by having large organised games sessions in the afternoon'.*[101]

Mavis went on to say that despite the pressure on the buildings, the schools eventually got on well together and began to do joint ventures such as school plays. She recalls that one of the biggest problems throughout the whole war was the lack of coal and having to teach in school buildings which were freezing cold during the winter. The headteacher got the staff, in turn, to lead the whole school in ten minutes of physical exercise every morning before school in order to warm up.[102]

Heating schools was always a problem. The log book of the Commercial Street school contains many entries made during the winters of 1940 and 1941 about lack of coal. On some occasions the school was closed because they had no coal at all and the fire had gone out.[103] Some small two or one room village schools relied entirely on open coal fires for their heat.

Entries in the log book of St. Matthew's Infant School, Buckley indicate that the school was always cold and coal was not being delivered. On 22nd January 1940 the thermometer registered 30 degrees of frost...inside the school! The heating boiler cracked...but school continued.[104]

An anonymous ex-teacher, evacuated with his school to a small village north of Newbury in Berkshire, describes the problems he had to face when sharing the facilities of the existing village primary school with only 19 on roll:-

'A muddy path led up past the churchyard to a brick Gothic school-house, with narrow pointed windows and an immensely high-pitched roof. There was a tiny dirt yard, divided by a fence into Boys and Girls, with rudimentary lavatories. The school had no water supply and every morning the bigger boys fetched buckets of water from a horse tough outside the church......It was to be one of the coldest winters of the century and even the autumn chills presented difficulties. The winter practice had been to gather the nineteen village children around the stoves, sending boys out 'sticking' to keep up the blaze, but with 50 children now in the school the outer rings were fated to shiver, though they sat in overcoats and gloves. Early in the new year an extended cold spell cut off the village for ten days. Every pump and many of the wells froze and food had to be brought from Newbury by sledge.

School was impossible; the boys could find no wood for the fires and even the ink froze in the inkwells. We gave up and took the children out for snow fights and sledging'.[105]

All these basic administrative and physical arrangements took precedence over everything else and allowed little time for educational reform to take place. Also it needs to be remembered that opportunities for change in curriculum areas such as science and nature study were already predetermined by the local environment and as such in many rural areas science would have been agriculturally biased.

Some schools actually encouraged pupils to work on farms in the local area but not necessarily from an academic or educational motive, more one of economics and giving the pupils something to do. Some of this extra work was 'suggested' by local authorities:-

'19th June 1940. Following instructions, enquiries were made at the farms in the neighbourhood, whether children can help with the work in the fields. One farmer accepted and a dozen older children went this morning to weed.

20th June 1940. 10 children worked in the garden of Buckland Vicarage weeding.[106]

6th June 1941. The senior children spent all week on the local farm planting potatoes.[107]

30th September 1941. The senior children spent a lot of time this month on the local farm picking and bagging potatoes.[108]

18th June 1942. The First team of 6 children over the age of 12 began work in agriculture. 3 hours per day every four days'.[109]

This introduction to agriculture must have been of some benefit to some evacuees as this newspaper snippet would indicate:-

EVACUEES CHOOSE FARM LIFE

Five evacuees from the London area who left school at Christmas are taking up farm work in the Okehampton district and have abandoned all intention of returning to city life.[110]

(It was not only the children who were wanted for work. As early as 8th September 1939 the following advertisement from various manufacturers in the area was placed in the Dorset Daily Echo asking evacuee adults to consider local work.

NOTICE TO EVACUATED PEOPLE

The Bridport Manufacturers Association feel that it would be the desire of all those capable of working to be given the opportunity to render service of National Importance rather than do nothing at this time of emergency. Work of National Importance is available for all able-bodied workers willing to learn. Will the general public please make this fact as widely known as possible?[111]

Despite Mavis Cordery's example of her school and the evacuated school working together, the general lack of cohesiveness between establishments was seen as a problem in Berkshire as early as October 1939 and the County Council issued the following statement about their education policy and billeting of evacuated schools:-

> *'Various adjustments have been made since the schools were originally reopened and efforts are now being made to arrange for full-time instruction wherever possible. For this system to be worked effectively, there must be a willingness on the part of the Berkshire and evacuated teachers to work together and so bring about the ultimate absorption of the London school children within our own school organisation. In this way, identity of the evacuated schools must disappear and this will be the logical outcome of the impossibility of retaining these schools as separate units'.* [112]

The authorities in Buckinghamshire took this one stage further and appointed evacuated teachers to their own county schools. The authority's own girls' school in Aston Clinton lost a teacher, Mrs Staples, in November 1939. It was suggested that because the evacuated boys' school had fewer numbers they could ask one of their staff to apply for the vacancy. This was agreed and a Mrs Webb joined the staff of the girls' school on the 11th December 1939, though, technically, she remained a member of the LCC Evacuee Party 941.[113]

In January 1941 the Executive of the National Union of Teachers issued a manifesto which stated that they had under review the impact of the existing war conditions on the educational system within the country. Through this document they wished to highlight specific observations for the consideration of all the people responsible for and interested in the welfare of schools both in the evacuated and reception areas. They were particularly concerned with the wide ranging demands now made:-

> *'...upon the public spirit and voluntary services of the teachers. The care of the children outside school, and the delicate work of billeting, the rest centre and registration office, the National*

Savings Movement and the ARP and Auxiliary Fire Service and the special police, the Home Guard and the nursing services and many other forms of national effort have already filled the daily programme of the teacher to overflowing'.[114]

By 1942 the same concerns were being expressed at the local level. There were specific worries about the additional tasks having to be carried out by teachers to the detriment of their actual roles as teachers. At a meeting of the Dorset Education Committee on Monday 26th January 1942, the teachers' representative, Mr J. M. Warren, was reported as being very outspoken on his views regarding the role of teachers within the County. He asserted that they were becoming 'Honorary Clerks to the Treasury, Assistants to Milk Purveyors, Housemaids, Cooks and Bottle Washers'.[115] He directed the attention of the committee to an administrative memorandum which referred to the anxiety of the Board of Education that teachers were being taken from their primary duty of teaching in order to attend to all sorts of things in school hours ....the classes which suffered the most were those in the charge of head teachers. Another member of the committee suggested that the WVS might undertake some of the administrative roles in school in order to release the teachers for other duties. There was no reply to this suggestion. However, it is perhaps significant that when, in July 1942, the Government issued a circular requesting that the Local Education Authorities made special arrangements for the care of school children during the holidays to enable mothers to continue in work, the Dorset Education Committee rejected it, albeit by the smallest of majorities. It was argued that teachers were already doing enough to assist the war effort and even if they attended schools during the holidays there was no guarantee that many, if any, of the children would be there.[116]

While many city school children and teachers were being sent to the country the school buildings they left behind were closed and remained so until November 1939, but even then 50% of the children in London were not to receive full time education until mid-1940. In the designated evacuation and neutral areas of England and Wales approximately 2000 schools were either requisitioned totally or used by various organisations at different times of the day... 1692 were used by the Civil Defence, the Auxiliary Fire Service had taken over 250 of these and 100 were designated as Wardens' posts, 213 by the military authorities. The rest, 70, were taken over by groups such as the Red Cross for first aid posts, decontamination centres, or in some cases, allocated as temporary mortuaries.[117] The figures were obtained in December 1939 when a survey of education provision was carried out in all areas of the country and, according to Titmuss, are not totally reliable hence the approximation.[118] It was estimated in April 1941 that 290,000 children in England and Wales were not receiving full time education. There had been a great deal of confusion over how many children attended school during the winter of 1940-41 and according to Titmuss, the Ministry of Health, Board of Education and the LCC could not agree as to a figure.[119] The LCC put the figure at 81,000 which was considered too low by the Minister of Health.

Where education was available, both in the cities and the reception areas, the question of class sizes became important and although, in general, they were considered by some of the host schools to be large they were usually no bigger than those pre-war classes which, in many inner-city schools had numbered more than 40 pupils. But there were of course exceptions. By October 1943, Liverpool had 600 classes in elementary schools with more than 50 children in each compared with 293 classes of the same size in 1938. Sheffield, which had had 2 classes containing more than 50 in 1938 reported 406 in September 1944, 60 of which continued with more than 60 pupils.[120] In the light of this evidence and the present 1990s debates on school class sizes, it is worth considering the recommendations made by the members of the Barnett House Study Group in 1947 who researched a group of London children billeted in Oxford. They suggested that 'the educational value of small classes was confirmed beyond a shadow of a doubt by the experience of evacuated schools'.[121]

It is also important to note that because of the general dislocation of the educational structures and practices, it was generally the less able pupils who suffered. This was due in no small measure to the fact that the 320 special classes in London County Council schools which had been established to deal with those pupils with special needs, were abandoned during the war years.[122] Also many more able pupils, such as the author Bob Holman, failed their examinations for the grammar schools because they were so far behind in their studies and in some cases were kept down a year in the Primary School in order to catch up with some of their contemporaries.[123] Others, including James Roffey and his brother John, returned to an education system in London sadly lacking in the basic necessities in terms of buildings, equipment and teachers. What teachers there were faced with was the task of bringing children from various ranges of experience up to a common level. No concessions were made to the pre-war examination system and pupils who had been away for some years now found themselves having to sit the examinations for the 'Central' school where they could stay until 16, or if they failed, leave school at 14. For many, unsurprisingly, the examination was a waste of time. In most cases the authorities refused to agree to the re-examination of those who had failed and the children were forced to leave school and find work. This had a very serious effect on the future lives of many evacuees. These children had been uprooted from their homes and schools, had their education disrupted through no fault of their own because in many areas no suitable provision had been made, and yet were expected to compete on equal terms with those who had not had their education interrupted and against examination criteria which had been established pre-war.

In a report to the Education (General) Sub-Committee on 13th September 1943, the Chief Inspector of Schools summed up the effect of four years of the war on London schools, although much of what he reported could easily have been said about many schools across the country. He stated that:-

> *'Many schools had lost their identity. Re-evacuation, the lack of continuity in school buildings, school staff and syllabuses had made educating the child very difficult'.*[124]

Under the circumstances it came as no surprise to the Inspectorate when a test given to a representative sample of 3,000, 13 and 14 year olds in 1943 when compared with results of a 1924 cohort, indicated that:-

'...while children could still write lively and intelligent compositions, spelling was definitely worse than corresponding pupils in 1924'.[125]

Despite the obvious problems of maintaining a continuity in education the BBC tried, as much as possible, to keep broadcasting programmes specifically for schools. The Spring programme for 1940, which commenced on 8th January, ostensibly continued the pre-war diet. Mondays were devoted to Herbert Wiseman's 'Singing Together', world history, book talks for the senior English course, the practice and science of gardening, preparatory concert broadcasts and English for the under-nines. Tuesdays included Physical Education, Science and the Community, and a programme called 'The River' specially designed for rural schools. There was also Senior English with play-writing and drama productions. On Wednesday the children heard Current Affairs from 'Alf' a lorry driver. There was also a programme called 'Home Listening' which was designed specifically for those children who, because of the war conditions, were working at home, either alone or in groups of not more than ten with or without the supervision of a teacher. These programmes centred on the exploits of a milkman from Northern Canada, who told stories about his life with the Indians, the lumberjacks of Canada and trappers. 'Music Making' also appeared on Wednesdays along with Biology and Junior English. On Thursdays the children could listen to 'Music for Every Day', the Senior Geography course, and British History, and on Friday they received a diet of Senior English called 'Rhyme and Reason' and topical talks for sixth formers. There were also broadcasts in Welsh Language for juniors and seniors.[126]

Programmes and material for courses in Modern Languages which had been established before the war were abandoned but, by 1944, thirty-one weekly series, a daily news bulletin and twice weekly religious services were available and the number of schools using them rose from 10,000 to 12,000 during the war.[127]

Some evacuees were lucky in terms of the education they received during the war and even today, when interviewed, consider themselves to have been privileged. The camp-school, established by West Ham council near Hemel Hempstead and opened in 1940, provided an excellent education for 200 boys from the West Ham area. In an interview conducted in 1996 Jim Bartley, a former pupil of the school, described the average school day and routine:-

'Wakened in the morning to walk to the ablution block to wash, return to the dormitory to fold blankets and make bed area tidy, then in dormitory order went to the dining area for breakfast, then morning school, lunch, afternoon school, tea. After tea there was free time but there were many organised activities especially between the hours of 8.00-9.00pm. Each dormitory was looked after by two teachers who took it in turns to read stories to the boys at bedtime which was usually 9.00pm. Jim considered himself fortunate for three basic reasons. He was getting an education when many of his contemporaries were not, he gained in self-confidence and self-sufficiency and, above all, for the first time he had access to a library which started him on a life-time's love of reading'.[128]

A camp-school established in Oxfordshire as early in the war as February 1940 was considered at the time to be an educational experiment. On the 19th February 1940 Beal Modern School, Ley Street, Essex (a Central School) became the first 'camp school' when seven coach loads of boys were taken to Kennylands Camp, Sonning Common near Reading. The School had originally been evacuated to Ipswich but 182 pupils and 12 Teachers were transferred to the camp in February 1940. The school was divided up into 5 houses; Wolfe, Drake, Clive, Blake and Scott and they competed against each other in all their activities including School work, Gardens, Games and the cleanliness of their dormitories.[129] The camp, built at a cost of £20,000, had central heating, its own hospital and sewage disposal plant, 20 acres of ground, an assembly hall with stage and dressing rooms, a dining hall, shower baths and tuck shop. The boys received four meals a day prepared by the camp chef. As well as a Headteacher the school also had a Camp Manager, Captain F. Mee, who had been a secondary schoolmaster. When interviewed Captain Mee explained the ethos behind the school:-

> *'Whatever the boys show a desire to learn we shall be glad to teach them. We are planting an orchard and ploughing up some land for the boys to work.....This kind of school is what I have been urging for years. It will make the boys self reliant and teach them the value of co-operation and the responsibilities of citizenship'.* [130]

Many of the boys studied for the School Certificate or the Royal Society of Arts but their academic studies were balanced by having non-academic interests for part of the day. These included not only sports but also such pursuits as bee-keeping and pig-rearing.[131]

The school was visited by the King and Queen on 30th September 1940 who inspected the dormitories, classrooms, piggeries and chicken houses.[132]

Education...The Extras

SWANAGE

THE COMMUNAL FEEDING CENTRE FOR EVACUATED CHILDREN

Voluntary help is urgently needed at the above centre opening on June 19th at the Congregational Schoolroom, High Street, Swanage. Any person willing to help with this war work please write to the County Canteens Organiser, Dorchester.[133]

School closure in the cities had other effects not often considered by social historians and certainly not referred to in text books and other resources available in schools. Those with jobs outside the classroom such as dinner ladies, caretakers and cleaners, were no longer required within the school system and this led to job losses, although in time many would have been re-employed in war related industries. Also the social services linked to the schools in effect ceased to exist and, during the initial stages of evacuation, there was no school meal provision which many of the poorer children remaining in, and returning to, London relied on for their daily nourishment.

In 1939 approximately 10,000 children in the London County Council elementary schools had school dinners and 60% of these were provided free. After some of the children were beginning to return during the 'Phoney War' period, school domestic science classes were used to provide meals. However, in September 1940, 1,700 daily meals were delivered by central kitchens to those schools which remained open or had not been damaged or requisitioned and were now conducting lessons, but because of the second phase of evacuation which took place during the Blitz on London, the numbers of dinners required fell to approximately 500 by November 1940. During the early part of the war the attitude of both central and local government towards school meal provision altered drastically. Before the war, school dinners were provided for those who were genuinely undernourished and who were thought to be in greatest need. Pre-war research carried out by Sir John Boyd Orr had shown that the diet of the poorest 10% of the population was deficient in nearly all the known vitamins.[134] In 1941 the Vitamin Welfare Scheme provided either free orange juice and cod-liver oil to expectant mothers and young children or Vitamins A and D as alternatives. There was a concerted advertising campaign throughout the war under 'The Kitchen Front', which was broadcast on the radio Tuesday-Friday at 8.15am, and 'Food Facts' which appeared in the newspapers. Both extolled the virtues of Orange Juice and Cod Liver Oil and explained to parents where they could get such commodities.

FOOD FACTS

MUM! MY ORANGE JUICE. MY COD LIVER OIL.
MEMO FOR MUM!

You can buy continued health for your child at any welfare centre or distributing centre. In exchange for a few pence and the coupons in your child's ration book you can get his orange juice and cod liver oil.

Don't get just the orange juice and forget about the cod liver oil - one is just as necessary as the other. Think of Orange Juice and Cod Liver Oil together as you think of pepper and salt, oil and vinegar, mustard and cress. Think of them as the two-part health scheme which your baby needs.[135]

(The practice of issuing Orange Juice was eventually banned in the early 1960s because there was thought to be too much emphasis on Vitamin D and many doctors were worried about too much absorption of calcium which could lead to hardening of the arteries).[136] After the first evacuation, during which they had provided those evacuees without food with packed lunches for the journey, the main school meals kitchens closed until January 1940. Four others opened later and by June, 2000 school meals were being supplied in 70 centres at schools.

However, in 1941 the School Meals Service was taken over by the Londoners' Meals Service.[137] The service started a successful campaign to persuade as many children as possible to eat at school. It is not an insignificant fact that the Londoners' Meals Service also ran the 'British Restaurants' where a three course meal, including soup, braised tongue and a pudding cost 9d.[138] Lord Woolton, Minister of Food, was photographed eating such a meal and the caption read 'Those who want luxury feeding in these days are outsiders.' Prices tended to vary slightly so dinner tickets were issued to those having school dinners which could then be exchanged for a meal at any of the British restaurants. By February 1941, 2,000 meals per day were being provided to children. Every child was now entitled to a school meal and, if parents were unable to pay, the whole, or part of the cost was returned to them.[139]

Figures for the period October 1941-February 1945 indicate the overall success of the scheme. Note that % is that of the total on roll.[140]

Date	Meals	inc. Free	Number of Roll
Oct. 1941	9,644 (7.25%)	350 (0,02%)	133,000
Oct. 1942	39,836 (17.9%)	2,355 (1.06%)	221,000
Oct. 1943	62,673 (25%)	3,951 (1.58%)	249,800
Feb. 1944	65,941 (26.5%)	4,415 (1.77%)	248,400
Feb. 1945	51,512 (27%)	3,279 (1,72%)	190,600

The significance of October 1941 lies in the fact that this is when it was decided that rest centres where meals were provided should be used as much as possible for the provision of school meals. At the same time the Londoner's Meals Service took over the central kitchen which meant that the education authorities were only responsible for the collection of dinner moneys and the supervising of pupils during meal times. Also the grant from central government for the provision of school meals increased to between 70-90% over the country, London receiving 70%. This resulted in a rapid extension of the service, helped additionally by the fact that all school meals equipment was provided free of charge.

In January 1942 the service was extended when a 'family rate' was introduced which meant that for those families in need, the first child would eat for 4d, the second for 3d and any subsequent children for 2d. In April 1942 all these prices were increased by 1d to cover the additional costs of specific ingredients within the meals.[141]

By 1944 almost 66,000 children were having school meals and the role of the teachers became a supervisory one, a role which incidentally was not relinquished until the change of teachers pay and conditions in the 1990s. The pressure on working mothers to be out of the house during the school holidays resulted in a limited school meals service in the London area during the recess. During the period 1940-45 the numbers of those children having free or subsidised meals rose and this could possibly be used as an indicator of positive social change whereby those in the community who were in need of help received it.[142] However, concerns were expressed in the Dorset County Chronicle and Swanage Times on 20th November 1941 about the anomaly of unaccompanied children not getting free meals and also inadvertently pointing out the fact that the poorer hosts were still bearing most of the responsibility for looking after evacuees. Under the headline 'End this Anomaly of Evacuee Payments' the correspondent, Frank Lloyd, questioned the scheme.

'Sir, I want to call the attention of your wide awake paper to the plight of a class of children who are getting a raw deal in the evacuation scheme.

In the hundreds of community feeding centres which are springing up all over the country with up to 90% of Government grant, children who are evacuated with their parents are given free meals if they cannot afford to pay. These children also get free milk in schools on the same basis.

Why then the strange anomaly in Government orders which expressly excludes the child evacuated without a parent from free meals and free milk?

The unaccompanied child, often lonely, and in many cases unwanted in its new home, is made inevitably unpopular and unwelcome by bringing with it a Government allowance as low as 8s 6d, 10s 6d for a single child. Parents remain responsible for clothing this war-waif, but everything else it needs is supposed to be found out of 8s 6d a week. Moreover, the Government claims that 3 shillings of this sum is a lodging allowance to put the child on par with the accompanied child for whom 3 shillings is drawn. We are thus left with the astonishing Government attitude that a child who is supposed to be fed on as little as 5s 6d a week must not receive free meals and school milk, however poor they might be.

The Government order says it is assumed that the householder who takes in such a child can afford to provide it with midday meals and milk. Why? The assumption in many cases is false and the 8s 6d child is a burden to many homes.

The child's food, washing and wear and tear of bedding and furniture cannot be met out of such a mean allowance in these days.

And this is the child who must not get a free meal at the community centre, although a child next door who may have a mother to see to its welfare can be fed for nothing, if there is poverty.

Surely all Government-evacuated children should be entitled to free midday meals at a time when it is declared policy to augment the rations of the poorer people by community feeding. At least if some of the poor are entitled to free food, all should be. Free meals and milk would bring that miserly 8s 6d to a more reasonable figure. It is well known to billeting officers that evacuees tend to congregate in poor homes. Many well to do people are able to evade their obligations, others deliberately make the evacuees so uncomfortable that they leave. I can quote cases of both.

The evacuee child is therefore often in a home where it is difficult to make ends meet before he came. And such a child, with no one to stand up for him, is supposed to be fed on 5s 6d a week'.[143]

Officials in some areas took their responsibility for providing meals for evacuees very seriously. As early as November 1939 the Dorset Education Committee established communal feeding centres in Dorchester and other villages in the County. The planning implementation was the responsibility of the County's Canteen organiser Miss A. M. Anderson who had been appointed on the 18th September at an annual salary of £200 plus travel. The idea behind the scheme was that those children whose foster parents were out at work all day, or had other reasons for being unable to provide a mid-day meal during the week, should be able to have a lunch at a communal dining room. By November approximately 200 evacuees living locally had used the centres. The cost per child was 4d a day or 1s 8d a week which came out of the allowance paid to hosts. For their money each child could receive two helpings of each course which included at least four ounces of meat per helping and, because the meals were done on a three week rota basis, there was not much chance of their getting tired of the same meals. The local paper did a special feature on the Mill Street Mission feeding centre in Dorchester, which was used in the main, by Infant aged children, and listed the menu for one particular day. It included: Topside Beef, Potatoes, Cabbage, Gravy, Rice and Raisin pudding.[144] A similar communal meal scheme was established in January 1940 at Bridport where 100 children ate their midday meal at the Technical Institute in Chancery Lane, again at 4d a meal.[145]

The school milk requirement also changed over the period of the war. Like school dinners, milk was provided pre-war to those children who would benefit from it, but after the war started there was an aim to prevent infant under-nourishment by making it available to all. From 1941 it was free to those children whose parents could not afford the cost. The distribution of school milk was problematic during the initial stages of evacuation but throughout 1940 there was a gradual improvement until every elementary school in London still open was having milk delivered. In addition the Government decided in July 1940 to give free or cheap milk to mothers and small children.[146]

The following advertisement, issued by the Ministry of Food appeared in local newspapers from the middle of July 1940 but the content is confusing. It initially gives the impression that free milk was available to all expectant and nursing mothers and children under five, but careful reading reveals that this was not the case and such provision depended on income. The information regarding individual applications is another good example of the bureaucratic procedures involved in obtaining what was due to these categories of people. Unwittingly it also reveals the numbers of bureaucrats which were needed to implement such a scheme.

CHEAP MILK
For Mothers and Children

The National Milk Scheme provides one pint of milk a day at a reduced price or free, for every expectant or nursing mother and every child under five not attending school.
* Get an Application Form from the Milk Officer at your local Food Office, the Post Office will give you the address, and through any Child Welfare Centre, Health Visitor or District Nurse.
* Fill in the top half of the Application Form and have it signed by a responsible person, such as a teacher or clergyman, who knows you well.
* In the case of an expectant mother, the form must also be signed by a Doctor, Certified Midwife or Health Visitor.
* Post the form to the local Food Office. It will be about ten days before you receive your Milk Permit.

MILK AT 2d PER PINT.

* All expectant and nursing mothers and children under five not attending school, will be able to get milk at 2d per pint.

MILK FREE OF CHARGE

* Mothers and children are entitled to free milk if the incomes of both parents together are less than 40 shillings a week, or if an only parent's income is less than 27 shillings and 6 pence a week. These limits are increased by 6 shillings for each non-earning dependant.
* Free milk will also be supplied to mothers and children in households where the householder is receiving public or unemployment assistance or supplementary old-age pension.
* When applying for free milk you must also fill in the lower half of the Application Form, after the top half has been filled in and signed as explained above.

KEEP THIS ANNOUNCEMENT TO HELP YOU FILL IN THE APPLICATION FORM[147]

The provision of free milk had not always been available in all reception areas. The following announcement appeared in the Isle of Ely and Wisbech Advertiser in September 1939:-

NO FREE MEALS FOR EVACUATED CHILDREN

The Board of Education consider that the payment of 10/6 or 8/6 to the billeting householder insufficient to provide adequate food. Also no free milk will be available except for special dietary cases.[148]

In December 1940, when the Ministry of Health had suggested that a subsidy might be required in order to prevent an inevitable rise in milk prices being passed on to those who already could not afford it, the Treasury had reacted against it, but new economic initiatives, brought about by a reappraisal of food policy, made significant changes so that... 'A social reform of the first magnitude, that at one time looked like languishing for months, if not years, was put into effect almost within days'.[149]

When, in 1943, milk to the general public was rationed, the school milk ration was cut to one-third of a pint, except for pupils getting free milk. They received two-thirds of a pint a day whereas normal householders received two pints per week in winter and three to four per week in the summer. This was supplemented by National Dried Milk.[150]

London children in reception areas also received their milk. Those who had got it free of charge when in London, continued to get it free, the cost being paid by the London County Council.

> '2nd September 1939. We adopted the Milk scheme today. The milk is supplied by the Tring Co-operative Society. The distribution, pending a medical examination, is on the London County Council basis; granting it free to those who had it free in London. Every child will have two bottles of milk a day. Four of the group were paying and nine were free'.[151]

Mary Nickerson (née Caw) remembers that in her reception school, Tenbury Elementary, near Ludlow, a crate of a third pint bottles of milk were brought into her classroom. Each bottle had a cardboard top with an indentation in the centre where pupils had to push with their thumb in order to get a straw through. As many of the children hated milk they bribed others to drink it for them because they were not allowed out into the playground until the crate was full of empty bottles.[152]

However, some evacuated schools in the reception areas were not to receive milk until a year after the war had started.

In 1941 the only requirement for free milk was the inability to pay for it, so the Government introduced a scheme of reappraisal to check that no child was precluded from having school milk through the inability to pay. The only way to do this was to use the parents' weekly contribution towards the billeting costs in the reception area as a guide to the 'ability to pay'. This scheme was not only bureaucratically cumbersome but also financially unviable. The amount of money collected did not cover the cost of the administration. In consequence the Government decided to ease the bureaucracy by allowing free milk to all unaccompanied evacuees who were in official billets, whether they could afford it or not.[153]

Number of children who received milk daily: (% of total on roll). [154]

Date	Number	Free	Roll
1939	263,186 (62.6%)	41,596 (9.9%)	420,000
Oct. 1941	83,743 (62.9%)	2,887 (2.1%)	133,000
Oct. 1942	136,065 (61.4%)	5,755 (2.59%)	221,600
Feb. 1944	151,821 (61.1%)	8,081 (3.22%)	248,000
Feb. 1945	113,869 (59.7%)	6,329 (3.32%)	190,600

Medical Provision

'Who pays for an enjoyed conception in London resulting in an expensive confinement in Dorset?!'[155]

School closure in the evacuated areas also brought about a decline in school medical series which, for some pupils, was the only form of treatment they received. This was taken up by the Minister of Health, Walter Elliott, who stated quite categorically that:-

'....the Government had no wish to undermine the welfare of future generations. They were determined that the school medical service should survive intact'.[156]

It was not only the school medical service that was required. A Ministry of Health Circular, No. 1882, dated 2nd October 1939, stated that all categories of evacuees were to have access to the local medical services. Questions about medical provision and payment were asked by the Councillors at the Wareham and Purbeck Rural District Council on the 26th October 1939.

'Who was responsible for payment to local doctors called when evacuees were ill and which doctors could be summoned? The Chief Billeting Officer said that in the case of unaccompanied children, a private Doctor could be called in, but in the case of others the Public Assistance Doctor should be sent for. It was pointed out that a local emergency committee comprising of Doctors, which met at Dorchester, arranged for payment of Doctors through a central fund'.[157]

In reception areas where the medical practice was rural the arrival of evacuees put an extra burden onto an already stretched service. This was particularly true of expectant mothers who were evacuated in the first groups. Some hospital beds in Maternity units in the cities, had been kept empty to allow space for the expected vast numbers of air-raid casualties which had been projected before the war. However, because these figures were inaccurate and over inflated, fewer beds were required. In August 1939 the Dorset County Council were told to expect around 800 expectant mothers and that arrangements were to be made to house them. In actual fact 244 were evacuated to the county, excluding the Poole area.[158]

'Who Pays?' seemed to be the most frequent question, especially where pregnancy was involved. In Oxfordshire the County Evacuation controller wrote to the Town Clerk in Chipping Norton:-

'I am informed by the City Almoner that a Mrs Phillips, an evacuee expectant mother.....is to be admitted to the Ruskin College Maternity Hospital on the 16th instant. I shall be glad if you will make the necessary transport arrangements and let me know when this has been done'.

The reply read:-

'I think it should be suggested that Mrs. Phillips uses the 'bus service to Oxford'.!!

This was agreed by the Controller.[159]

Did the reception area pay for the confinement, or did the evacuating authority? No issue seemed to promote such anger as an 'enjoyed conception in London leading to an expensive confinement in Dorset'.[160] Alderman Oliver, in the Weymouth Council in September 1939, noted that the Greenhill residence of Captain Hamblin had been requisitioned as a home for one hundred evacuee expectant mothers at a cost of £1,300 per year, excluding rent and rates. He wanted to know if this expense would be met by the Ministry of Health and the Town Clerk assumed that it would.[161]

The information had obviously taken time to reach the reception areas as this issue of cost had been resolved in late August 1939 when the Ministry of Health agreed to guarantee any payment. Once this had been agreed, the reception areas were able to find an extra 1,003 maternity beds by the 2nd September and a further 2,679 by October, in 137 Maternity homes. During this time 2,881 confinements took place.[162]

Having found the extra accommodation, the biggest problem was where to find the much needed staff. Of greater concern was that once the babies had been born, the mothers and children needed extra welfare care. This was even more important under their new circumstances because they were away from their extended families who would, under normal circumstances, have been around to help, either with the new baby or with other dependant siblings. There were other attendant problems. Between 1939-45 illegitimate births had risen by 300% and billeting officers found it very difficult to house them on moral grounds. This resulted in their being sent to local workhouses where their 'public assistance' costs had to be paid by the evacuating authority. Some areas were adamant that the costs should not be borne by them and Holman cites one case where the Public Assistance Department in Somerset put two young unmarried mothers back on the train to London.[163] This whole issue does raise the question of confidentiality and the rights of the individual. Why did the Billeting Officer have to tell the hosts about anyone's personal circumstances? Surely a mother and child were simply a mother and child. The fact that the child was illegitimate should not have been a significant factor.

Some areas were a little more sympathetic and, realising that the Workhouse was not always the best place, appointed social workers to help the mothers. This created a worthwhile service which had not been readily available before the war and is one of the more positive 'spin-offs' of the evacuation scheme.

The Drift Back

'600 evacuees gone back to London!'[164]

By the 5th December 1939, 30% of previously evacuated unaccompanied children and 49 % of accompanied children, together with 50% of the mothers had returned to London.[165] Figures for January 1940 show that only 55% of unaccompanied children and 12% of mothers with children remained in the reception areas.[166] All the time they were returning, some reticent hosts were becoming more frustrated at having to retain their charges in line with Government policy but against the wishes of the children and adults. However, some of the blame for the return had to be apportioned to the billeting authorities. The tone of the content of the following letter from the Secretary for Education in Exeter to his colleagues responsible for billeting, would suggest that in some areas there was even severe disagreement between local government departments in the same authority!

```
Dippas-Wadden Evacuation Party
Mount Pleasant Hall,
Exeter,

28th March 1941

Dear Sir,

I am concerned over the rather large numbers of children who have
ventured to Croydon from this Unit during the past week or two. I have
continually impressed upon the children the advisability of remaining
in this reception area and realising that satisfactory billeting is one
of the most vital factors in children's lives here, I have paid very
special attention to that and in most cases have obtained alternative
billets for the children.

Unfortunately, the billeting authorities have either refused to
re-billet children or their action has been so tardy that their parents
have withdrawn them from this area. I know quite definitely that
practically all the children who have returned from this school have
done so because their billets have been unsatisfactory.

If something could be done to ensure greater co-operation between the
billeting authorities and ourselves, who are better acquainted with the
needs of the children, I am confident that the evacuation scheme would
operate better than it is now.

J.M.N.Francis.[167]
```

It was estimated that 98,500 of all unaccompanied children, 408,930 of mothers with children and 154,167 accompanied children had returned home by the end of September.[168] Teachers, concerned that a lot of these children were now walking the streets, reacted vociferously and suggested that the Boards of Education should either close the schools in the home areas or open them up and admit that the scheme was not working. According to a national evacuation count taken in the reception areas in England and Wales on 8th January, a total of 44% of all unaccompanied children, 88% of the mothers, 86% of the accompanied children, 81% of other designated groups and 55% of teachers and helpers, had returned home.[169]

In December 1939, a headteacher evacuated to Haslemere in Surrey wrote:-

> *'We should be glad to be informed whether the Government really considers education of any importance whatsoever and whether they really intend the evacuation of schools to continue or not. The action of almost all their officials right through this business leads me to suppose that neither matters very much either way'.*[170]

It is fair to say that in some areas there was a compromise. Some city schools were reopened during the latter end of 1939 but with limited hours and usually with a severely curtailed curriculum. Initially schooling was made available to children of over 11 who lived within a mile of a specific neighbourhood school, but as war progressed and some pupils returned from the reception areas other ages were catered for as the following timetable from a West London school illustrates.

Date	Notes	No. On Roll	No. Of Classes
29.i.40	Opened for Seniors only	12 half-time	1
29.iii.40	After Easter all ages	177 half-time	6
7.iv.40	Before Evacuation	383 half-time	12
21.iv.40	After Evacuation	352 half-time	10
27.ix.40	During Battle of Britain	289 full-time	9
6.xii.40	After intensive bombing	137 full-time	5
7.iii.41	Return of children from reception areas	237 full-time	6
4.vii.41	Return of children from reception areas	342 full-time	9
10.x.41	Return of children from reception areas	400 full-time	10
24.x.41	Reorganised as Mixed and Infants	433 full-time	10 [171]

Once schools did open in target areas the pupils were in danger, not only from raids but from structural defects in some buildings as a result of earlier raids. Despite attempts to get the returning children into school, poor attendance was very common and was as low as 2% in some areas of London. Although these figures rose considerably from the end of 1940 the overall decline in numbers attending school was not as low as one would suppose considering the circumstances. Attendance statistics show how the percentage of full attendance at school fluctuated during the period December 1940-1941 and again from March 1942-45. Unfortunately, no figures indicating the percentage of attendance are available before July 1941, but there are significant factors which are worth highlighting; that few months were drastically lower than the pre-war average attendance of 87%, hop-picking was still a popular pastime which affected school attendance, despite the rigours of war, the drastic decline in attendance during the V1/V2 attacks on London when, coincidentally, there were a high number of schools open to receive pupils.[172]

The comments made by the headteacher from Surrey, were echoed in many quarters and there was a genuine concern that the problems in the education system, highlighted by evacuation, were simply a continuation of the education policies and general apathy of the 1920s and 1930s during which time expenditure on education was cut, free grammar school places were reduced and, despite advice from educationalists, the leaving age remained the same. The raising of the school leaving age to 15 had first been discussed in 1918. Ironically, its implementation had been timed to take effect from the 1st September 1939 but was of course postponed and not introduced for another eight years.

Problems of Social Class

'I had settled down quite well in my billet until my mother came......Once she had met my mother, my friend was cool to me because she realised that I was from a different class. My foster mother told me that the parents of my friend were paying extra for her keep so I was not to be too disappointed if she received more treats that I did....I think that was the worst thing that ever happened to me'. [173]

It is reasonable to state that although evacuation relieved the urban areas, it did place extreme burdens on the host localities and all too often it was a case of the poor and underprivileged housing the same from the cities. Titmuss remarked that the wealthier classes evaded their responsibilities quite effectively. [174]

Crosby reinforces this when reporting the findings of the Women's Voluntary Service:-

'We find over and over again that it is the really poor people who are willing to take evacuees and that the sort of bridge-playing set who live at places such as Chorley Wood are very difficult about it all'. [175]

In 1939, one clergyman in charge of a small country parish outside Warwick offered to find billets for child evacuees in the local village and 'tramped many weary miles over muddy fields, getting refusal after refusal, especially from many of the richer people'. [176]

A teacher from Sheffield wrote to the Times Education Supplement in 1941:-

'....Evacuees were willing to stay in pleasant billets. These were mostly in smaller houses. Larger houses, well known to have plenty of rooms, consistently refused to help. Until the well-to-do can be induced to take their responsibility seriously and accept the billeting of children of all kinds as a war time duty or an essential form of National Service, parents could not be expected to participate whole-heartedly in the evacuation programme'. [177]

A letter to The Times on the 15th September 1939, provides an indication of disagreement with some aspects of the evacuation scheme by this particular correspondent who, from other evidence, was not alone in his, or her, beliefs. It also demonstrates the problems of simple Public Relations faced by the authorities:-

'Sir, As an emergency plan for a few weeks the evacuation of all city children to country homes would be beyond criticism. As a scheme to be carried through several years it simply bristles with difficulties.

Take the middle-class home where the income largely disappeared from the moment war was declared. Here the billeted children have meals with the kitchen staff if we are fortunate enough to have one. But we cannot feed our maids on 8s 6d a week per head. The children must have some food, and they eat more.

But our kitchen staff has probably gone home, either because their own mothers have children billeted on them, or they do not like the extra work in our homes. Many of us are either elderly, not over strong, or busy with our own small children, and unable to do the extra work of cooking, cleaning, washing and mending, unable to afford the extra expenses and the wear and tear to our homes and gardens for more than a short time.

Yet many fathers of evacuated children are in good jobs and the mothers are now free to go out to work. Might not the broadcast appeals to the charitable public for clothing also remind parents to do their share at any rate in this respect?

Then, where the mothers are billeted with smaller children, in some cases they do not lift a finger to help, and expect to have everything done for them, and the women naturally dislike being in other people's houses. The teachers, too, are not at all easy or contented.

Now that the children are safely out of the cities, is it not possible to organise empty houses or camps, with teachers, mothers and children running them themselves with voluntary helpers? Happy billets could be left undisturbed, but a heavy burden would be lifted from many homes where the strain of living is already great.

Yours &c E.M.Curtis

Alton House. Redhill'[178]

In some areas of the country this action by the upper and middle classes was actively supported by local regulations. An area in Wiltshire refused to take evacuees because:-

'...the servant problem in the large houses is so acute that it would be unfair to billet children on the owners'. [179]

This lack of servants seemed to be a common concern with some of the correspondents to The Times:-

'...my own and other local experience suggests that the evacuation authorities should explain to parents that good manners are the least return they can make for the very real effort and unselfishness on the part of the householders of all conditions, especially in houses where there is a trained and often reduced domestic staff and where the extra work has been cheerfully undertaken and where children live on a scale above the 8s 6d and generally above their own home standard...'[180]

Before the war this lack of cohesion between the classes would not have been a problem worth considering by the voluntary services hierarchy. When asked to appear before the Anderson Committee on the 21st July 1938 to give her opinion on evacuation planning, Lady Reading, Head of the Women's Voluntary Service, stated:-

'Evacuees would be quite happy to live in barns or garages in the countryside, especially if they were next door to a middle class house'.[181]

A note below this comment in the minutes says:-

'...this view was fully endorsed by the Chairman of the Women's Institute, Lady Denman'.[182]

To her credit, Lady Reading did change her opinion and told Mass Observation in 1940 that:

'Evacuation had been a terrible fiasco.....not nearly enough use had been made of the big houses of England'.[183]

This had also been noted by the Ministry of Health in a Circular issued in September 1939 in which regional officers were informed that certain local authorities had not included the really 'good class' residences in the billeting lists.[184] Even when the use of such houses was shown in propaganda and feature films the unwillingness of the film characters to welcome evacuees was often apparent. In 'Cottage To Let' made in 1941 and distributed by Gainsborough Pictures, one of the central characters, 'Lady Barrington', when informed by a billeting officer that she was to have evacuees, told her Butler to 'get the spare blankets and eiderdown from the attic...you know, the one with the holes in it', implying that this was good enough for an evacuee.

Some housekeepers looking after country properties for absentee or weekend owners were sometimes put in very difficult situations. One evacuee describes the general conversations when arriving at his first billet with his sister:-

'Soon we were being driven along a lane that took us right out of the village and then along a bumpy track. The driver didn't say very much except to tell us he was not the billeting officer. The car stopped near a cottage that looked like a picture on a chocolate box, except the garden was overgrown and weedy. When a women opened the door our driver said 'I've brought you two temporary foster children'.

To which she replied...'Well you can just take them away again. I never said I would have any evacuees'.

Undeterred he pushed us into the house saying....'According to our lists you have a spare room with a double bed. By law you cannot refuse to take them'.

With that he ran to his car and drove away quickly leaving us standing there miserable.

The woman was very angry... 'They have no right to dump you on me. I have no food and the shops are miles away. What he will say when he finds out I don't know!'[185]

In fairness this unwelcoming experience, although difficult to comprehend by young children, was not necessarily the fault of the housekeeper. Many in similar circumstances reacted in the same way. This housekeeper obviously had no authority to accommodate evacuees. True, billets in this area at the time were hard to find but surely the billeting officers could have gone about their task in a manner which was a little less authoritarian. As it happened the children were in the cottage only a short time and the owner did in fact do a lot to make their stay enjoyable. However, one could imagine a similar situation where the housekeeper's job could have been put in jeopardy!

But it was not always just the upper classes who were unhappy to provide billets for evacuees. As late in the evacuation process as July 1941, the Incorporated Association of Head Masters had gathered evidence from Headteachers of evacuated grammar schools that the more well-to-do people, superior artisan and the clerk class have tended to shirk their responsibilities.[186]

It was reported in the Dorset County Chronicle and Swanage Times on 1st August 1940, that a man from Owermoigne was fined £5 for refusing to take evacuees. This was a great deal of money, but the courts also had the power to imprison people for non-compliance. In this particular case the defendant told the court that he preferred to go to gaol rather than pay, what he considered to be, an excessive fine. Unfortunately, the final outcome of the case was not reported.[187]

Some of the upper classes of course took in evacuees but as this diary entry from John Colville would suggest in some instances they were tolerated as long as they did not upset the status quo:-

> *'Saturday. September 23rd: After lunch I went by train to Stansted to spend the week-end with the Bessboroughs.....There were also sixty or more orphans, who played cricket happily on the lawn in front of the house who were carefully excluded from the main part of the house itself, which remains as cheerful and comfortable as ever'.*[188]

Some evacuees were not even allowed in the house. A visit by a host and her evacuees to a friend resulted in the following situation:-

> *'We had been shown the grounds by a girl of 15. Then we were taken to the house, but before we went in we met the girl's mother who asked...'Where are you taking them?*

> *'To meet Daddy,' was the reply.*

> *'Oh darling! I don't think that is a good idea. I'm sure your little friends are very nice but we do not want them in the house do we? I'll have the buns and barley-water sent out'.*[189]

Others obviously took their responsibilities more seriously and either made over their whole house to the evacuees or made their stay as comfortable as possible.

> *'Sunday September 17th: After lunch and a game of billiards I motored Philip to Middleton via Stoney Stratford and Banbury. The house is occupied by a horde of Roman Catholic children, in charge the of a dozen nuns, and the family are living in cottages'.*[190]

Joan Faulkner described her first placement with a Mrs Sayers, an American, who was a daughter of a Woolworth magnate and who owned a large house in Wentworth. Joan was given a bedroom which contained full size models of Snow White and the Seven Dwarfs and was chauffeured to school in a limousine.[191] Her second placement was not so luxurious. Joan and her family were billeted on a family in a small council house where she had to share a bed...four children of both sexes sleeping width ways! [192]

And 'Dolly' remembers in a letter to her first host, Nella Hughes-Smith, how her billets were at either ends of the social scale both in terms of care and experience. It has been reproduced in full as an excellent example of where evacuation had a significant influence on a child's life. It illustrates what a different carefree experience 'Dolly', her 14 year old sister Mary and 5 year old brother 'Tiddler' had until they were taken away by their stepmother because 'they were too comfortable'. (Two other brothers had been billeted with another family.) One can only speculate how life might have changed for 'Dolly' and her siblings had they been allowed to stay in the billet.

'We drove down the long drive and the door was opened by a maid in uniform. As we went in I tripped on the step and fell into the hall. Instead of the expected clip around the ear for being clumsy, you and Mona, the maid, were very concerned. Thus started the only happy memories of childhood and I have treasured them all my life. I remember you always bathed Tiddler and me yourself although you had two maids. We were bathed, put to bed and you read to us until the dinner gong went.

We had a delightful bedroom, very clean and comfortable, a complete contrast to our home where we slept 'top and tail', 6 in a bed with no sheets and pillow cases. The place was infested with bugs and we had paraffin sprayed on the walls each night, no windows open; you can imagine the smell!

I have many happy memories of playing in the woods near the house, the local hunt, the Garth, scrumping apples from the austere looking house up the lane, in fact not scrumping but openly taking your gardener's wheelbarrow and stripping a whole tree. I came back triumphant to Sallie the cook and presented them to her. I remember when we threw porridge out of the nursery window onto the nectarines and when Albert the gardener complained you did not punish us but you set up a little plot of our own. You bought us Wellingtons and a fork and trowel and we spent happy times digging in our own garden. When Christmas came we had toys for the first time ever and we were surrounded by love and happiness.

When we heard we were leaving I remember going down the lane and lying in a field of cowslips and crying. Apart from a few months spent in a children's home where life was quite pleasant, my time with you and your family was like a wonderland and a happy release from a very traumatic and unhappy childhood.

You said you thought we went back to London but in fact I went to a couple called Roberts in a bungalow. My stepmother told me years later that she had asked for us to be moved as we were too comfortable. Later I went to a children's home in Maidenhead. I went back to London when I was 13 as my stepmother had had a baby and I was needed to queue for food. When the Blitz started in earnest my father, stepmother and the baby went into the country and left me there alone, having turned off the water and electricity. I wasn't afraid, just glad to be free and I just went into the Anderson shelter when the sirens went and to a neighbour's house for a wash.

I left at 16 and went to Cornwall to work in a children's home. I didn't see my brothers and sisters again'.[193]

It would be wrong to assume that although in some areas the responsibility for housing evacuees fell on the poorer classes they would offer a more caring environment for evacuees from similar deprived backgrounds. Lilian Evans has made a collection of reminiscences of ex-evacuees from a poor area of Liverpool. They were all evacuated to Wales and it would seem from their comments that there had been a significant amount of anti-evacuee propaganda to warrant the same measures being taken by hosts when their evacuees arrived. Out of 35 evacuees 15 of them, mostly girls had had their heads shaved.

'The man had a chair ready. He said 'Sit here Julie'. He cut and cut and my hair fell on the floor. He then got hair clippers and shaved my head.

'You're next', he told Ann. She was crying. The lady brought a tin from under the sink with a bottle of purple Gentian Violet and started to paint my head with a little brush. I now had a bald head with purple dots all over and so did Ann.'[194]

Many of the hosts, when asked by the evacuees who were having their heads shaved replied 'Children from Liverpool bring lice, scabies and sores'.[195] Those who were not shaved had their hair washed in disinfectant and many had their clothes burned. Some of them were wearing new clothes!

Blodwyn, (the daughter of the house) said to me 'Come on, take your clothes off'.

I said 'No!'

'Mama, she won't take her clothes off'.

Mrs Davis came and told me to undress. She look at me with staring eyes, so slowly I started to take my clothes off. Then I was put in a bath.....The lady got a poker and started to throw my clothes into the back garden. She said to the girls, 'Whatever you do don't touch them!'

I felt dirty, the girls kept looking at me as I got out of the bath. I was glad, it smelled awful. Then I was told to kneel on the floor. The woman came with scissors and cut off all my hair then she got some clippers and went over my head. I was bald. I had been in the house twenty minutes.

She passed me with the pillowslip with all my clothes in. She threw them in the garden and set them alight'.[196]

'First let's get you undressed'.

I went to sit on a chair. There was a scream so loud that I jumped. I thought I had sat on the cat. It was the lady.

'Go in the back and take all your clothes off ready for a bath'.

I know why she screamed....'I had sat on a chair and not had a bath first. Evacuees were alive with lice bugs and I don't know what else she said they had been told. We were washed in Dettol and our hair was shaved off".

(I thought I had sat on the cat.)[197]

Julie, Hilda and the others were seven years old. One can only imagine the trauma that she and their peers went through.

These incidents raise an important question. Why did these hosts assume that the evacuees coming to their area would be dirty and lice-ridden!? One can only speculate that such assumptions had been gleaned from someone in authority because so many of the hosts in this small area of Wales adopted exactly the same policy. However, detailed research in the documents relating to this area resulted in very little concrete evidence except a comment stating that:-

'...While some voiced their disgust at the condition of the children some hosts chose rather to accept the situation and apply themselves zealously to the task of cleaning up their charges'.[198]

If the hosts were rather 'zealous', where were the billeting officers when all this was going on? Why did they not do something to stop it? However, any blame for allowing such situations to arise cannot be directed entirely at them. It may be that they simply did not have, or were not given, enough time by the organising authorities to check what was going on. The following statement would suggest that some local councils were unaware of the responsibilities of Billeting Officers and the amount of time needed for them to do their job effectively despite having been sent various Ministry of Health Circulars, including No. 1857 on 27th August 1939, which stipulated the frequency of visits to evacuees in their billets. The Clerks of the Amlwch RDC and Nant Conway RDC told their respective councils that the 'Billeting Officers will be able to complete their work in 2-3 hours. The Billeting Officer in Penmachno was told:-

'...should occasion arise it is not anticipated that this particular work will involve more than one day release from your duties while ensuring this defence'.[199]

No consideration was given to follow up work or visits. Such ignorance of the amount of time involved in doing the job properly could only lead to some billeting officers having to pay lip-service to their role, especially if they were responsible for a large geographical area. Under such circumstances, any host wishing to take advantage of their situation in terms of abuse, using evacuees as servants, generally ill-treating them, was in an ideal situation to do so.

Finally, why were there no complaints from the evacuated teachers? Even today many of the group ask why they did nothing to help. A quote from a teacher, mentioned by some of the group, would suggest that she was not too sympathetic:-

'Just be thankful that these nice people took you into their homes. You could be in Liverpool with all the bombs'.[200]

In fairness it has to be said that despite this initial treatment a number of this group of evacuees were then well looked after in their billets and did enjoy the remainder of their stay.

Not all people were prepared to countenance the billeting of evacuees on private householders. An anonymous correspondent to the Windsor Express on the 25th October 1940, seriously suggested the building of Concentration Camps in order to house evacuees and some town councils in reception areas discussed the possibility of putting evacuees in segregated communities.[201] The use of the words concentration camp could have been forgiven as merely identifying some sort of holding area for evacuees, similar to the use of such camps in the Boer War for prisoners. However, even in local papers, journalists were writing articles describing life in the camps. In August 1939, under the title 'Concentration Camp for Women' the reporter described the Ravensbrueck as having:-

> *'...the usual drastic measures to prevent escape. The whole camp is surrounded by a barricade of high-tension wire and a detachment of S.S. men is always on guard. At their work the inmates are perpetually watched by women warders, who are most strictly forbidden to exchange a single word of private conversation, with their charges...'* [202]

Although, when in October 1939, the Government had produced and published a White Paper on German Concentration Camps, it was obviously not taken too seriously by John Colville who, in his diary, described the Paper as:-

> *'...a sordid document calculated to appeal to people's lowest instincts, and reminiscent of the 'Corpse factory' propaganda in the last war. It does shed a lurid glow on the bestial sadism of the Germans at their worst; but after all, most evidence is produced from prejudiced sources, and it is in any case undesirable to arouse passions before the war has begun in earnest'.* [203]

By the end of 1939 many people were aware of the possible sinister implications of the development of concentration camps.

Although the concentration camp suggestion was an isolated one, there were communities which objected to having evacuees billeted in their area. The following letter was sent by members of the Lychett Minster Parish Council to the Chairman of the Dorset Civil Defence Emergency Committee on the 24th November 1939:-

> *'Sir,*
>
> *We strongly protest against the billeting scheme for evacuated families who have been sent unexpectedly to this area and billeted upon country families regardless of the differences in the standards of living and of the insurmountable difficulties occasioned by forcibly overcrowding country homes, with the result that many families have returned to London. We suggest an alternative scheme that the Authority responsible take over empty houses and buildings and recondition them to take these families'.*

The reply from the Chairman implied that it was a Government and not a County matter. However, later in the war Dorset County Council did in fact refurbish houses for use by evacuee families at its own expense.

These statements and actions tend to contradict the Canadian diplomat Charles Ritchie's comment in August 1940 that:-

> *'English men and women of different classes, localities, sets and tastes are for the first time talking to each other'.*[204]

Angus Calder recently made the comment that:-

> *'...the bombing mixed classes together. Well-off travellers in the London Underground could not miss the thousands of poor people sleeping on the platform'.*[205]

It is true that in this situation they could not help seeing each other, but evidence would suggest that in many reception areas the 'classes' did not necessarily get on, nor, in many cases did they tolerate each other. To a certain extent this was brought about by a notable condescension of the voluntary services in some of the reception areas and ignorance and misunderstanding on the part of both evacuees and hosts. Despite legislation appearing before war broke out, few authorities had thought enough about the social consequences of such an evacuation scheme. Therefore, in hindsight, it is not surprising that problems relating to mutual suspicion and disregard occurred. Local authorities did not help the situation by using billets that were unsuitable, either from the inadequacy of the building or of the hosts. Also, in some cases the reception areas were expecting either large numbers of people or a preponderance of a specific category. Berkshire County Council were told to expect evacuees as follows; 50% schoolchildren, 30% mothers with children under school age, and 20% cripples, blind helpers, teachers and expectant mothers. As it turned out these figures were not adhered to and in East Berkshire a considerably larger number of women and children arrived than anticipated with the result that many host families who had volunteered to take a school child were called upon to provide lodging for a category of person they had previously declined. This obviously created great difficulties for the reception and billeting officers. In other examples whole company workforces were moved en bloc to safer areas and this caused great problems to all aspects of evacuee administration.

> *'21st March 1941. The staff and families of Folland Aircraft were moved to Exeter from Hamble near Southampton today'.*[206]

There is a great deal of evidence to support Crosby's view that the poor took the brunt of housing evacuees.[207] It must also be said that some agreed to take evacuees either through ignorance or a naive sense of well-being. The following letter was written to the billeting officer in Exeter by an 80 year old man and one can sense that it is almost apologetic and humble in its tone.

'Our evacuees, a woman and 2 children under 3 years of age, have been with us since November 11th. During all that time my wife has been ill on account of her severe heart trouble. (Angina Pectoris). I shall be glad if you will be good enough to give permission to move them as soon as possible....' [208]

There was no evidence of any reply or outcome. But the letter does beg the question why did the authorities use 80 year old hosts?

Some people did their utmost to avoid having evacuees and used all manner of means and excuses to do so:-

1.12.40

From Doctor.

With reference to Lady Davy: On medical grounds it is not good for her to have ten evacuees in a house with only five bedrooms and 2 living rooms. Because of her public duties Lady Davy requires more than just her bedroom.

This request was turned down by the evacuation authorities on two separate occasions. But the fact that the letter was sent and worded in this fashion does suggest that Lady Davy did have ten evacuees in her house. [209]

There was a certain amount of abuse concerning the issue of medical certificates to help people avoid having evacuees. These could be easily obtained from some Doctors and, in some cases could be purchased for 2/6d. [210]

However, some excuses may have backfired, as this letter would suggest:-

28th October. 1940

Dear Madam,

I understand that in response to the billeting notice served upon you, you stated as a reason for being unable to receive evacuees that your daughter has been in bed for three years with tuberculosis.

I am unable to trace any record of this in the City Health Department so I would be glad if you will inform me of the name of your medical practitioner in order that I may ascertain further particulars which will enable me to consider whether you can be exempted from billeting or not.

Yours faithfully

C.J.Newman [211]

And, as this letter from the billeting officer in Chipping Norton to the Town Clerk indicates, even senior personnel in the local authorities were becoming very frustrated by some people's lack of co-operation:-

'Dear Mr. Morris,

Mrs.....of....will be in, I expect, with an appeal. She has no reason to appeal, she is actually a miserable, wicked old woman, and if the people are moved it should be stressed that it is for their sakes and not for hers. She absolutely abused them last night so much that Mrs Watts was trying at a late hour to find alternative accommodation for a very nice superior sort of woman and her two small children.

Please give it to the old girl hot and strong, as a witness I can say she deserves it. In fact, could we but direct the bombs, some would do good.

Yours sincerely... '[212]

There was an appeal procedure, Ministry of Health Regulation 22. Defence Regulations 1939, through which hosts could go if they had any grievance about the evacuation process. But others relied on the good will and sympathy of neighbours and some local politicians to inform the authorities of problems.

'21.2.41 5.35pm. Councillor Pedlar 'phoned.

One of his van drivers, Moore, lives at 16 Hazel Road. Man, wife, 4 children of his own and two evacuee children.

Billeting Officer has called today and says that two more evacuated boys will be billeted upon him tomorrow. The house is a non parlour type.

Mr Pedlar thinks this is damnable as one class of person seems to be carrying all the burden. He does not wish to mention the matter in Council if possible, but points out that houses on his own road and in other roads of similar class do not appear to be taking their share.

He also says that he knows of a case where the husband is on service and his wife has eight children, some of her own and some evacuees'. [213]

This anonymous letter was sent to the Town Clerk's Office in Exeter in mid-1940:-

'...It has come to my notice that childless women resident in Beacon Lane, Whipton, retire to their back rooms when the evacuation authorities are in the district. Alternatively, they go out of their houses.

Is this equality or sacrifice? What do you propose to do about it? What chance does this country stand of pulling through if this is permitted?

Signed. JUSTICE' [214]

The Clerk of the Bradford-on-Avon reported the same problem in 1941:-

> *'...Occupiers have deliberately left their homes during the period of Billeting in an attempt to avoid having to provide accommodation'.*[215]

After the Council in St. Ives, Cornwall had introduced compulsory measures to house evacuees, the editor of the St. Ives Times wrote, in June 1940, under the headline 'It occurs to me'...

> *'Tonight loyal inhabitants of this ancient borough will extend a welcome to little evacuee children driven from their homes and their parents' side as a result of war. Others will look on and do nothing.*
>
> *I gather that those who have had the task of finding volunteers to house these children have had no light job. A number of people who a short while ago were moaning that they had no seasonal bookings this year were apparently full up immediately the question of evacuees arose. Perhaps we are to have a season after all. I hear that the number of people who have developed heart trouble and kindred ailments this week is staggering. I suppose we must expect to see these poor souls wheeled along the Wharf Road in bath chairs.*
>
> *One man is alleged to have said he would as soon house Hitler as evacuee children. If this attitude was general he would probably have Hitler and the Gestapo with him sooner than he expected. Perhaps he anticipates becoming a local dictator under the Nazi regime. As I said last week, I consider the fact that the Council had to adopt compulsory measures a serious reflection on the Borough.*
>
> *I hope that adequate measures will be taken by the authorities to see that children billeted compulsorily are properly and kindly treated...'*[216]

This problem of non-compliance with the scheme was recognised as early as September 1939. The Revd. R.W. Sorensen, Labour M.P. for Leighton West, agreed that the behaviour of evacuees in reception areas was a psychological problem, ignorance of the other lifestyles and withdrawal from a stable home life. Also 'working class women used to their own homes and practices would naturally find it difficult to share the home of a stranger'.[217]

However, the problem of billeting did not go away. At a meeting of the Wareham and Purbeck Rural District Council on 30th October 1940, the Chief Billeting Officer, Mr A.T. Selvey, asked the Council if they were prepared to authorise action being taken against those persons who refused to comply with the requirements of the billeting. Supporting the proposition, a fellow councillor, Mr. I.S. MacDonald was quoted as saying that 'those people who had definitely refused to take evacuees were sitting back laughing at those who had taken them'. The Mayor, Councillor A.T. Moss, warned that there was a statutory duty on the part of householders to comply with billeting notices and that in the event of further people coming we shall exercise our powers if we encounter difficulties'.[218]

There were particular problems with housing expectant mothers and one example from Wiltshire where such an evacuee, described as 'a lady of very superior type' was not allowed to stay in her 'superior type of billet' generated an interesting response from the Clerk of the Bradford-on-Avon UDC. He raised the very important issue that if the 'well-to-do' were infringing the Defence Regulations and could be so easily relieved of their obligation to house evacuees, this would put undue pressure on those who were willing to take in evacuees. Also it would make the whole scheme very difficult to manage because he would have no response to any other householder refusing to comply with the regulations.[219] But even MPs and even members of the church had misconceptions about the type of person being evacuated. The M.P for Caenarvonshire, R. Owen, stated:-

> *'It is ludicrous that evacuees should be sent to the beautiful Welsh valleys which only have quiet country pubs'.* [220]

In February 1942 the Vicar of St. Mary's Church, Dorchester commented on the 'heathen' upbringing of many evacuated children.

> *'We have witnessed the return, unwise as it has seemed to many of us, of many of the evacuee children to their homes. Many of them have been brought up in a manner one could call anything but heathen. They had never been to any place of worship or Sunday School and had never been taught to say their prayers...'* [221]

However, despite this concern for the lack of religious practices and morals, in some areas the locals, well known for their religious enthusiasm, did not extend their own Christian values towards the evacuees. On 8th September 1939 the following article appeared in the North Wales Chronicle under the headline 'Something I shall never forget'.

> *'Last Sunday evening (the day war was declared) I saw something I shall never forget. A little crowd of homeless schoolboys evacuated from Liverpool, sat huddled on the pavement in one of the most well-to-do roads in Bangor, outside the house of a married couple who refused to take them. The Billeting Officer had argued and begged. You have seven empty rooms and no responsibilities. You are only taking one grown up. Can't you manage even two of these tired children?*

> *'No I can't!', snapped the woman, and closed the door.*

> *While the Billeting Officer discussed what to do with the children the garden gate opened and the 'lady' of the house emerged followed by her husband. They were going to Church!*

> *They stepped daintily through the pathetic little bundles, the haversacks and gas masks and the children watched them....saying nothing'.*[222]

Despite obvious problems in accepting evacuees in rural areas, some individuals took in more than their fair share. It was reported in February 1940 that a Mrs Price of Oxford House, Abbotsbury Road, Weymouth, mother of nine children, also had seventeen evacuees. Also a Mrs Allard of 6

Verne Road, Weymouth, mother of three, had sixteen evacuees.[223] Mrs Dine of the Grosvenor Hotel, Weymouth had 24 evacuees from the Notre Dame Convent High School, Southwark.[224]

Some people who had accepted the proposal of having evacuees, recognised potential problems early in the scheme and were genuinely concerned that some screening should have taken place in order to put the correct combination of evacuees into suitable households. A correspondent to the Bedfordshire Times and Standard in September 1939 is only one example of concerns expressed by a number of responsible hosts.

> *'Sir, After reading your account of the arrangements made for the reception of evacuees in Bedford, I was resolved that we must meet our obligations and take them in whether we wanted to or not.*
>
> *Therefore, on Friday, I felt that common humanity demanded I should take these people under my roof and make them as happy as possible, but I could not live up to my ideals when the Billeting Officer brought me a mother and two children. To have taken them in would have been disloyal to my wife and children. Why were these people not graded?'* [225]

However, it did work both ways. One interviewee from a reasonably well-off family, was indignant that she was billeted with a very poor couple who had no bathroom and she had to wash in a tin bath in the kitchen with people, including neighbours, walking through.[226]

Teachers must have found the situation arising from poor or ineffectual billeting procedures just as frustrating, as the following entry in a school log book, dated 28th July 1941 would indicate:-

> *'When every pressure is brought to bear on parents to leave their children in the reception areas, it seems a great pity that billets cannot be found. I wish to quote the case of Arnold Cohen, aged 8, whose parents came to report to me yesterday that they were obliged to take him home as they had been told by the billeting officer that there was no other billet and he suggested that they took him home. The reason given for his being sent from his billet here was that his head was dirty. This may be true but his head was quite clean on June 26th when he was inspected by the school nurse. If his head is infected now, it has happened only during these last four weeks and surely the foster parents could have found it out quickly!'* [227]

Any unwillingness on the part of a householder to take in an evacuee and then be forced to do so could only have had a detrimental effect on the relationship between the two. A number of correspondents have described the cattle market situation which occurred in many areas. The fact that so many remember this aspect of the scheme suggests that it had a traumatic effect on their initial, and perhaps later, well-being:-

> *'There were some seats but many of us had to sit on the floor or stand with our belongings until we were chosen by a foster parent. ....With the foster parent standing in front, the billeting officer would call out 'two girls' or 'one boy'. Sometimes he might say 'Which boy would like to live on a farm?' or 'Is there a girl here who likes horses?'*

Each time a forest of hands would go up and it quickly developed into a competitive situation in which the children vied with each other to be chosen'.[228]

Some people in authority also managed to use this system to their own advantage. A teacher from Liverpool reported in his anonymous memoirs the following incident which occurred when he had first been evacuated to North Wales with his school:-

'The billeting officer drew me to one side and asked if I could recommend one nice, clean little girl as his wife would be pleased to take one evacuee....I selected a victim....the 'market' was then declared open'.

He went on to describe the rest of the billeting procedure:-

'To my fellow teacher and I the procedure of adoption was just guesswork, as neither of us could understand a word that was being said. The local helper stood at the door allowing the foster parents in one at a time. She was armed with a 3ft blackboard ruler which she held 'at the slope' considering this an appropriate attitude to adopt in a state of national emergency. When a new customer was admitted the sound of high words and a scuffle came from the waiting room. Obviously, there was a common desire to be the first in the queue and 'bag' the cleanest child'.[229]

New Initiatives

'Many of them, evacuee mothers and children, have drifted back to London. Much ill-feeling has been caused. But the interesting thing is that this feeling is not between the rich and the poor but between the urban and rural poor. This is a perplexing social event. One thing that they say is that these children were evacuated at the end of the holidays and were therefore more verminous and undisciplined than if they had been taken in the middle of the term. But the effect will be to demonstrate to people how deplorable is the standard of life and civilisation among the urban proletariat'. [230]

The Government was very concerned about the rise in discontent and the return of evacuees to the cities at the end of 1939. At a meeting of the Dorchester Council in early December the Chief Billeting Officer, Admiral W. de M. Egerton stated that 600 evacuees had returned to London. This created problems as many of the parents had removed their children without informing the authorities. As a result the Council sent a formal complaint to the Minister of Health about this practice but the reply simply informed them that the letter would receive consideration. However, evacuees had been returning home earlier in the year. As early as October it was estimated that in the Dorchester area twenty per cent of the 1,642 evacuees had left and that billeting officers were having to deal with the problems their absence had created. One was the question of debts which the evacuees had left behind and it was suggested that where the billeting officers had the home address of such people they should be contacted and asked for any moneys outstanding.[231] It was reported on 2nd November 1939 that:-

'....evacuees are fast leaving the Wareham Rural District area'. [232]

Christmas of that year, 1939, was seen by many as the watershed of the scheme 'unless Hitler played up with a bomb'.[233] In the small village of Ashley Green, 15 out of 20 evacuees registered from the 12th September had returned by the 4th December 1939.[234] It was reported that Parliament was to discuss the question of 'What kind of Christmas are the evacuated children to be given?' in a debate on 14th November 1939. There was never any suggestion that children should be sent home for the holidays so the debate was to centre on what could be provided in the reception areas. 'Santa Claus' trains and coaches taking parents to visit their children were considered along with home-grown entertainments.[235]

Programmes of special events such as film shows, Pantomimes and concerts were set up in reception areas in an attempt to keep children in the country. £15,000 was raised in London, £5,000 from the general public, to provide the finance for these Christmas parties in some of the reception areas, and in Liverpool £2,000 was allocated to providing Christmas gifts for evacuees.[236] Some evacuees organised their own Christmas entertainment as a report from the Retford Times of 15th December 1939 indicates:-

TOWN HALL CROWDED FOR CONCERT

Since they became Retford's guests the evacuee children from Leeds have won a well deserved reputation in the staging of public entertainment. The Town Hall was packed on Thursday evening for another of their concerts during which the senior boys sang a special song...

'When Retford was invaded by troops of evacuees,
the good folk of Retford were somewhat ill at ease.
But now the invasion's over
and the troops have settled down,
they're as happy as bees in clover,
living in Retford Town'

West Leeds High School for Boys gave a detective sketch and there were items from Patrick Behan, a senior boy, after which a vote of thanks was given by the Mayor on behalf of the people of Retford'.[237]

There is evidence to suggest that some evacuated schools provided entertainment for their hosts very early in the scheme. A newspaper article of 21st September 1939 in the Dorset County Chronicle reported that the local villages around Stratton had been entertained by Section 4 of the Haberdashers School billeted in the area. The headline 'Evacuees entertain Again' suggests that this was not the first time they had done this.

In Dorset, the County Council's Chief Billeting Officer considered that there were only three parishes which needed any sort of organised Christmas events and he was very concerned that many visiting teachers had had a very hard time working on the evacuation scheme since July and many had not had a holiday at all, or had been recalled from them in the summer. He felt that under the circumstances it was important that they should have a break over Christmas. In order to do this he suggested that some voluntary arrangements should be made in the parishes concerned whereby the teachers could rest. He suggested that instead of parties, the evacuees could be taken to the cinema in Weymouth or Dorchester.[238]

In Buckinghamshire, the County Education Board were not so benevolent towards the evacuee teachers. They requested that evacuated school staff should carry out duties in their host schools over the Christmas period, including Christmas Day and Boxing Day so that even one child who was unable to stay at their billet during the holiday period could go to the school where there would be some connection with someone from London. Head teachers of evacuated schools were therefore asked to draw up rotas to cover the Christmas break.[239] The same arrangements were made in Weymouth:-

'There was a great deal of heated debate at the town's Education Committee when it refused to allow evacuated teachers to have an extra half-day's holiday on 22 December for travelling home. It was reported that the Chairman and Clerk had met with teacher's representatives with whom it had already been agreed that schools should close for instruction during the Christmas holidays, but that schools would remain open and a sufficient number of evacuated teachers would arrange

activities for schoolchildren from other districts as well as their own and teachers remaining on duty would stagger their holidays before and after Christmas. It was pointed out by one Councillor that non-evacuated teachers were getting the extra half day!' [240]

The Christmas holiday was not the only time that teachers had to give up. There are numerous accounts of teachers losing their holiday to provide recreational facilities for children in the billets and to find the time to deal with social and pastoral aspects with foster parents. The following can be found in the Commercial Rd. School log-book:-

> '*8th August 1940.*
> *Although the school is officially closed I am attending at school in the mornings to supervise the children who attend. I am also taking the opportunity of dealing with the clothes problem, reporting on it and taking measurements in necessitous cases. I have visited foster parents for the purpose of enquiry before reporting to the Secretary of the Care Committee in Stepney Green East'.* [241]

And at the Ashley Green School:-

> '*10th August to 7th September 1940.*
> *During the summer closure their doors were opened each morning at the customary time. About 30 children arrived each day and stayed in the charge of two members of staff until 4pm. Sometimes the children played organised games in the playground, or painted pictures or played with various toys or in the sand pit. They all had a jolly holiday. At the same time 30 seniors worked in the fields harvesting for the farmers'.* [242]

In a deliberate attempt to keep evacuees in the reception areas in December 1939, no special trains were laid on to take the children back home for Christmas and in Scotland the school holidays were shortened to relieve the pressure on hosts.[243]

However, according to the analysis of the national evacuee returns estimates of 5th December 1939 and the actual count made on 8th January 1940, 16% of evacuees still remaining in the reception areas returned home and there was a greater rate of return of mothers and children.

Christmas seemed to be a very important influence on the rate of return.[244]

Travel for evacuees, their teachers and visiting parents was a problem throughout the war and not only during the Christmas period. Demands were made early in the evacuation process for cheap train fares to allow parents to visit their children. There was a great deal of concern over the amount of money such a journey could take out of the family budget, especially as one of the first acts of the railway companies after war was declared, was to abolish cheap day returns for long distance journeys. There were meetings between the LCC and the rail companies. The LCC argued that a flat rate fare to any destination in the reception areas should be introduced. It was agreed that since parents had no say in the final destinations of their children they should not be expected to bear disproportionate costs, especially as some had been evacuated to areas within a short distance of the capital and others to the rural villages of Wales and the North. However, the railway companies found the proposal unacceptable and it was not until November 1939 that the Minister of War Transport announced a programme of limited concessions whereby day trips on Sundays at reduced rates were to be provided to a limited number of destinations, none of which was to be more than 160 miles from the centre of London.[245] This concession was later extended to further distances. Between 1941 and 1945 the Ministry of War Transport made reduced rate tickets available to parents and relatives wishing to visit evacuated women and children. However, these were usually only allowed to be used for one journey a month for each person and they could not be used at certain times including Christmas, holiday periods and during troop movements. The following Circular issued jointly by the Ministry of Health and the Board of Education in November 1943, indicates that there was often a need for curtailment of travel facilities.

> 'Government Evacuation Scheme: Travel facilities for teachers, helpers and other transferred staff.
>
> The Ministry of War Transport has stated that it is of paramount importance that passenger traffic on railways during the coming winter should be reduced to a minimum. It is accordingly necessary, as part of the general reduction, to apply the same restrictions as were in operation last winter to free and partly-free journeys allowed to evacuated teachers, helpers and other transferred staff during the period 1st October 1943 and 31st March 1944 ....
>
> Full or partial reimbursement of travelling expenses may therefore not be made in respect of more than 2 journeys in all undertaken by an individual teacher or helper during this period....'[246]

A memorandum had also been issued the previous Easter from the Ministry of Health stipulating that there was to be no cheap travel on the trains between the 22nd and 27th of April 1943.[247]

As children were increasingly being sent to the more remote areas of the country the cost of visits became prohibitive for some people and a number of ex-evacuees have expressed their concern that it was for this reason they had received very few visits from parents and had lost contact with their families. Contact which, for some, took a long time to redevelop after the war. [248]

Others were a little more fortunate. Some reception areas took the initiative and arranged parental visits. An appeal was launched in the Weymouth area to persuade people with the accommodation who could not take evacuees on a permanent basis to volunteer to house the parents of evacuees over the Christmas break.[249] On 11th December it was reported that over 300 parents of evacuees arrived in Weymouth by special train. They were either met at the station by their children and hosts or were taken on by car to the outlying villages or to Portland where they were entertained and fed. This had been arranged by the WVS. The same happened in the Isle of Purbeck just before Christmas and again on the 28th January 1940 when special evacuee trains arrived at Swanage.[250] These arrangements were so successful that it was announced locally in February 1940 that further trips at special reduced fares for friends and relatives of evacuees in West Country reception areas were to be arranged for 25th February and 3rd March with connections arranged with local bus companies to isolated villages. Other evidence suggests that there were further trips arranged in May but, as meat rationing had come into force by then, hosts were advised not to share their Sunday roast with the visitors. The parents had in fact been informed of this and were told to make their own arrangements by taking sandwiches etc.

Not all these visits went according to plan. Just one example to illustrate the problems of many is recounted by Margaret Harrod who had been evacuated to Sway in Hampshire. She was visited by her parents who were not impressed by the fact that she had moved billets and nobody, including Margaret, had told them. They therefore spent a great deal of time searching for her! However the situation was resolved and her mother managed to visit every six weeks.[251]

With all these visits it was the intention that parents should relieve the hosts of the responsibility of looking after the children, at least for the day, and that no hosts should feel duty bound to incur any additional expense, although implementing this was not very easy.[252] In August 1940 concern was expressed in the Dorset Emergency Committee about parental visits. A letter had been received from the Centre Leader of the WVS for the Wareham District referring to arrangements made for the frequent visits from parents to evacuated children. Whilst she thoroughly appreciated reasons for them she did point out that they often had an unsettling effect on the children. She indicated that foster parents felt duty bound to offer hospitality which, in many cases, they could ill afford. It was suggested that the Committee wrote to the Southampton Education Committee, where the majority of the evacuees had come from, explaining the situation in the hope of restricting the visits.[253]

These visits also had an effect on some evacuees. James Roffey recalls that he and his brother and sister were to receive a visit from their mother who had booked a place on one of the fleet of coaches organised to take parents down to Sussex from South London:-

> *'After what seemed a lifetime the convoy of Argosy coaches came slowly down Church Hill and stopped outside the Swan Hotel. All the children were cheering and pushing forward, trying to see which coach their parents were on so that they could be at the right doorway. ....Our mother could only stay at Pulborough for a few hours before she had to rejoin the coach and go on to Shoreham to visit our brother Ernest....We sadly watched the coach leaving and then wandered off feeling very despondent and homesick'.*[254]

For many evacuees like James these visits were a disappointment and an emotional wrench. Parents and children tried to relate to each other sometimes in very difficult circumstances and in many ways the situation was false. There was a hope on the part of some evacuees that the relationship between them and their parents would be the same as it had been at home, but of course this was impossible. It has to be said that some parents treated these visits as an excursion and an excuse for a visit to the coast or countryside where seeing their children was low priority. Not all parents went off to visit their children's foster parents. Some got straight off the coaches into the local pubs leaving their children outside. This must have been particularly difficult for the evacuees and foster parents to comprehend and in a way added to the anti-evacuee feeling and the thought that such children were just being dumped in the country to be looked after by others.

On the 17th November 1939, the Ministry of Health issued a Circular authorising evacuation authorities to pay the fares for parents and husbands wishing to visit any member of their evacuated family who was sick. However, in order to be eligible for the ticket, the person travelling had to produce a Doctor's Certificate and had to be means tested and the money for the fare, wherever and whenever possible, had to be recoverable.[255]

This was not a great deal of help to those families already struggling with their domestic finances.

Between January and February 1940 the Civil Defence Committee held a number of meetings in order to devise a new policy which would redirect propaganda away from the evacuee and more towards the rural householder.[256] This view was supported by delegates at the Headmasters' and Headmistresses' Conference in January 1940, when they recommended that:-

> *'...the Government should call upon householders in the reception areas for a generally wider spirit of forbearance and understanding in their acceptance of the children's presence'.*[257]

In January 1940 the Civil Defence Committee, under the Chairmanship of Sir John Anderson, held an evacuation conference which took evidence from Government Ministers, representatives from local authorities, including the LCC, and members of the National Union of Teachers. [258]

After considerable debate, the advisory committee to the Minister of Health came up with three broad strategies.

a. New evacuation scheme to be brought in when raids actually started but it would not include the aged, crippled, and mothers with young children because it was thought that these latter categories were more easily housed.

b. A new propaganda campaign in the reception areas.[259]

c. Measures to deal with the growing number of children within the reception areas.

Elliot, Minister of Health, said in Cabinet on the 21st February 1940:-

> *'A persistent stream of propaganda was being maintained and almost every householder was getting something through the letterbox'.*[260]

And, on the 7th February the Minister of Education, De la Warr, had announced that compulsory education would be imposed as soon as the necessary buildings in the cities were available or made safe.[261]

The second strategy included the announcement of increased billeting allowances for evacuees over 14 years of age to 10/6d per week. In 1939 hosts had received 10/6d for the first child and 8/6d for every subsequent child, and 5/- for teachers. Parents who could afford it, were asked to pay 9/- but the Government were prepared to take 6/-, and those receiving unemployment benefit were not asked to contribute but deductions were made from their assistance benefits, if any of their children were evacuated. All these figures and categories were based on the Poor Law provisions.[262] These figures had been calculated on the cost of the services provided by evacuation, excluding travel which had been paid for by the Government. In return for these allowances the hosts were expected to 'provide lodging, access to water and sanitary arrangements and, if required, cooking facilities'.

A further increase was announced on 14th May 1940 by the Minister of Health, Walter Elliott. With effect from 31st May children aged between 10 and 14 would receive 10/6d per week, 14-16 12/6d per week and 16+ 15/-.

Some hosts felt that the first allowances had been inadequate and as early in the scheme as 4th October 1939 a group of fifteen Weymouth householders who had evacuees billeted on them got together to press for an increase in payment especially for evacuees over the age of 10. The Secretary of the group, Mr. Winter, stated that:-

> '...it was unanimously felt that the allowances are inadequate, especially in the cases of boys and girls tens years old and over. Some people seem to think that you can provide food for children at a ridiculously low figure, but these growing children between 10 and 17 eat as much in many cases as a full grown man'.

They all claimed that they were having to subsidise the scheme in order to provide the children with proper meals.[263]

The responsibility for assessment and for the collection of money was placed on the County Councils.[264] The Poor Law authorities would collect the money from parents and pass it on to the evacuating authorities who, in turn, would pass it on to the Government. Despite the administrative procedures, the amount of money collected was a small percentage of that spent by the Government. Government expenditure on unaccompanied evacuees for the financial year 1939 was £6.7 million of which £559,950 was collected from parents. From 1939 to 1941 local authorities were able to deduct 1/6d per child per year. (1/9d after March 1940) for administrative expenses, plus 7.5% for collection fees (8.75% after March 1940).[265] The average amount of money collected from parents throughout the war was 2/3d per child per week. 2% offered more than the acceptable 6/-, 40% gave 6/-, 11% were on unemployment assistance and 14% were unable to pay and were therefore given a zero assessment. This 'nil payment' differed geographically, 18% in Birmingham, 27% in London, 40% in Sunderland and Liverpool.[266] Specific arrangements were made for those people who could not afford the 6 shillings. The householder had to complete a form providing details of income and normal expenditure plus exceptional expenditure. Rent, travelling expenses to work and statutory insurance contributions were deducted from the family income and allowances were given for the personal needs of the family remaining at home:-

25/- per week for a father and a mother or:

15/- per week for one parent

10/- per week for a dependant adult aged 16 or over

6/- per week for a dependant child under the age of 16.

When these deductions had been made, half of the remaining sum was regarded as available for the repayment of billeting charges. If these figures came to less than 6/- per week, the people concerned were permitted to pay the sum lower than 6/-.[267]

There was also concern from some quarters about how money earned from housing evacuees affected those hosts who were receiving outdoor relief. In February 1942 the Dorset Public Assistance Committee was asked to clarify the matter by the Dorchester Rural District Council. The County Public Assistance Officer explained that when the evacuation scheme started a lot of evacuees were billeted on relief recipients. The Committee maintained that there were two forms of billeting. In one a householder was required to provide accommodation for which a rental allowance was paid and the other in which the householder was required to billet and maintain the evacuee, for instance in the case of unaccompanied children. In the case where the billeted person was maintained, the amount received was not taken into account for the assessment of relief. In the case where rent was paid it was regarded as sub-letting and the usual course was taken of disregarding the first 2/6d and one third of the remainder and taking the balance into consideration. The District Council considered this to be grossly unfair and that the rental should not be taken into account at all. The Public Assistance Officer explained that out of the 5/- rental the householder would get 3/4d and they took into account the remaining 1/8d as additional income and the reduction in relief was for this amount. However, the R.D.C's concern must have been listened to because the P.A. Committee did agree to disregard the 5/- rent allowance when assessing relief.[268]

Payment for housing evacuees was considered to be one of the problems why hosts were not coming forward in the numbers expected. This was an ongoing problem throughout the war and there are many examples of local concerns such as the points from a letter dated 20th November 1941 from Frank Lloyd of Spetisbury, Dorset referred to earlier.

General concern about the effect lack of payment was having nationally was also highlighted in a letter sent to all reception areas by the Town Clerk of Carmarthen in 1943:-

> 22 November 1943
>
> To all Reception areas.
>
> Billeting allowances are considered to be totally inadequate therefore the Town Council has passed the following resolution:-
>
> That the Council, in recording its grave concern at the meagre and totally inadequate billeting allowances paid by the Government for the accommodation of evacuees, feels that this is one of the root causes of the immeasurable difficulties which have arisen and are still arising

```
in billeting, particularly in relation to unaccompanied children, as
the allowances are insufficient to meet the financial burden thrown
upon the householders by the presence of such evacuation, and with a
view to alleviating the distress thus caused this council urges HMG in
the strongest possible terms to increase the present billeting
allowances to such amounts as are adequate to maintain the unfortunate
billetees....

Howard White.

Town Clerk[269]
```

Despite protests from many quarters payments were not revised again until June 1944, under an Amendment to the Defence Regulations:-

```
Defence Regs. AGD (B1)24

Amendment to Form E. Incentives to Occupiers.

As from the first pay day in the week commencing Saturday 1st July
1944, the weekly rates of billeting allowances for unaccompanied
children are as follows:-

Under 5 years of age    10/6 per week.
5 & Under 10   .  .  .  11/6 per week
10-12   .  .  .  .  .   12/- per week
12-14   .  .  .  .  .   13/- per week
14-16   .  .  .  .  .   14/- per week
16   .  .  .  .  .  .   16/6 per week
17+   .  .  .  .  .  .  17/6 per week[270]
```

Other methods were used to appeal to hosts and evacuees alike. Throughout March and April 1940, there was an intense programme of newspaper propaganda in the reception areas. A series of advertisements appeared in local newspapers under various headlines:-

'Thankyou, Mrs Ruggles...we want more like you!'   14th March 1940.

'Who'll give a promise to keep this child safe?'   21st March 1940.

'Who'll help Mrs Harrison?'   28th March 1940.

'Someone here is going to need your help.'   4th April 1940.

'Will you share a small burden with your neighbour?'   11th April 1940.

'You've been splendid, Mrs Johnson, and you deserve to have some help.' 18th April 1940.

All these appeals showed smiling children in the foreground with a hint of the danger of them staying in the cities in the background.

In 1941, the Ministry of Information released a film called 'Living With Strangers', in which they attempted to address the issue of conflict between the evacuees and their host families and for once looked at the problems from both sides.[271] Unfortunately, it is not possible to ascertain how well the film was received at the time because it was not researched by Mass-Observation. But audiences today comprised of people who were evacuated find the content very amusing and patronising. The film, made by the 'Realist Film Unit', is so obviously staged that it loses much of its credibility and the script still portrays a distorted image of the evacuees. For example the commentator on the film talks about:-

> *'They will now have to do without their fish and chip shops and cinema and rely on their own entertainment'.*

It also creates the impression that the host families are better educated and more socially adjusted than their guests:-

> *'...the local WI set up needlework classes to show the women evacuees how to make clothes for themselves and their children'.*

This implies that they had never done this before which of course was not the case. It was apparent however, that some mothers found it difficult to buy the material required for these clothes out of their income as this transcript of a telephone message from a reception area trying to establish such a sewing circle would suggest:-

> *'8.2.41. Miss Jenkinson telephoned.*
>
> *I told her about the £5 5s. She suggests that she be allowed to lend mothers money out of this sum to buy materials to make clothes for their children. Mothers will repay if and when they can.*
>
> *Does the town Clerk agree?*
>
> *(Answer..Yes)'* [272]

The film is also useful for another reason. It has an excellent example of how women were treated at the time and, considering this film would have been shown in the cinemas, what women were prepared to accept. A rather authoritarian billeting officer, who is portrayed as nonetheless being sympathetic, has to deal with two women, host and guest, over a problem of the ownership of a child's toy. At the end of a long conversation, in which he basically tells them off and suggests there is more to worry about than 'a kiddie's toy' he sends them away saying:-

> *'...I have more to do with my time than standing around listening to you all day. Be off with you before I set about you both!!!!'* [273]

Some evacuees, when interviewed, are still rather upset by the patronising attitudes of some of their hosts. One, Maureen Stephens, describes how her mother who, although from the East End prided herself on her general manners and her standards of dress, 'always wearing hats and gloves'. They were taken to a large detached house in St. Albans where the host immediately produced a list of rules and regulations about behaviour and cleanliness. She had preconceived ideas about East Enders. The host made things so difficult for the family that they were prepared to risk the bombing in London and they returned home.[274]

The contemporary Ministry of Information films created an unrealistic image of evacuation. 'Westward Ho!'[275] made in 1940, reinforces an atmosphere of romantic adventure when dealing with the journey of evacuees. There were only a few tears in sight and everyone, children, billeting officers and foster parents are seen in a relaxed, jovial and genial manner. This was pure propaganda issued at a time when the Government was attempting to persuade people to leave the cities in the second evacuation in 1940. However, this image is one which has been perpetuated until very recently and has contributed to the mistaken belief that all was well with the scheme.

It is difficult to evaluate objectively the value of this propaganda, but the movement back home would suggest that it had limited success. It can be said that the failure of these visual tactics, first of all to ensure people left the target areas and then, later, to stay in their reception areas, was due partly to the misunderstanding on the part of the film makers and the Ministry of Information about the depth of antagonism in some areas or, more importantly, the pull of family and community ties.

This host-evacuee conflict became a serious problem in some areas. Had there not been a 'Phoney War' period perhaps the evacuees would have been tolerated in the spirit of 'doing one's bit'; however, as this period of relative 'inaction' continued, tolerance was replaced by intolerance, resentment and ill-feeling in many of the reception areas. This, in turn, led to countless requests, from both sides, guests and hosts, for evacuees to be moved. Some parents demanded that their children should be moved. The Town Clerk in Chipping Norton, Oxfordshire, was sent the following letter by a Mrs Reading from Plaistow after she had visited her children in their new foster homes during the first weekend of the war.

> *'I went to see my two children today, (Sunday September 10th), and I found Ethel very comfortable and happy with Mrs Webb at No 3 Spring Place, but I am sorry to say I could not say the same for Johnny, he did not complain but I cannot leave him where he is, so I am asking you if you could find somewhere else for him.*
>
> *I know Mrs Pickett of No.4 Spring Place would have him and he would have better care taken of him. His father has been called up for the Navy so I haven't him at home to speak about it, and if he isn't found somewhere better I shall have to bring him back to London......'* [276]

This example is typical of the sort of correspondence received by billeting officers in the reception areas.

Other moves were requested on medical grounds although some were very confusing. One can assume that the writer of the following letter was trying to secure accommodation for herself because of her son's illness. (The letter is transcribed verbatim. It was addressed to the Town Clerk. Chipping Norton.)

'3/1/40

Dear Mr. Morris,

I should have written you Before But have been waiting to see if I could possibly manage to get Back. But I find I cannot do so as Mr Benham is having a run of Bad Luck he is in shipping and there is not much Doing in His Line, and I cannot afford to Be in Chipping without the Allowance he has been making me. If I make enquiries this end could you Keep me on the List of Helpers, as I want to see if under the circumstances I can get any Pay as I am very worried as it means Keeping my Boy at home here with me and he is Delicate Has Congenital Heart, and I could not expect any one in Chippy Norton to take the risk of having him without I were there. That was my reason For coming with the School But as you know I did all I possibly could to Help in whatever way. If you can Keep me on your List Whilst I make enquiries I can Be Alright for a Billet.

Trusting you will Understand My Position.

Yours sincerely

J. Benham. (Mrs)' [277]

During the first six months of the war in the reception areas of Berkshire, there were fifty transfers of billet per week in Newbury and two hundred and fifty a month in Maidenhead![278] Transfers from one area to another were usually allowed provided that both local authorities agreed. The cost of the transfer had to be paid by the parents unless the move took place for educational reasons, when the costs were charged to the evacuation account.[279] Under the law, it was the local Mayor's duty to appoint three people to act as a tribunal to hear complaints, so that a householder had the right to make a complaint in writing to him and if necessary go before the tribunal. Evacuees also had the right to put their case. The Town Clerk in Dorchester, speaking at a special meeting of the Town Council on 7th September 1939, was very concerned even at this very early stage of the war, about changes of Billets. He made it known that he was the Chief Billeting Officer with a very able team of billeting officers under him, and only these people were allowed by law to interfere in any billeting whatever. He went on to say:-

'I am not going to stand any interference. I want to make it clear to people who are changing billets in the town or 'swapping' children and that sort of thing that they are guilty of an offence. Although I have been patient up till now the time may come when I have to prosecute, and that will mean a fine or imprisonment. Unless a householder desires, no one other than a billeting officer has authority to go into a house. I have come across cases where the people who would like to get out of their commitments have taken children around the town trying to find billets for them. For this they render themselves liable to prosecution'. [280]

The Chief Billeting Officer in Weymouth officially announced on 26th September that all billeted persons in Weymouth had to remain in their present billets without exception until 7th October. Mr Warren stated that:-

'The authorities have been very tolerant and have made great efforts to assist the evacuees to settle down. A tremendous amount of work has been done to try and correct the more obvious misfits. But there must be a limit to the unrestricted movement which appears at present to be taken for granted.

Billeting cannot be changed at will by people who profess to be satisfied with what has been provided for them at the Government's expense. Cases of real necessity will still be dealt with by me, but I am determined to put a stop to unnecessary movement amongst the evacuated population and for that reason 'standstill' must be maintained.

People who, after this warning, take the responsibility of leaving the billets which have been allocated to them and seek accommodation elsewhere without the consent of the Chief Billeting Officer run the risk of having to pay for their lodgings from their own resources. If for no other reason that the National Register is in process of being taken the standstill order would appear to be entirely justified'.[281]

In support of this, the following notice was placed in the Weymouth local newspapers on 28th October:-

CHANGE OF BILLETS

The attention of evacuees and others is again drawn to the necessity for obtaining official sanction BEFORE removing from the billets in which the former have been placed.
Failure to observe this will deprive both evacuees and householders of the benefit of a billeting allowance.
No change will be sanctioned in future, unless fully warranted by some exceptional circumstance.
Any person aggrieved by a refusal of resettlement may appeal to the Billeting Tribunal.[282]

This annoyance and frustration was also evident in other areas. In a letter to the Town Clerk of Chipping Norton dated 18th November 1939 a billeting officer, Mr. R.J. Brandum, wrote:-

'Dear Mr Morris,

...Lastly - it is no use any more people requesting transfers even if they have 20 Doctor's Certificates. We have come to the end of our tether. They must produce the necessary accommodation if they wish for a transfer. We have no more <u>willing</u> (sic) householders with accommodation. Mrs Benham and Mrs Nelms have walked and walked. We have not yet moved the boys from Pembridge Terrace, but that will be done this week. King's have gone and the Mayor's. And still I can name many deserving cases which cannot be moved'.[283]

Some transfers were deemed not to be necessary and some evacuees played the system. Town Councillors in Dorchester, in October 1941, were of the opinion that some of the adult evacuees were 'not playing fair' and they were using the billeting scheme for their own purposes, changing from area to area as their 'private conveniences directed'. The abuse of the scheme in Dorset was halted when the authorities were given the power to withhold billeting notices. This meant that if evacuees wanted to leave their temporary homes they had to satisfy the billeting officers that their reasons were good. If they moved without such authorisation they became ineligible for financial assistance.[284]

Some evacuee mothers with children moved from place to place and chose the areas they wished to go to. These were called 'twicers' and were in effect getting a 'guided tour' of the best reception areas in the country.

On the 18th September 1939, the Dorset Echo reported:-

EVACUATED WOMEN GOING HOME
A CHEAP FORTNIGHT'S HOLIDAY

Women evacuated from London appear to be returning home in increasing numbers from the south coast although they are not being encouraged to do so by local authorities.

Many of the women were in excellent billets and expressed themselves well satisfied with their reception but stated that they were returning home with the consent of their husbands.

It appears that a number of them have treated the evacuation scheme as an opportunity for obtaining a fortnight's holiday at very very little expense.[285]

The attitude of the evacuees in one area was considered to be having such a detrimental effect on the morals and behaviour of the local children that an article in a local church magazine asked:-

'Is there any necessity for the spoliation of decent homes and furniture, the corruption of speech and the moral standards of our own children?' [286]

Not a very Christian attitude considering the state of the war!

In a Memo. for Wales entitled 'Problem after evacuation is completed' the Deputy Regional Commissioner wrote:-

'...a number of evacuees from Liverpool and Birkenhead would appear to be of a very undesirable type and it is anticipated that their habits and customs will be resented by Welsh householders, especially in rural areas. For example, some of these women are in the habit of frequenting public houses and several cases of drunkenness have already been reported. Today the County Council has been notified that a number of Irish women from Birkenhead, billeted in Eglwysbach in the Urban District of Hiraethog, applied to be billeted in an institution adjoining a public house, or in

Llannwst where there are public houses available, and stated that otherwise they would return home. Permission has been refused and it is hoped that they will carry out their threat'.[287]

There was an inherent disbelief in some reception areas that the deplorable accounts of the living conditions, morals and social behaviour in the areas evacuated were true, and surprise that such poor physical condition and moral well being of some of the evacuees could exist in a seemingly well off and modern society. This disbelief may also have been a result of simply not wanting to admit that such a situation could arise in a 'caring society'. One letter to The Times on 22nd September 1939 suggests that not all people were so uncaring that they did not see the benefits of evacuation for the poorer classes and felt that something needed to be done to relieve the plight of the children from the poorer areas, but the text and tone of the letter is patronising in the extreme and is further evidence of the upper classes dictating the terms:-

'Sir,

While from all my friends in the country comes praise of many town-children evacuees, and, without exception, praise of all the secondary schoolchildren, complaints are pouring in about the half-savage, verminous and wholly illiterate children from some slums who have been billeted on clean homes. Stories with which one cannot but sympathise are told of mattresses and carpets polluted, of wilful despoliation and dirt that one would associate with untrained animals. The authorities, with plenty of time to prepare, seemed to have failed both in the physical and psychological examination of the evacuees, although the mechanics of the great trek have been so well ordered. Now one hears that both women and children of the roughest and uncleanest types are going back to their own homes. At present time, when Britain is fighting for liberty, no Briton would suggest dictatorship methods , but surely something short of these can be evolved to prevent these unfortunate children from being allowed to return to the appalling conditions whence they have been rescued. It is not fair that they should disrupt small houses; but is it not possible to cause, to coin a phrase, grass orphanages under the care of skilled and sympathetic teachers, to come into being? Let the mothers go back if they will. It does not matter so much what happens to adults, but surely children should not be allowed to go back to conditions which shame a nation fighting for civilisation....'

Yours faithfully, F.Tennyson Jesse.

11 Melina Place. NW8 [288]

As an estimated 900,000 of the original 1.5 million evacuees returned during the 'Phoney war ' period,[289] the Government Scheme was being undermined and it received a great deal of criticism from many quarters, including the Press and Teachers Unions. The Joint Consultative Committee of the NUT in Weymouth and Evacuated teachers sent a resolution to the Government in April 1940 stating that they could not stop the drift back to the evacuated areas and the collapse of the scheme. They also expressed their opinion that the proposed new evacuation plans would only add chaos to the existing arrangements and they were dismayed about 'the lack of any progressive facilities for rationalising the existing evacuation scheme before bombing begins. Councillor

Ronald Gould of the NUT National Executive highlighted the three main aspects of evacuation...transport, billeting and education which were of serious concern to teachers and he suggested that Education had been forgotten, despite warnings from the NUT. He thought that the main issue was the fact that in many cases the billeting authorities and the education authorities were not identical and often there was little co-operation or co-ordination between them'. He urged the Government that when the next phase of evacuation was introduced no place should be called upon to take evacuees unless it 'possessed adequate billeting and educational facilities'.[290]

After the Government conferences in early 1940 had introduced incentives for evacuees to stay in the reception areas, a second official evacuation started in 1940 which required the registration of potential evacuees. However, by April 1940, only 95,000 had registered, 220,000 had refused to do so and 842,000 had not replied. This apathy, combined with the local difficulties such as finding host families and the resignation of many billeting officers, put a great deal of pressure on the evacuation scheme. It was not until May 1940, when Malcolm MacDonald was appointed as Minister of Health and Herwald Ramsbotham to the Board of Education, that the situation changed.

On the 31st May, MacDonald stated that:-

> '...in the light of the latest war developments the Government regard the danger of air attack in the near future as so real that we should have plans for the evacuation of schoolchildren as complete as possible by the beginning of next week. Parents who do not register their children by Monday evening run the risk of not having them taken away'.[291]

They devised several experimental schemes which removed children and non-essential persons from within 10 miles of the Norfolk coast southwards towards Sussex, re-evacuated some of the children who had returned from the original scheme of 1939 to South Wales and the Midlands, persuaded people to move inland from all eastern and south-eastern coastal areas, (60% children. According to MacDonald 97 trains were to be used to transport 47,000 children) and implemented a 'special' evacuation scheme between 13th-18th June 1940 when 103,000 children left London.[292] This number was less than expected. Throughout the week the Minister and various Ministry spokesmen had been talking in terms of 120,000 leaving on 180 trains. An L.C.C. official at Paddington Station simply stated that about 25% of the children who had registered under the new scheme had not turned up. He was quoted as saying 'Probably the parents changed their minds'.

During each of the six days an average of 15 trains ran on the Great Western and Southern Railway. This time there was 1 teacher or helper to every 15 children. It is interesting to note that this scheme, although lower key than the first, still attracted the same jingoistic reporting as September 1939:-

> '...As the trains drew out of the stations there were wild cheers from the children. Boys leaned out of the windows waving their caps and the girls blew kisses to the porters'.[293]

LONDON EVACUATION

Going Like Clockwork

Everything is going like clockwork and the children are behaving admirably. This was how one official of the L.C.C. described the working of the great six-day evacuation scheme from London.........
"I have not heard of a single case of a child forgetting either gas-mask, identity card or ration book," said the official'.[294]

Others left the cities voluntarily, but at a slower rate of exit. This was referred to as the 'trickle evacuation' although in some areas the exodus was more like a flood. Unlike the first phase in 1939 this was not an evacuation before the event, this took place throughout the Blitz and, in consequence, some panic did occur. After the Blitz had started many Londoners crowded into the main-line railway stations to catch a train to anywhere away from the city. So many East-Enders arrived in Oxford, around 6,000, that the authorities had to take over the Majestic Cinema, ironically showing 'Babes in the Wood', in order to house them.[295] The following account from the Mayor of Stepney, Councillor Frank. R .Lewey describes in some detail the problems faced in the target areas.

'We resolved to occupy the People's Palace , the theatre in the Mile End Road....this place was big enough to give us elbow room in handling the masses of homeless who were already tramping in like a retreating army, seeking our assistance...When we first set up business at the People's Palace...our very first task was to arrange for the evacuation of mothers and small children who had been rendered homeless, and, after those, for the mothers and children who wished to leave London....

I myself, dog tired after a terrific day's work, dragging wearily out of the People's Palace and seeing in front of me a great area of deserted prams in the evening light, with the drifting smoke of nearby burning houses dimming them....The mothers had brought their babies in prams, and, of course, we had not foreseen that, and, as they could not take the prams with them on the overcrowded trains, they just had to leave them there in front of the building, so that it was by evening, hardly possible to get in or out except by climbing over a great expanse of them...' [296]

The Mayor of Stepney was very concerned to visit the reception areas and thank people for looking after evacuees from his area. The following log book entry supports this:-

'7th November 1939. The Mayor and Mayoress of Stepney visited the Aston Clinton Evacuee Boys School after being received, at his request, at the Headteacher's billet in Buckland. Arrangements were made by the Headteacher whereby the Mayor met the principal people of Buckland who had been instrumental in welcoming and sending in schools from London'.[297]

There is evidence to suggest that this evacuation phase was much better organised. Although the overall organisation remained the responsibility of local authorities, the Ministry of Health had provided advisers to help local officers. In some cases this came down to simple 'trouble-shooting' as this description by Lucy Faithfull, who as a regional welfare officer in the West Country from 1941 would indicate:-

> *'...I also had problems in Ilfracombe where people just refused to take any foster children. The children had arrived and were staying in schools looked after by teachers and volunteers. I had to live in Ilfracombe for three months and eventually, by visiting and persuasion got them to change their minds.'* [298]

This second evacuation scheme did provide a necessary link between central and local government which was to become very useful in the post-war development of social services. However, even within the scheme there was a continual flow of evacuees returning home. This became such a problem that in June 1940 the Minister of Health, Ernest Brown, sent a copy of a hand-written letter to parents of evacuated children advising them to keep their children in the reception areas:-

> *A MESSAGE FROM THE MINISTER OF HEALTH TO PARENTS WHO HAVE EVACUATED THEIR CHILDREN.*
>
> *'You are among the many fathers and mothers who wisely took advantage of the Government's Scheme to send their children to the Country. I am sorry to learn that some parents are now bringing their children back.*
>
> *I am writing to ask you not to do this. This is not easy for family life has always been the strength and pride of Britain. But I feel it my duty to remind you that to bring children back to the Congested towns is to put them in danger of death or what is perhaps worse maiming for life. You will have noticed that the enemy is changing his tactics.*
>
> *He is now concentrating heavier air raids on one or two towns at a time, leaving others alone for the moment.*
>
> *Nobody knows which town he will attack next so don't be lulled into a false sense of security if your home district has been having a quieter time lately.*
>
> *Remember that in April over 600 children under the age of sixteen were killed and over 500 seriously injured in air raids. So keep your children where they are in the reception areas.*
>
> *Don't bring them back even for a little while. This is your duty to the children themselves, to the ARP services in your home town, to those who are working so hard for them in the country, and to the nation.*
>
> *Please read the message as the sincere words of a friend both to you and the little ones.*
>
> *Yours sincerely*
>
> *Ernest Brown'* [299]

It is impossible to calculate what effect this letter had on keeping evacuees in the reception areas.

Endnotes

1   Dorothy Lofts. cited in 'Innocents Abroad'. Edward Stokes. Allen and Unwin. 1994 p4

2   Dorchester Rural District Council Minutes. 31st May 1939.

3   Dorset Daily Echo. 25th August 1939.

4   Dorset County Chronicle and Swanage Times. 31st August 1939.

5   ibid.

6   ibid. 21st September 1939.

7   From 'Welsh Rarebits' the anonymous and unpublished account of a Liverpool teacher evacuated to North Wales. 1939-45. cited in Wallis op.cit. p131

8   Dorset County Chronicle and Swanage Times. 21st September 1939

9   T.L.Crosby. Impact of Civilian Evacuation in the Second World War.. Croom Helm. 1986. p28

10   ibid. p97

11   Dorset Daily Echo. 31st August 1939.

12   ibid.

13   ibid. 1st September 1939

14   Crosby. op. cit.

15   Dorset Daily Echo. 25th August 1939.

16   Joan Faulkner. Englefield Green. Surrey. Letter to author and oral testimony. Nov. 1996

17   Lyn Mendlson. Letter to author 29th January 1997.

18   Angus Calder. The People's War.. Panther. 1971 p42

19   Welsh Nationalist Party. Memorandum. February 1939. cited Wallis. op. cit. p265

20   Gerald Wasley 'Blitz. An account of Hitler's aerial war over Plymouth in March 1941 and the events that followed'.. Devon Books. 1991. p49

21   Dorset Daily Echo. 9th September 1939.

22   Purley Rural District Council Minutes. September 1940

23   Bradfield C.of E. Primary School. Log Book. Berkshire Record Office. D/P/22/28/3

24   James Roffey. op.cit. Personal Archive.

25   E.O.Humphreys. Education Officer. Anglesey. Report The Education of Evacuated Children. University College of North Wales. Archives. V.4594

26   Wallis op.cit.p173

27   P.E.Owen. The Development of the Bilateral System of Education in Caernarvonshire 1903- to date (1961) University College of North Wales. 15234.

28   Imperial War Museum. Compiliation Video. Keep the Wheels Turning. 'The Village School'. Ministry of Information 1941.

29   Ashley Green C.of E. Primary School Log Book. Buckinghamshire Record Office. E/LB/6/3.

30   For a full list of the schools see Appendix 14.

31   'The Evacuee' Journal of the Evacuee Reunion Association. October 1996.

32   Dorset County Chronicle and Swanage Times. 29th June 1944.

33   Anon account lent by P.Farley-Rutter from family papers.

34   J.Roffey. Letter to the author. 9th June 98.

35   Alfred Sutton Primary School. Wokingham Rd. Reading. Log Book. 1934-62

36   J.Roffey. Letter to the author. 9th June 1998

37   Sylvia Rose. Letter to the author. 29th Jan. 1998.

38   Commercial Street. London County Council School. Log Book. Bucks. Record Office. E/LB/6/3

39   Mr. Foster, Didcot Parish Council, in response to a report that a Domestic Science Laboratory in a local school was being used as accommodation for evacuees. The Minute was undated but would be around September to October 1939.

40   Titmuss. op.cit. p112

41   From Monday to Friday evacuee children and mothers were required to have their lunches in this building. One ex-evacuee recalls that the diet consisted entirely of minced rabbit and vegetables. The rabbits were skinned each morning by a Dr. Scott but the meals were considered to be rather dangerous because they contained slithers of bone. Dr. Scott also served up Rook. Letter to the author from John O'Connor. March 1998.

42   John Rawlins. Private Papers. 1989.

43   This particular problem was identified by a number of ex-evacuees during taped interviews.

44   Exeter Blitz. Box 12. ARP/Evacuation. Devon Record Office.

45   Hampshire Evacuees. The Wartime Diary of Eric Wyeth Gadd. cited in 'The Children's War.' Ruth Inglis op.cit.p57

46   Ruth Inglis. The Children's War. op.cit.p79

47   Berkshire County Council Minutes. May 1940.

48   Purley-on-Thames. Parish Council Minutes. July 1940

49   Berkshire County Council Minutes. April 1941. As it turned out the Rev. Skuse's predictions were correct. Purley was not hit, however, this does not excuse the original decision. In 1940 he was not to know with any degree of certainty that the inhabitants would be safe.

50   Berkshire County Council Minutes. November 1939

51   Dorset Daily Echo. 7th September.1939

52   Dorset County Chronicle &Swanage Times. 1st August.1940

53   Berkshire County Council Education Sub-Committee Minutes. November 1939.

54   Dorset County Chronicle & Swanage Times. 15th February 1940

55   St. Matthews Infants School. Log Book. Hawarden R.O E/LB/11/5.

56   Dorset Daily Echo .23rd September 1939

57   H.C.Dent.Education in Transition. London 1944 cited. P.H.J.H. Godsen. Education in the Second World War. 1976.

58   PRO.ED 136/205

59   Brian Simon. Education and the Social Order 1940-1990. Lawrence and Wishart. 1991.p35

60   Ministry of Education estimate. February 1946. cited Titmuss op.cit. p406

61   House of Commons Debates. 19th October 1944 vol.403 col.2511 cited Titmuss op.cit. p407. The number of male teachers in grant-aided elementary and secondary schools in the UK fell by over 30% between 1939 and 1944. The Impact of War on Civilian Consumption. HMSO 1945. p63

62   E.O.Humphreys. Education Officer Anglesey. Report. The Education of Evacuated Children. 27th Nov 39. Univeristy College North Wales. Archives V4594.

63   Dorset Daily Echo. 13th October 1939. As well as cultivating flowers and vegetables the children also raised poultry and kept bees.

64   Evacuation Group. Prince Rupert School. Liverpool 1941. Log Book Caernarfon RO.

65   Cambridge County Records. CES/66C/3. Ely Market Street School. I am indebted to Dr. Penny Starns. University of Cambridge, for bringing this to my attention.

66   Letter to the author from W. Elliott and Sylvia Lewis. June 1998. See Appendix 2.

67   Wallis. op.cit. p147

68   M.T.Perks. letter to J. Stace-Masey. 21st July 1939. Shaftesbury File DC/SYR Dorset Record Office.

69   M.T.Perks to J.Stace-Masey. 24th July 1939. DC/SYR. Dorset Record Office

70   Miriam Ward. Evacuation. A Reception Area in Berkshire. unpublished account. Undated

71   Miriam Ward. op cit.

72   Berkshire County Council Minutes. August. 1939

73   Billeting Officers were appointed under Regulation 22 of the Defence (General) Regulations 1939 by Mayors of Boroughs and County Boroughs and by Chairmen of the Rural and District Councils. The Ministry of Health had delegated the power of appointment but local authorities were able to appoint anyone who was a person of tact, judgement and had common sense. Titmuss op.cit. p391

74   Mavis Cordery. Retired Headmistress of Alfred Sutton Girls School. Green Rd. Reading. One-time Billeting Officer. From an interview recorded March 1996.

75   This has been supported by evidence gathered from oral history sources by Peter Cunningham and Philip Gardner.....see Oral History and Teachers' Professional Practice: a wartime turning point?. Camb. Journal of Education, Vol 27 No 3 1997 pp 331-341.

76   The Boys Evacuated School. Aston Clinton. Bucks. School Diary. Bucks Record Office E/LB/8/1

77   Dorset County Chronicle & Swanage Times 23rd October 1941.

78   Commercial Street. LCC School. Log Book. Bucks. Record Office E/LB/8/1

79   ibid.

80   Exeter Blitz. Box 76. Devon Record Office.

81   James Roffey. op.cit.

82   E/LB/8/1 op.cit.

83   Letter to the author from Win Elliott and Sylvia Lewis. April 1998.

84   WRO/F2/850/1-12. Wiltshire Record Office

85   ibid.

86   Evacuation Box 1. File E. Mass-Observation Archive. cited in Wartime Women ed. Dorothy Sheridan. 1990 p65

87   WRO/F2/850/1-12

88   PRO.ED.138/34

89   E/LB/8/1. op. cit. 17th October 1939.

90   ibid. 30th September 1939.

91   Idbury and Fifield C.of E. Primary School. Log Book. Oxford Record Office.

92   Letter to author from John William O'Connor.

93   WRO/F2/850 1-12.

94   Denbighshire County Council File 35/4. Letter to W. Brookes Parry to William Jones. 24th Jan 1941.

95   Clerk of Nant Conway RDC to C.F.Mott. Evacuation File. 23rd April 1940 Caernarvon Record Office. cited Wallis p165.

96   Padley & Cole. Evacuation Survey. London.1940. p236-7.

97   Denbighshire County Council.File 8/1. Letter from W.Jones to E. Evans 13th November. 1939. Caernarvon Record Office.

98   North Wales Chronicle 12th May 1939.

99   Dorset County Council. Education Committee 31st October 1939.

100   Caernarfon British School. Log Book 1910-1942. 19th February. 1940. CRO.

101   Mavis Cordery op.cit.

102   ibid.

103   E/LB/8/1. op cit. 31st March 1941

104   E/LB11/5 Flintshire Record Office. Hawarden.

105   Anonymous Account. Lent by P. Farley-Rutter from family papers.

106   E/LB/8/1 19th & 20th June 1940

107   ibid. 6th June 1940

108   E/LB/6/3 Bucks.Record Office. 30th September 1941.

109   ibid. 18th June 1942.

110   Dorset County Chronicle & Swanage Times. 15th January 1942.

111   Dorset Daily Echo. 8th September 1939.

112 Berkshire County Council. C/CL/C1/1/42

113 Aston Clinton Girls School. Log Book. Bucks.Record Office. E/LB/8/1. 28th November 1939.

114 Quoted in the Dorset County Chronicle & Swanage Times. 2nd January 1941.

115 ibid. 29th January 1942.

116 ibid. 9th July 1942.

117 T.L.Crosby. op.cit p93

118 ibid. p94

119 Titmuss op.cit.p58

120 ibid. p406

121 Barnett House Study Group. London Children in Wartime Oxford. pub. Oxford University Press. London. 1947. p112. For more forward looking educational recommendations from this group see Appendix 13.

122 Titmuss. op.cit. p409

123 Bob Holman. Former Professor of Social Administration. University of Bath. Lecture at the Imperial War Museum. 18th October 1996.

124 Report to Education (General) Sub-Committee. Ed. No. 208 (addendum) 13th September 1943. cited. Titmuss. op.cit. p408

125 ibid. p408

126 Dorset Daily Echo. 22nd December. 1939.

127 Tom Hickman. What did you do in the war Auntie? BBC. 1995. p79.

128 Jim Bartley. Former evacuee. Taped Interview. November 1996.

129 Kennylands School Log Book. 26th February 1940.

130 Dorset Daily Echo. 19th February 1940.

131 From a report by R.L.Arkell. Home and Country. September 1942. p138. cited in London Children in Wartime Oxford. op.cit. p50

132 In March 1946 the 'Beal' boys returned to Ilford but the Education Authority continued to rent the property from the National Camp Corporation. Groups of children were sent for short spells from all over Essex. Eventually it became a full-time boarding school until it was closed down in 1980. Letter to the author from Joyce Goddard who taught at Kennylands until 1950.

133 Dorset Daily Echo. 15th June 1940.

134 Bob Holman. The Evacuation. A Very British Revolution. Lion.1995.p117

135 Dorset County Chronicle & Swanage Times. 27th January 1944.

136 Interview with Dr. Robin Borthwick. Theale Medical Centre. 21st September 1996.

137 2,160 had opened by September 1943, a long way short of the intended 10,000. They served approximately 6000 meals a day. A. Calder. People's War. op. cit. p446

138 Philip Ziegler. 'London at War' Sinclair-Stevenson. 1995. p90

139 Samways. We think you ought to go!. GLRO. 1995 p39

140 ibid.

141 ibid.p40

142 'Health of the School Child: report of the Chief Medical Officer at the Ministry of Education, for the years 1939 - 45. HMSO. London. 1947. p23

143 Dorset County Chronicle and Swanage Times. 20th November 1941. See Appendix 1.

144 Dorset County Chronicle & Swanage Times 23rd November 1939.

145 Dorset Daily Echo 12th January 1940.

146 Angus Calder. Peoples War. op.cit. p132

147 Dorset Daily Echo. 16th July.1940

148 The Evacuee. October 97.p6

149 Angus Calder. op.cit. p132

150 ibid. p440

151 E/L/8/1. Bucks Record Office. 2nd September 1940.

152 Mary Nickerson. unpublished account entitled 'Happy Evacuee' sent to Author. May 1996.

153 Samways. op.cit. p41.

154 ibid. p53

155 Dorset County Council. Minutes. Sept.1939. Unattributed statement.

156 PRO.ED 50/207. 26th October 1939

157 Dorset County Chronicle & Swanage Times. 2nd November 1939.

158 Dorset County Council. Public Health Minutes October 1939.

159 Chipping Norton Borough Council. Doc. 113/4

160 Anonymous Quote. Dorset County Council Minutes. September 1939.

161 John Murphy. Dorset at War. pub. DForest Pub. Co. 1979. p32.

162 Holman 'Evacuation' op.cit. p124

163 ibid. p125

164 Dorset County Chronicle and Swanage Times. 7th December 1939.

165 Titmuss. op.cit. p544

166 See Appendix 10.

167 Exeter Blitz. Box 12. Devon Record Office.

168 Titmuss. op.cit. p545

169 ibid. p544

170 PRO.ED 134/74

171 Samways. op.cit. p35

172 See Appendix 15.

173 Edith Green. Taped Interview. June 1995. Edith was evacuated from Walthamstow to Wellingborough in September 1939.

174 Titmuss. op.cit. p372 et al.

175 Crosby. op.cit.p56

176 Norman Longmate. Air Raid. Hutchinson. 1976 p20

177 Crosby. op.cit. p56

178 The Times. 16th September 1939.

179 Crosby. op.cit. p50

180 Letter to The Times from Beatrix Crofton. Berwick St. John Manor. Wiltshire. 5th October 1939

181 PRO.HO/45 17635

182 The National Federation of Women's Institutes represented 338,000 countrywomen and in total approximately 148,000 members of the Women's Voluntary Service helped with the organising and implementation of the evacuation and its aftermath. Holman. Evacuation op.cit. p143. However, they were not the only interested groups. For full list see Appendix 12.

183 Mass Observation. Topic Collection 5. Evacuation Folder 2/A. 20th February 1940. cited Crosby op.cit p66

184 Titmuss op.cit. p392

185 James Roffey. Letter to Author. 9th June 1998.

186 Titmuss op.cit.p393

187 Dorset County Chronicle and Swanage Times. 1st August 1940.

188 Colville op.cit. p27

189 James Roffey. 'Is he being a good boy?' The Evacuee. August 1996.

190 Colville op.cit. p23

191 Joan Faulkner. Letter to the Author. December 1996.

192 ibid.

193 It was only by chance that Dolly was billeted with Nella Hughes -Smith. When Nella collected Mary she found her cutting a piece of soap in half to give to Dolly because they were being separated. Nella did not want this to happen so took Dolly as well. Letter to Author. June 1997

194 'Aliens'. Anonymous extract from Yesterday's Children. compiled by Lillian Evans.

195 ibid.

196 'You have burnt my dad!' Anonymous account Yesterday's Children op.cit.

197 'Hilda'. Lilian Evans. op.cit.

198 Wallis op.cit. p84

199 Nant Conway RDC. Letterbook Evac 1939-41 letters 17th and 26th May. Also Amlwch RDC Evac. File 1939-41 letter sent 28th July 1939.

200 Lilian Evans. Letter to Author. July 1998.

201 Crosby op.cit. p53

202 Dorset Daily Echo. 8th August 1939.

203 Colville op.cit. p46

204 Charles Ritchie. The Siren Years. Macmillan. 1974

205 Angus Calder. The Myth of the Blitz. Cape. 1991. p34

206 Exeter Blitz. Box.16. Devon Record Office.

207 Crosby op.cit. p56

208 Exeter Blitz. Wartime Correspondence. Devon Record Office.

209 ibid.

210 Titmuss op.cit. p393

211 Exeter Blitz. Wartime Correspondence. Devon Record Office.

212 Chipping Norton Borough Council Doc 78.

213 Exeter Blitz. Wartime Correspondence.

214 ibid.

215 WRO F2/850/1-12.

216 The Evacuee. October 1997 p9.

217 Hansard. Vol 351 14 September. cited Crosby. op. cit. p88

218 Dorset County Chronicle & Swanage Times 31 October 1940.

219 WRO F2/850/1-12. For full text of the letter see Appendix 16.

220 Hansard. op.cit.

221 Dorset County Chronicle & Swanage Times.5 February 1942.

222 North Wales Chronicle. 8 September 1939.

223 Dorset County Chronicle & Swanage Times 29 February 1940 & 14 March 1940.

224 Dorset Daily Echo. 15 July 1940)

225 Bedford Times and Standard. September 1939.

226 Jane Macauley. The Evacuee. September 1996.

227 E/LB/8/1 op.cit.

228 James Roffey. Letter to the Author. 9 June 1998.

229 Extract from Welsh Rarebits. unpub. memoirs of a Liverpool Teacher evac. to Caernarvon . cited Wallis. p82

230 Harold Nicolson. Diaries and Letters. Vol.2 1939-45. 14 September 1939. Collins. 1967 p33

231 Dorset County Chronicle & Swanage Times. 5 October 1939.

232 ibid. 2 November 1939

233 PRO/ED 136/125

234 E/AR/6/2 Bucks.Record Office

235 Dorst Daily Echo. 11 November 1939.

236 Titmuss op.cit. p144

237 <u>The Evacuee</u>. October 1997. p6.

238 Dorset County Chronicle & Swanage Times. 7 December 1939.

239 E/LB/8/1. Log book entry. 25 December 1939.

240 Dorset Daily Echo. 30 November 1939.

241 E/LB/8/1 Commercial St. School. op.cit. 8 August 1940.

242 E/LB/6/3. Ashley Green School. op.cit. Log Book. 10 August - 7 September. 1940

243 Titmuss. op.cit. p144

244 ibid. p544

245 ibid. p178

246 Exeter Blitz. Box 12. Ministry of Health Circular. November 1943. Devon Record Office.

247 Exeter Blitz. Box 12. Ministry of Health Circular.2593E

248 Letters to the Author.

249 Letter from A.T.Grubb. Dorset Daily Echo .6 December 1939.

250 Dorset Daily Echo. 29. January 1940.

251 Letter to author from Margaret Harrod. 1 March 1997.

252 Dorset Daily Echo 15 February 1940 & 9 April 1940.

253 Dorset County Chronicle & Swanage Times 8 August 1940.

254 Letter to Author from James Roffey. June 1998.

255 Ministry of Health Circulars. 1913 & Ev.6. 17 November 1939. cited in Titmuss op.cit. p178 and Exeter Blitz. Box 12.

256 Crosby. op.cit. p96

257 GLRO EO/WAR/1/65. 22 January 1940 cited Crosby op.cit. p96

258 ibid.

259 PRO.CAB 73/1. 21 February 1940. Ministry of Health Circular 1965. 15 February 1940.

260 PRO CAB.73/1/ 21 February 1940.

261 Crosby op.cit. p98

262 Defence Regulations 22(5), 31(A), 32 (6) Section 56. Civil Defence Act.1939. cited as Footnote. Titmuss. op cit. p157.

263 Dorset Daily Echo.4 October 1939.

264 Titmuss. op cit. p157 (Footnote)

265 ibid. p160

266 ibid. p160

267 ibid. Footnote p158.

268 Dorset County Chronicle & Swanage Times. February 19.1942.

269 Exeter Blitz. Box 12. C51945. Devon Record Office.

270 ibid.

271 Film <u>Living with Strangers</u>. Produced by the Ministry of Information 1940.

272 Exeter Blitz. Box 76.

273 Extract from soundtrack. <u>Living with Strangers</u>. op.cit.

274 Maureen Stephens. Taped interview. November 1996.

275 The film <u>Westward Ho!</u> was produced in 1940 by the Ministry of Information and was an attempt to persuade parents to evacuate their children.

276 Doc. 10 Chipping Norton Borough Council papers. Town Clerks Office. There are no reference numbers except the number of the Document.

277 ibid. Letter to Town Clerk from Mrs J. Benham 3 January 1940.

278 Crosby op.cit. p32

279 Guide for Billeting Officers. Exeter Blitz. Box 5. Devon Record Office.

280 Dorset County Chronicle & Swanage Times. 14 September 1939.

281 Dorset Daily Echo. 26 September 1939.

282 ibid. 28 October 1939.

283 Doc. 24. Chipping Norton Borough council. Town Clerks papers. No reference numbers.

284 Dorset County Chronicle & Swanage Times. 2 October 1941.

285 Dorset Daily Echo. 18 September 1939.

286 Crosby op.cit. p35

287 Denbighshire County Council. File 36 Ruthin R.O Z1352.

288 Livesey. Are we at War? op.cit. pp28-29.

289 Titmuss op.cit. p17

290 Dorset Daily Echo. 20April 1940.

291 ibid. 1 June 1940.

292 Angus Calder. People's War. op cit. p148

293 Dorset Daily Echo. 13 June 1940.

294 ibid. 15 June 1940.

295 Holman 'The Evacuation' op.cit. p48

296 Ruth Inglis. Children's War. op.cit. p77

297 Aston Clinton School. Log book. 7 November 1939.

298 Holman. op.cit. p51

299 WRO F2/850/1-12.

Overseas Evacuation

'Went along to CORB after getting a certificate of evacuation from Cook's. She fixed everything up for me quickly, including the 66 coupons which I am allowed for clothes for each child and of which I am the first recipient. But total value of all parcels sent during the year, including birthday gifts must not exceed £10 per child.'[1]

Some of those who had the money to do so sent their children to safety abroad, and by the beginning of the war thousands of evacuees had fled to the USA and other countries.[2]

This was not only restricted to children. It was estimated that immediately pre-war at least 5,000 left Southampton for the USA in 48 hours.[3]

The following description is an indication of the type of person who was leaving the target areas:-

> *'....a constant stream of private cars and London taxis driving up to mother's front door in the Thames Valley in the September of 1939, filled with men and women of all ages in various stages of hunger, exhaustion and fear, offering absurd sums for accommodation in her already overcrowded house and even for food. This horde of satin-clad, pin-striped refugees poured through for two or three days, eating everything that was for sale, downing all the spirits in the pubs, and then vanished'.*[4]

The original cost of £15 for the travel limited this 'escape' route to those who could afford it and it came to be seen by many as an elitist scheme. To put this into the context of the time it must be remembered that £15 was an average month's salary for 75% of the British population in 1939.[5] By the spring of 1940 this perceived elitism was severely criticised by MPs, especially those on the Labour benches, and the Government established a scheme to increase the availability of overseas evacuation to other sectors of the population.

Offers to take evacuees had already been received from various Dominion Governments. In early 1939, Southern Rhodesia had offered refuge, and a number of Canadian Women's Organisations offered homes for the under 16s and over 60s, and Australia offered to take orphans for the duration of the war.

These early offers had been rejected by the Government as not being necessary, 'the idea is good hearted but impracticable'.[6] They were also dismissed because there was serious concern that this type of evacuation might encourage panic and defeatism, an opinion which was to affect the course of the overseas evacuation plan throughout its short life.

Other questions regarding the scheme also needed to be resolved before it could be considered seriously. Voluntary evacuation by those who could afford to do it obviously created resentment and this was recognised, but it was also apparent that any Government scheme could not compete on the same level because there were fewer ships available to take Government sponsored evacuees abroad. Also, it was not clear what would happen if the allies ever got the upper hand and yet were not able to actually win the war. Some of these children might never return. However, after lengthy discussions at Cabinet level, it was agreed that the threat of invasion outweighed these negative concerns.

Geoffrey Shakespeare, who had been MP for Norwich since 1929 and Parliamentary Under-Secretary in the Dominions Office, was asked to chair an inter-departmental committee to 'consider offers made from overseas to house and care for children, whether accompanied or unaccompanied, from the European war zone, residing in Great Britain, including those orphaned by the war and to make recommendations thereon'.[7]

Shakespeare approached his task with energy and patriotic fervour and without this energy and leadership it is doubtful whether the scheme would ever have gone ahead.[8] He presented his final report to the War Cabinet on the 17th June 1940, but while doing so was interrupted by a messenger informing Churchill that France was surrendering. Although the Cabinet Minutes show that the scheme had been endorsed, Churchill himself was so preoccupied with the situation in France that he had not realised a decision had been taken. Had he done so it would seem from comments he made in meetings and in the Commons later, that he would have opposed it.[9]

Shakespeare established the Children's Overseas Reception Board (CORB) which, in collaboration with other interested parties, the Ministry of Health, Board of Education and Ministry of Pensions, was to oversee an evacuation scheme which was to include participants from all stratas of society. This egalitarian aspect won the support of many Labour MPs and the overall scheme was also supported by those with other motives. Some for instance stated that the scheme would reduce the number of 'useless mouths'[10] and others because... 'the soldiers would fight more happily if they knew that their wives and children were safe'.[11] (These are exactly the concluding words used in the propaganda film 'Westward Ho!' which deals with evacuation within the UK.) There was also a feeling that the witnessing of the plight of these children might induce the host countries to join the conflict on the side of the allies. 'The United States Committee for the Care of European Children' had applications from foster parents to take 5 million evacuees! Lord Lothian, the British Ambassador in Washington, was in favour of the scheme. He felt that the USA were out of touch with British war aims and, in consequence, reluctant to make contributions in the manner of arms and ammunition. He hoped that the plight of these children would help sway United States public opinion. This figure of 5 million seems to be rather inflated. On the first day after her election as chairman of the U.S. Committee for the Care of European Children Mrs Roosevelt received 2,000 offers from U.S. families anxious to adopt children. These were in addition to those made direct to Washington and other cities.[12] The big New York daily papers had taken the lead in this appeal. The 'Herald Tribune' asked the U.S. Government to issue an invitation to young evacuees to go to the United States as 'guests of the nation'. The 'New York Daily Mirror' which had one of the largest circulations in America, made a moving appeal under the headline 'This nation's duty to England's future':-

> '...Hitler may hurl hell towards England at any moment and certainly he will strike soon. America must act instantly. America must say to England 'Our bars are down to your children. Send them by the thousands, it is our duty and privilege to give them a home. There is no conceivable reason for not taking 60,000 children if England wants to send them to the new world, and more too'. [13]

The CORB recommendations and criteria were accepted by the Cabinet on June 17th 1940. They included:-

- Children should be aged between 5-15.

- The children should be attending school.

- A minimum of 90% of those selected for evacuation had to be from grant-aided schools.

- Parents of these children would have to pay the normal rate of 6/- per week for maintenance, the same amount applicable to British based evacuees, but the fare for the ship transportation would be free.

- Parents of children from independent schools had to pay £1 per week maintenance and £15 towards travel costs.

- Preference would be given to children from areas considered to be most dangerous.

- Preference would also be given to children from less affluent families.

- Children would be fostered by Host families or relatives.

- Parents had to accept the warnings that children were to be evacuated for the duration of the war. They would only return to Britain as soon as possible after the cessation of hostilities.[14]

(Although it was generally the case that children stayed for the duration some, like Sir Martin Gilbert, managed to come home earlier from Canada. In a letter to 'The Evacuee' in December 1996, he states that:-

> *'It was Churchill himself I later learned, who had noted, in his regular scrutiny of ships in transit and in port, that the ocean liner 'Mauretania', then a troopship, was sailing from New York in the summer of 1944 with several hundred empty berths. He at once suggested that several hundred children be rounded up and brought back........Churchill specifically asked the Admiralty to ensure that there were enough life jackets on board for all the children'.)*[15]

Circular 1515 outlining these proposals was sent, secretly, to Local Education Authorities on the 17th June with instructions that they had to be distributed to grant aided schools attended by the less well off. The Circular was also sent to private schools.

On 19th June, Clement Attlee, as Lord President of the Council, tabled the CORB recommendations and report in the House of Commons. The following day the written information reached the relevant parents at the same time it was announced on the radio and in the Press. By mid-morning the response was so great that more than 3,000 people were queuing outside the CORB offices in Berkeley St. London.

This response, which revealed to some extent the deep current of public apprehension and fear for the future, concerned the Government so much that they instructed Shakespeare to issue a statement in an attempt to calm things down, 'drawing attention publicly to the dangers and difficulties involved'.[16] He therefore issued a press statement on the 1st July:-

'The Government has no intention of shipping large numbers of children overseas. Any idea of mass migration is absolutely contrary to the wishes of the Government concerned. For scores of thousands of children to be transferred in a few weeks, as suggested in some quarters, is outside the bounds of any practical scheme and would be an extremely dangerous process'.[17]

The message was an echo of a radio broadcast which Geoffrey Shakespeare had made on Sunday 23rd June:-

'Any notion of sending hundreds of thousands of children overseas in the space of a few weeks was both dangerous and stupid...The scheme could only operate subject to the limitation of shipping and offers made by each Dominion'.[18]

Churchill was very much against the scheme and on 21st June 1940, he had told the Cabinet that:-

'...a large movement of this kind encourages a defeatist spirit, which is entirely contrary to the true facts of the position and should be sternly discouraged. It is one thing to allow a limited number of children to be sent to North America, but the idea of a large scale evacuation stands on a different footing and was attended by grave difficulties'.[19]

He referred to this again in a Cabinet meeting on 1st July before the issue of the Press release.

'The Prime Minister drew attention to the scheme for evacuation children to North America. Many people were now expecting the scheme to develop on a considerable scale. A large movement of this kind encouraged a defeatist spirit, which was entirely contrary to the true facts of the position and should be sternly discouraged'.[20]

In reality, the true facts were actually different from that implied in the 1st July statement. On the 4th July, Churchill stated:-

'We consider large scale raids on the British Isles involving all arms, may take place at any moment. A full scale invasion is unlikely to take place before the middle of July'.[21]

At the end of June 1940 articles such as the one below appeared in some local newspapers outlining the rationale behind the Overseas Scheme and explaining to parents what their responsibilities were:-

WEYMOUTH CHILDREN
CAN GO OVERSEAS FOR SAFETY
PROBLEMS FOR PARENTS

Very soon all Weymouth mothers and fathers will be confronted with perhaps the biggest problem of their lives. Should they keep their youngsters by their sides in Weymouth, so-called safe area, or send them overseas to a safe land?

They must decide whether they will face the pain of not seeing their own children for perhaps years, when at the most important stage in their young lives, but knowing that they are growing up safe from Nazi bombers, from death, injury, and that the youthful minds will not be for ever contaminated by total warfare.

All parents in Weymouth are to be sent two forms, dealing with the evacuation of Weymouth children from five to 16 years of age to Canada, USA, Australia, New Zealand and South Africa.

Parents with children attending grant maintained schools should send their replies to the Local Education Authority, Municipal Offices, Weymouth. Those with children attending secondary schools to the Director of Education, Dorchester...and other schools to the Secretary of the Overseas Reception Board c/o Thomas Cook and Sons Ltd., Berkeley St., London W1.

It is explained on the sheets that before going overseas the children will have to pass a medical examination, which will probably be held in Weymouth.

They will travel under suitable escorts and, on arrival, be boarded with private families and not institutions.

They will receive as good an education as the children in the neighbourhood to which they are sent and their welfare afterwards will be carefully watched.

Extra clothes will be issued to them free, and when the war is won they will return home again.

Travel will be free. Parents will be expected to contribute for the maintenance of each child as much as they would have contributed had the child merely been evacuated to a receiving area in this country. If they offer to pay more than 6/- a week or more, no enquiry will be made; if not, they will be assessed according to their circumstances.[22]

(In September 1940 an invitation was received from a Mr. Vic Latty who had lived in Weymouth and was now a successful businessman in New Zealand. He offered accommodation in 'Dorset-like Southland, where he and other organisations would look after them 'especially well'.)[23]

It is no wonder that after such positive advertising many parents thought it worthwhile to apply. By the 4th July the total number of applicants was 211,548. Of these 11,702 were from Independent Schools, and 199,746 from Grant Aided Schools. Almost 50% fulfilled all the criteria.[24]

As a consequence of the vast numbers of applications, the Cabinet called a halt to the scheme 'without killing it and to ensure that it was kept to quite small proportions,' [25] and closed the lists on the grounds that they had more names than they could cope with. They also ordered Shakespeare to once again diffuse the panic.[26]

'Diplomatic' announcements were placed in newspapers:-

> *'It has now been announced that in view of the adequate response already received from parents wishing to send their children overseas it will be impossible for any more applications to be entertained until further notice.*

No further applications from parents should therefore be made to either the local education authorities or the Children's Overseas Reception Board. Similarly, no further applications should be made for employment as escorts'.[27]

This limitation on shipping was becoming a serious concern for members of the Admiralty. They stated that there were three factors which would make it impossible to move all but a handful of children:-

- Few ships were available and capable of carrying large numbers of children.

- Most of the available passenger ships were needed to transport enemy aliens to Canada.

- General safety. U-boats were operating in the Atlantic and the Western Approaches and the Luftwaffe was also attacking shipping. This led to a shortage in Convoy escort vessels.

This lack of Naval escort forced the Government to suspend the whole overseas evacuation scheme on 4th July, much to the annoyance of some Labour MPs who protested that private evacuation was still going on. A question was raised in the Commons. 'Was the scheme merely a camouflage to get out the well-to-do?' [28]

There was a certain amount of substance to this claim as some of the evacuation offers to the USA were seen to be elitist. On 1st July 1940, Mr. Frank Aydelotte, American Secretary of the Rhodes Scholarships, appealed to American Rhodes scholars throughout the USA to help to house 'one or more children of Oxford and Cambridge dons, or those children of dons from other universities'.[29] Although a few days later the suggestion that only the children of the titled and wealthy were wanted by American hosts was refuted by the 'American Committee in London for the Evacuation of Children'. The chairman, Mr. Justice Weddell, blamed exchange restrictions for the fact that the children so far sent to the USA belonged to families who had travelled and made well-to-do friends in the States. He was quoted as saying:-

'We are arranging to take all kinds of children. Cities have said 'Send us all you can, poor and well-to-do.' He also stated that some American sponsors were paying for the passage of poorer children'.[30]

On 9th July 1940 Mrs Roosevelt formed the 'National Child Refugee Committee' in New York, in order to raise $5m, (at the time £1m) to provide homes for refugee children. She addressed a large audience of welfare workers and stated that speed in raising the money was vital. In answer to the question of whether or not American Red Cross could send ships to collect the children, Mrs Roosevelt stated that:-

'...it would be a very grave responsibility, and might get us into the war. The USA, in all probability, would not feel that they could assume that responsibility'.[31]

In an oral reply to the Commons on 18th July 1940 Churchill stated:-

'His Majesty's Government have been deeply touched by the kindly offers of hospitality received from the Dominions and the United States. They will take pains to make sure that in the use that is made of these offers there shall be no question of rich people having an advantage, if advantage there be, over poor'.[32]

This had already been said by Clement Attlee in a debate in the House of Commons on Tuesday 3rd July. He pointed out to the House that although the overseas evacuation scheme was part of the national defence there was no intention to clear out of the country everybody except fighting men and those engaged in war industries. 'We are going to defend invasion and neither the Government nor the country is facing the situation in any sense of panic'. He felt that it was important to stress this as there was a great deal of difference between sending children to places of safety and the mass movements of the population which had never been contemplated. He also stressed that there was no class privilege in the scheme, a fact reinforced by Geoffrey Shakespeare in the same debate. He made it quite clear that the Government were opposed to the uprooting of public schools and settling them overseas. Nothing, he said, would undermine public morale more than the granting of such facilities to the privileged few.[33]

The scheme went ahead despite Churchill's reservations and its detractors, who were concerned that they had got tied up in a scheme driven by crisis and emotion rather than rational thought, having just cause to stop it.

Parents were asked to nominate the Dominion they wished their child to go to and they had to sign an indemnity form releasing the Government from responsibility for their children's safety at sea. Throughout this time the CORB administrative staff increased from 30 to 350 and reached a peak in September 1940 of 620.[34]

On the 9th July the Admiralty again warned the War Cabinet that the Navy could no longer provide adequate naval protection and on the 16th and 18th of July both Attlee and Churchill told Parliament, in answer to a series of questions, that the scheme had again been suspended.

In the Commons on the 18th July 1940 Frederick Cocks, Labour MP for Broxtowe, Nottinghamshire, asked the Prime Minister whether:-

'...in view of the fact that the large scale evacuation of children overseas was an important factor in the military defence of Britain, will he reconsider the decision to postpone the scheme, bearing in mind that children can be evacuated in ships which are already convoyed?'

Churchill replied:-

'It is most undesirable that anything in the nature of a large scale exodus from this country should take place, and I do not believe that the military situation requires or justifies such a proceeding, having regard to the relative dangers of going and staying. Nor is it physically possible....[35]

The scheme has been postponed, not abandoned, but any further emigration that may be possible, as opportunity serves, will be regulated, with a view to restoring the balance between classes, and not in pursuance of any policy of reducing the number of persons in this well-defended island. Furthermore, the scale of movement must necessarily be small in number and dependent in time upon naval facilities'.[36]

This was taken up by the Labour MP Benjamin Smith, who asked the Prime Minister whether he would, at some later date:-

'...reconsider the possibility of evacuation of children by neutral and American ships'.

Churchill answered:-

'Yes, of course; if a movement to send United States ships to these shores were set foot from the other side of the Atlantic, it would immediately engage the most earnest attention of His Majesty's Government'.[37]

Reading through the debates of the time one can sense Churchill's displeasure about the whole scheme. His concerns expressed in the Press release of 1st July were reiterated in this debate on 18th July:-

'I must frankly admit that the full bearings of this question, (Overseas evacuation) were not appreciated by His Majesty's Government at the time when it was first raised. It was not foreseen that the mild countenance given to the plan would lead to a movement of such dimensions, and that a crop of alarmist and depressing rumours would follow at its tail, detrimental to the interests of National Defence...' [38]

Despite the official postponement, the scheme continued and Churchill must have been aware of this situation when he sent a memo to Sir John Anderson on the 18th July 1940 questioning the relevance of Geoffrey Shakespeare leaving his post in London to see off 100 evacuees departing from Liverpool. [39]

Those selected for evacuation began to arrive in Liverpool where they were put up in schools, hostels and orphanages while awaiting embarkation. Those who were private evacuees stayed at the Adelphi Hotel.[40]

However, despite the difference in accommodation, most of them spent all their nights underground sheltering from the Luftwaffe attacks on the city. Margaret Wood, who was to sail on the Llanstephan Castle to South Africa on the 23rd August stated that the only thing she can remember about her in two days in Liverpool with her fellow evacuees was spending the time in a shelter and 'being dosed with Castor Oil...all 302 of them!'[41] (There seemed to be concern for the bowel movements of evacuees. Brian Maystone recalls being introduced to 'Senna Tea' when billeted in Pulborough!)[42]

The daily dose of castor oil!

During their stay the evacuees were contacted by their ship board escorts and each was given a metal identification disc with their CORB number inscribed on it. In general it could be said that these children faced a more difficult time than their counterparts who had been evacuated internally along with friends and teachers.

Unlike internal evacuees the overseas ones were 'screened out' if they had any form of disorder and medicals were carried out at the port of departure. Also, those with extreme homesickness were sent home. Those who lacked proper clothing were issued with it before departure and lessons in etiquette and information about the country they were going to were provided both immediately before departure and on the outward journey.[43]

Homesickness was a serious and, under the circumstances, not an unnatural occurrence. Geoffrey Shakespeare attempted to visit as many of the evacuees as he could and he adopted a paternalistic attitude towards his charges but even he stated in his memoirs that he saw:-

> *'...homesickness as a strange disease; it comes suddenly like a virulent germ, and such is its physical effect on the child that it lowers all power of resistance. But the same child within an hour is laughing and joking again'.*[44]

On board ship there was an escort for every fifteen children, one doctor and 2 nurses for every 100 and Ministers of leading denominations in every large group. Many Salvation Army Officers went as escorts with the evacuees and ensured their well being. The Government was anxious to secure the help of a considerable number of leaders and helpers and it was thought that, among others, the Salvation Army would be able to help. An appeal went out in the June 1940 issue of the International War Cry asking for volunteers but stipulating certain criteria. They had to be:-

- Experienced in controlling children.

- Not more than 55 years of age unless possessed of exceptional health and other qualifications.

- Available at short notice.

- Good sailors.

- Persons with experience as leaders of Young People's Groups such as Life-saving Guards and Young People's Corps'.[45]

The total number of applications to become escorts, from all sources, reached more than 19,000.

The first evacuees to Canada sailed on the 21st July 1940 on the 'Anselm' in convoy OB 189. The convoy was attacked by U-boats on the 27th July, but despite four vessels sinking, the 'Anselm' survived.[46]

Between July and mid-September 19 ships sailed. Ninety percent of the 3119 evacuees left during August and by September, 16 ships had reached their destination. It is interesting to note that only 8 of the 19 ships could take more than 100 passengers.[47]

Three ships sailed for Australia. On the 5th August the 'Batory', a sixteen thousand ton luxury liner of the Polish Gydnia American Line, sailed with Convoy WS2 with a compliment of 1,340, including 477 children and 51 escorts and medical staff. It had originally been designed to carry only 300.[48] On the 24th August, the 'Nestor' of the Alfred Holts Blue Funnel Line, sailed with Convoy OB203 with 82 children and 8 escorts and medics. On the 17th September the 'Diomed' sailed with 18 children.[49] Margaret Wood was to travel from Liverpool to Gibraltar in convoy with some merchant vessels, together with an evacuee ship going to Australia. All the ships steamed east into the Mediterranean whilst the Llanstephan Castle struck out alone into the Atlantic, zigzagging its way to Cape Town hoping to avoid the U-boats. The journey lasted five weeks instead of two weeks because of these evasive measures. In her diary Margaret describes conditions and life on the ship.

> *'On Friday, 23rd August 1940, we boarded the ship Llanstephan Castle. We were very well looked after on the ship. Each morning for about an hour and a half, we had lectures on travel, South Africa and divinity. There was a church service every Sunday. There were two concerts, one was*

given by the escorts and the other by us. I sang duets with Olwyn Gibson, 'The Indian Love Call' and 'Somewhere over the Rainbow'. The voyage was quiet and the only port of call was Freetown in Sierra Leone. We all had to drink quinine, ugh! - and plaster ourselves with ointment if we went out after sunset because we were in a malaria infested area. When we crossed the line, the equator, we had a big party. It was very riotous and ended by putting bread and jam down each other's backs'.[50]

The Llanstephan Castle had been converted into a troop ship so Margaret and her fellow travellers slept in three tiered bunks. They bathed in hot sea-water and used a 'rough chunk' of soap which was supposed to lather. The food on board was very good and in marked contrast to the sleeping arrangements. The restaurant was run on pre-war style and they even provided printed menus. Some were devised to make them fun. For example the tea provided on September 3rd 1940 comprised: 'Filleted Fitness, Soused Hasty Words with Toasted Tempers and Bright and Breezy salad'.[51]

What the majority of parents did not know, or realise, was that when these ships and convoys travelled from Britain they only had a naval escort for 300 kilometres west of Liverpool. At that point the convoy scattered and the individual ships took their chance against the U-boats. This was because:-

- The USA had not entered the war and, in consequence, there was no provision for refuelling in ports on the east coast of America.

- The Naval escorts were required for coastal protection in the Western approaches.

In 'Children of the Benares', Ralph Barker describes the pattern of the convoys:-

'Arrayed on a broad front three miles across in eight columns of two vessels each, with an asymmetrical ninth column of three to vary the pattern, their generous spacing allowed them to zigzag in concert either side of their mean course to a prearranged schedule. This was their only defence, passive and ultimately unpredictable, against the submersible enemy.....'[52]

An indication of how dangerous the journey could be can be found in the number of U-boat 'kills' confirmed during the summer of 1940; 58 in June, 38 in July and 56 in August as well as 15 other vessels sunk by the Luftwaffe.

The quote below indicates that civilian as well as naval and merchant vessels were possible targets even though, as in the case here, they were flying a neutral flag.

'Friday. October 20th 1939.

Received a letter from Gay, who still seems uncertain about coming back from America. Her father, Capt. David Margesson, tells me he consulted Winston about the safety of returning on an American ship: 'Perfectly safe,' said Winston, 'but of course there is a risk of their being torpedoed or mined!'.[53]

On the 1st August 1940, the liner 'Volendam' carrying a total of 606 passengers, including 321 evacuee children, was torpedoed in the Atlantic. Fortunately a second torpedo did not explode so she did not sink and was towed back to England by tugs.[54] However, little was learned from the experience. The 'Volendam' had been the leading ship in the centre column thus visible to other vessels, including the enemy. Also she was carrying a cargo of wheat to sell in America, thus making it a legitimate target. It is surprising that such a cargo was on an evacuee ship!! [55]

On 17th September a similar prominent position in the convoy, together with, in this case, lack of escort protection, possibly contributed to the sinking of the 'SS City of Benares'. She was part of the Ellerman's City Line and sailing in Convoy OB213. She was torpedoed by U48 commanded by Heinrich Bleichrodt. This attack resulted in the loss of 77 children and 179 adults and crew, including six escorts.

It is ironic that until 1am on the morning of the 17th the Convoy had been supported by the destroyer HMS Winchelsea, which had used her submarine detection echo sounders (ASDIC) to monitor U-boat activity in the area. At that time she had to leave to rendezvous with an incoming Convoy (HX71) from Halifax, Nova Scotia, carrying stores and ammunition vital for the British war effort.[56] Therefore, at the time of the attack Convoy 213 remained unprotected.

Forty six of the surviving children spent 8 days in an open lifeboat before being rescued.[57] This was partly due to the fact that the Admiralty had ordered all ship's officers in Convoys not to attempt to pick up survivors from sinking vessels if it involved endangering the safety of their own ships. In this case all the ships were in danger. Despite the human cargo some of these ships were now having to carry, it is a surprise that nobody considered countermanding the order to take account of the loss of life that could occur and the potential damage to morale at home if such a tragedy should take place. In fact this was raised by Shakespeare himself at the subsequent Departmental enquiry. He wrote: 'I understood from the Admiralty that in a convoy one or two ships were told off to act as rescue ships and were charged with the duty of stopping to rescue survivors of any ship that was torpedoed'.[58] This had been the understanding of everyone involved with CORB. When the Admiralty replied to the findings of the enquiry they quoted the orders that had been given to all vessels regarding the rescue of victims of enemy attack:-

> *'When other considerations permit the rear ships of columns should be detailed to act as Rescue Ships for their respective columns.*
>
> *Rescue ships may go to the assistance of vessels damaged by enemy action when a local escort is present. If the local escort is not present a Rescue Ship should not act unless this can be done without undue risk'.[59]*

Therefore as soon as the 'Winchelsea' went off to meet the incoming convoy she had in effect neutralised the ability of any other vessel to act as a rescue vessel.

Had the 'Benares' been allowed to go at her own speed of around 15 knots rather than go with the slowest ship of the Convoy as ordered, travelling at 8.5 knots, she might have had a better chance of survival.

This event prompted Churchill to say to the Defence Committee on the 28th September:-

> *'In view of this recent disaster to the ship carrying women and children to Canada, the future of evacuation overseas of children must cease'.*[60]

On the 3rd October 1940 the scheme was officially abandoned and the four groups of evacuees waiting to embark were sent home. Although there were suggestions up to March 1941 that it should be resurrected, to all intents and purposes it finished on the 17th September 1940 with the sinking of the 'Benares'.

After the evacuation of 2,664 children, of whom 1532 went to Canada, 577 to Australia, 353 to South Africa and 202 to New Zealand, the official scheme was now dead. It had become politically unacceptable.

It is interesting to note, but in the circumstances understandable, that there was no public enquiry into the 'Benares' disaster. It was used merely as a forceful piece of anti-German propaganda. The initial enquiry advised the Minister of Shipping that although such a loss of life would have merited an enquiry in peacetime, if only to satisfy the public that safety measures were available in ships, the 'Benares' was a war casualty 'resulting from Germany's unrestricted warfare at sea and the essential facts were clear'.[61]

The Overseas Reception Board itself did remain in existence, albeit with reduced personnel. They had responsibility for maintaining contact with those children who had been evacuated abroad. This need to keep in touch was supported by Princess Elizabeth and Princess Margaret who made their first broadcast to evacuated children at home and overseas on 13th October 1940:-

> *'In wishing you good evening, I feel that I am speaking to friends and companions who have shared with my sister and myself many a happy Children's Hour.*
>
> *Thousands of you in this country have had to leave your homes and be separated from your fathers and mothers. My sister, Margaret Rose, and I feel so much for you as we know from experience what it means to be away from those we love most of all...*
>
> *All of us children who are still at home think continually of our friends and relatives who have gone overseas, who have travelled thousands of miles to find a wartime home and a kindly welcome in Canada, Australia, New Zealand, South Africa and the United States of America...'*[62]

Although the official overseas evacuation scheme was halted, there was nothing to stop private individuals or companies making similar arrangements and after June 1940 it is estimated that 17,000 were evacuated under private schemes. Professor Barbara Shawcroft, of U.C. Davis in

Berkeley, California, was one of 25 children who were evacuated to Canada in 1940 on the 'S.S. Duchess of Atholl', under the sponsorship of the Ford Motor Company. Her father had been an executive with the company and because of his position she was sent to Windsor, Ontario until July 1944, when she returned to the UK to a much different and quieter reception than that she had experienced on the outward journey. She remembers that this had been accompanied with a great deal of flag waving and an outward show of gaiety.[63]

The private schemes remained extremely elitist, either for the reason of position, as in the case of Barbara, or in simple financial terms. Those with money could afford to send their children away. In his diary the MP 'Chips' Channon described the scene at Euston Station on 24th June 1940 as the boat train for Liverpool was ready to depart:-

> *'There was a queue of Rolls-Royces and liveried servants and mountains of trunks. It seemed that everyone we knew was there'.*[64]

When Sir John Anderson suggested the suspension of exit permits to avoid any suggestion of class distinction and privilege the Cabinet opposed it:-

> *'The proposal virtually to ban the sending abroad of any further children by private arrangements was considered unduly drastic'.*[65]

Before both the private and Government schemes ended, 13,000 children had been settled in Canada and the United States. Some of them, for a variety of reasons, never returned and eventually became American or Canadian citizens.

Endnotes

1   Vera Brittain. <u>Vera Brittain's Diary. 1939-45</u>. 25 June 1940. pub. Thorpe 1993. p167

2   Angus Calder. <u>People's War</u>. op.cit. p36

3   The Times. 1 September 1939.

4   Constantine Fitzgibbon. <u>The Blitz</u>. Wingate. 1957. cited in Calder. People's War. op.cit. p41

5   PRO.DO131/29

6   PRO.DO 35/259/B277/4: PRO.DO 35/529/B305/8: PRO.DO 35/529/B305/4 cited in <u>Imperial Identities and Social Mobility: Class, Empire and the British Government</u> <u>Overseas Evacuation of children during the Second World War</u>. Patricia Lin. unpublished PhD thesis. University of Berkeley, California.

7   Report on Inter-Departmental Committee on the reception of children overseas. Cmd.6213: CAB.67/7/172. Minutes 15 June 1940: Official CORB History. PRO.DO 131/43.

8   Edward Stokes. <u>Innocents Abroad</u>. Allen & Unwin. 1994. p32

9   Ralph Barker. <u>Children of the Benares. A War Crime and its Victims</u>. Methuen. 1987. p28

10   Parliamentary Debates. Commons 5th Series. Vol.363.1939-40 col. 358. 17 June 1940: PRO.CAB. 65/7/170 17 June 1940: PRO CAB. 65/8/179 1 July 1940 cited in P.Lin. op.cit.

11   Parliamentary Debates Commons 5th Series vol.362. 1939-40 cols. 5-6. 18 June 1940. and <u>Westward Ho!</u>. MoI Film soundtrack. 1940

12   Reuters.

13   Reuters

14   PRO.CAB.65/7/170. 17 June.1940. cited Lin. op.cit.

15   Sir Martin Gilbert. Letter to <u>The Evacuee</u>. December 1996.

16   PRO.CAB. 65/7/174. Minutes. 21 June 1940. M.Gilbert. <u>The Churchill War Papers</u>. <u>Vol.2 May 1940 - December 1940</u>. Heinemann. 1994. p391

17   E.Stokes. <u>Innocents Abroad</u>. op.cit. p35

18   ibid. p36

19   Pro.CA. 65/7/174. 21 June 1940. Gilbert Churchill War Papers. op.cit.p 391

20   Gilbert. Churchill War Papers. Vol 2. op.cit p451

21   PRO CAB. 65/9/244 4 July 1940. cited P.Lin. op.cit.

22   Dorset County Chronicle & Swanage Times. 27 June. 1940.

23   ibid. 12 September 1940.

24   PRO DO.131/39. March 1941. P.Lin op.cit.

25   PRO.CAB.65/8/179 Minutes. 1 July. 1940

26   ibid.

27   Dorset Daily Echo. 6 July 1940.

28   Parliamentary Debates. Commons 5th Series. Vol 363. 1939-40 col. 21.23,355-62

29   Reuters. 1 July 1940

30   Dorset Daily Echo. 6 July 1940.

31   Reuters. 10 July 1940.

32   Martin Gilbert. Churchill War Papers. Vol 2. op.cit. p543

33   Dorset Daily Echo. 3 July 1940.

34   P. Lin op.cit.

35   Martin Gilbert. Churchill War Papers. Vol 2 op.cit. p542

36   ibid.

37   ibid.

38 ibid.

39 ibid. p546

40 R. Barker. <u>Children of the Benares</u>. op.cit. p9

41 Margaret Wood. Letter to the author. September 1997.

42 Brian Maystone. Letter to author February 1997.

43 M.Fethney. <u>Absurd and the Brave</u>. The Book Guild. Sussex. p105 & 113

44 G.Shakespeare. '<u>Let Candles be brought in</u>'. Macdonal. London. 1949. cited in Stokes. Innocents Abroad. op.cit. p56

45 <u>International War Cry</u>. 6 June 1940. Salvation Army Publications.

46 Stokes. <u>Innocents Abroad</u>. op.cit. p49

47 ibid. p50

48 ibid. p62

49 ibid. p68

50 Margaret Wood. Letter to the author. September 1997.

51 ibid.

52 R. Barker. <u>Children of the Benares</u>. op.cit. p1

53 Colville. <u>Fringes of Power</u>. op.cit. p43

54 Holman. <u>The Evacuation</u>. op.cit. p31

55 Barker. op cit. p43

56 ibid. p20

57 Holman op.cit. p37

58 Barker op.cit. p147

59 ibid. p149

60 PRO.CAB 79/6 folio 323 Gilbert Churchill War Papers. Vol 2 op cit. 23 September 1940. p862

61 Barker op.cit. p147. One positive thing to come out of the sinking was the introduction of small fast vessels for the sole purpose of rescuing people from the sea. There were only 12 but they rescued over 4000 seamen. It meant that escort vessels did not have to endanger themselves in a rescue mission but concentrate on engaging the enemy. Barker p153.

62 For full text of the broadcast see Appendix 3.

63 Interview with Barbara Shawcroft. Professor of Pottery. University College Davis. San Francisco. California. 10 July 1994.

64 Robert Rhodes James. (ed) '<u>Chips. The Diaries of Sir Henry Channon</u>. Weidenfeld. 1993. p259

65 PRO.CAB 65/8WM (40) 199th conclusions. 10 July 1940.

The Return Home

'Perhaps the only solidly real place we ever know is the place in which we spent our childhood and youth. It's there that there are genuinely real streets, shops and houses, and their only fault is that they have a trick, like the queer cards that conjurers use, of appearing diminished every time we go back'.[1]

One important aspect of evacuation which is almost always overlooked is the return of the evacuees to their homes. In some cases this was just as significant as leaving them in any of the Government schemes. As early as August and December 1943 a Departmental Committee in the Ministry of Health submitted a report on the eventual return of evacuees from the reception areas. Detailed planning took place in the Spring of 1944 but the V1 and V2 attacks on London, with the resultant damage, meant that the scheme would be implemented first in areas other than the capital. On the 10th April 1945, the Ministry of Health distributed Circular 68/45 to all local authorities and County Councils which had taken part in evacuation.[2] By April, the Ministry had considered the arrangements that needed to be made for children returning to the Metropolitan areas, the Medway Towns and those along the Thames. Even as late on in the war as this, the Government still did not consider that the time was right for implementing a return, but they were concerned that local authorities should be ready to act on any given order from central Government. This Circular 68/45 was the vehicle through which outline plans were given. It was suggested that immediately the decision to return evacuees to their homes was put into operation the Minister would notify all areas by means of a telegram which would simply state 'Operate London Return Plans'. On receipt of the message local authorities were to adhere to the timetable appended to the Circular.[3] In the end the telegram was sent on the 2nd May 1945.

The outline of the plan was to ensure the organised return of all evacuees who had homes to return to and who were not prevented in any other way from going back to them. It was stressed that because of acute difficulties in the housing situation in parts of London, it was very important that evacuees who did not have adequate accommodation to return to were to be given no assistance or encouragement to leave the reception areas. Houses, or parts of houses, which had been damaged and were in need of repair to make them habitable, could not be regarded as being immediately available for occupation. It was thought that many of this group would remain in the reception areas for a considerable time and that the local authorities were to ensure that social and welfare services dealing with evacuees would remain in place. For instance some pregnant women who had made arrangements to have their babies in the reception areas were to be billeted for up to four weeks after the birth, should they wish to stay. If, however, adult evacuees stated that their reason for not returning home was simply that there would be a shortage of bedding and equipment or that nobody would be available to open the house, they were to be informed that they would return as normal but be accommodated for a few days in a Rest Centre while the problems were investigated.[4] A note of these was made on the registration card which the evacuees had to complete before departure from the reception areas. In the event the WVS were prepared to make temporary loans of bedding to families in difficulty and they also provided help in opening up houses and preparing them for occupation.[5]

The whole scheme involving the London areas was to be co-ordinated by the London County Council working with the senior regional officers in the Ministry of Health. They in turn appointed an officer in the reception area to take charge of the assembly, entraining and departure of the evacuees in their area. The LCC also appointed a 'train-marshal' for each train with the

responsibility for the actual journey. Both of these people were additionally respon
making sure that the arrangements for overnight stays of evacuees and escorts, luggage and
feeding were in hand, although technically it was a 'Food Executive Officer' who was in charge of
the feeding of evacuees. Food and luggage were very important considerations. On arrival in
London all evacuees were to be given a meal, but for the journey they, and their escorts, were
provided with packed lunches. Drinks were to be provided at stopping points along the route by
members of the WVS and other voluntary organisations. Food and drink for unaccompanied
children was loaded onto the relevant trains and handed out during the journey. Adult evacuees had
been given notices about the movement of their luggage during the time leading up to the actual
journey and also when they were asked to complete the registration cards. After these cards had
been returned to the Senior Regional Officer they were collated and specially coloured labels,
representing the first dispersal centres in London to which the evacuees were to be taken, were
returned to the evacuees' billets to be attached to their luggage. It was very important that the
correct colour corresponded with the addresses on the evacuees' home address.

As far as possible, the plan was to move the evacuees in organised parties travelling by special
trains or alternatively in reserved seats on regular trains. The local authorities were informed of the
stations where the evacuees in their areas were to travel from. Notification of these details, plus the
times of departure and the names of those due to travel, were sent out a week prior to the journey.
During the seven days, the local officers were to ensure that all persons were made aware of the
travel arrangements and where they were to assemble. In some cases the stations were a long way
from the reception areas so Civil Defence, Private cars and other vehicles were used for
transportation. Where this was not possible, the Senior Regional Officers were able to organise
transport as long as they had at least four days notice. Where the travelling distance was vast, it was
necessary for the groups to stay in the area of the stations. Suitable buildings in the area were
requisitioned for this use and the billeting authorities used the equipment and bedding previously
provided in the evacuation scheme. Some were able to use the local rest centres and these were
staffed and supervised by existing personnel.

Alternative arrangements were made for those who, for various reasons, were unable to travel by
rail. Free travel vouchers were to be given for those who wished to travel independently only when
they could not be included in an organised group or where insufficient numbers in a specific area
warranted an official organised party. Evacuees whose return had to be delayed were eligible for
free travel. The vouchers could only be used during the weeks as the railway companies were not
prepared to allow their use at the weekends. The parents or designated guardians of
unaccompanied children who could not be included in the organised travel could also apply for
free vouchers in order to collect their children. This also applied to people acting as escorts to the
blind, disabled and elderly. The reception areas were asked to provide escorts for adults and
accompanied children at a ratio of 1-40. Again the WVS provided many of them and they were
usually co-ordinated by the local WVS centre organiser who liaised closely with the authorities.
The ratio for unaccompanied children was 1-12, but in this case the escorts provided by the

reception areas were only responsible for them up to the entraining stations. Supervision on the journey and in London was provided by the LCC.

The actual scheme, like its predecessors, was bound up in seemingly endless bureaucratic red-tape, but the plans were designed to overcome any disorganised evacuation from the reception areas. As it was, when evacuees did eventually arrive at the main-line stations in London, the sheer numbers of people and the luggage they brought with them, caused a great deal of dislocation to the day to day running of the stations. It was a very difficult task to organise in advance the movement of a large group of people of indeterminate numbers and from locations situated in a vast area of the United Kingdom .

In March 1945, a count of the evacuees remaining in the reception areas showed that during the previous six months 600,000 had returned home independently. This was out of a known total of 1,040,200.[6]

Most of these returnees were Londoners so the overall plan was scaled down to account for the decline in numbers, which amounted to a total of 453,200, including 134,000 unaccompanied children. The LCC had to arrange its scheme to recover their children from around 1,000 different billeting areas, sort them into travelling parties, take them back to London, sort them into the original eighty evacuation districts and accompany the individuals back to their homes.[7] In order for this to happen specific measures had to be taken.

During the week immediately after the delivery of the order to move, the billeting officers had to visit every adult evacuee in their area and get them to complete the record card giving personal information including home address. These were to be completed with details of any children in the adults care. Where the adult was not accompanying children the word 'priority' was to be written on the card where space had been left for the children's names. The card also included a code number for the reception areas so that the receiving authorities knew where the group had come from. These cards were returned to the Senior Regional Officer in the Ministry of Health, together with a full list of names of those able to travel. After 22 days from the original order these cards were sent back to the reception areas with numbered lists of the evacuees and their home addresses.

Cards were also issued to hosts looking after unaccompanied evacuees. The same information was required and the same sequence of events took place, except that when the LCC received the cards from the SROs they ascertained whether or not the individual domestic circumstances made it possible for the evacuees to return. Any important details concerning individuals were included on the card to make the authorities in London aware of specific difficulties. As there had been previous correspondence between the authorities some of these problems were already known to the relevant agencies. Registration cards were not issued to groups of special children including those who were disabled or mentally ill, the under-five's in nurseries and children in camp schools or self-contained secondary schools established by the education authority for the evacuation area.

Special arrangements were made for these groups. Some of this latter group and secondary age individuals were due to take the School Certificate and Higher School Certificate examinations at the end of the summer school term and because it was thought that the upheaval would jeopardise their chances of success they were to remain billeted until the end of the summer term subject to the confirmation of the local Education Authority. If this child was part of a family group then the mother and siblings were to travel in the organised party and the examinee was to be billeted unaccompanied.

The London scheme was completed and the evacuees returned home by 12th July 1945, three days later than originally scheduled. By then 115 trains had taken a total of 24,317 evacuees back to the capital including 29,701 unaccompanied children, 21,127 mothers and children and 3,489 other adults.[8] However, despite all their good intentions the Government again had not reckoned on people's independent thoughts and actions and many of the 'organised' trains returned only half full because people had made their own arrangements.

All this was fine for those evacuees who had homes to go to, but it was different for those who had to remain behind in the reception areas, reckoned in August 1945 to be around 76,000 people.[9] For reasons of Government planning, this group was divided into two separate units: Mothers with children and Unaccompanied children, and then into two further sub-divisions... those who wanted to remain in the reception areas and those who wanted to return home.

The Government was concerned that householders in the reception areas should be relieved of the burden of housing evacuee mothers and children who wanted to stay and, where possible, the latter were encouraged to seek accommodation of their own through a local authority housing procedure. There were also emergency arrangements which could be used if:-

- The person had been rendered homeless as a result of enemy action,

- The rehousing after such an event was inadequate,

- They had given up their homes in the evacuated areas before being moved to the reception areas.

It was the responsibility of the authorities in the reception areas to check that those wishing to stay were in fact genuinely homeless, had not had previous housing or had given theirs up at the beginning of the war.

The second group, those who wanted to return home, were also sub-divided into three distinct categories:-

a. Those who had been made homeless as a result of enemy action.

b. Families who had never had a home of their own. This group consisted primarily of young mothers, often the wives of servicemen, who had lived with their parents before the war and had never had the opportunity to rent or buy a home of their own.

If the parents or other relatives had lost their home it rendered the people in this group homeless and it was considered apposite that they should be given the same opportunity to gain accommodation as home owners who had lost their property. There was also the additional problem that families may have grown in numbers during the evacuation and would no longer fit into the existing house.

c. Families who had given up their home in the evacuation area. The number in this category was substantial. One reason why free accommodation had been provided under the Government evacuation scheme was to ensure that some of the expenses on housing would be avoided and thus enable the evacuees to meet the demands arising from the retention of their home in the evacuated area so that they could return to it as and when enemy action ceased. The Ministry of Health made it quite clear in a Circular[10] that preference for accommodation should not be given, except under exceptional circumstances, to those families who voluntarily deprived themselves of any accommodation to return to. If however, these people genuinely were not able to re-house themselves their names were to be added to the local authority list for housing.

In all three categories the authorities in the reception areas forwarded lists of families to the evacuated areas. The information on these lists included:-

- The number of persons in each family and the ages and sexes of the children.

- Their present address in the reception area.

- The address in the evacuation area to which the family state that they are unable to return.

- The reasons why the address in the evacuation area was now unavailable for reoccupation.[11]

There were problems in making these lists accurate especially where families and evacuated groups had been billeted over a large area and in some cases in more than one official reception area. In the case of a mother and children being accommodated in one area and other unaccompanied members of the family in another it was recommended that they should be listed as being with the mother, but with a note indicating that there were children elsewhere. It was thought that this would be enough information for both the reception areas and the authorities in London to make sure that families were eventually united. However, administrative oversights made the plan very difficult to implement and a great deal of confusion resulted especially where the billeting officer had not kept an accurate record of evacuee movements in the reception areas.

When the lists had been received and the 'homeless' situation had been verified, the local authorities in the evacuated areas were duty bound to either provide temporary accommodation, housing through normal authority channels or use emergency powers available to them.[12] It was particularly important to find accommodation for those who had not had it before or had lost their homes owing to enemy action because, being in the reception areas, they had not had the chance to find any housing of their own in their home area.

Although these details concerned those who had been evacuated under the Government scheme, there were families who had made their own temporary arrangements within the reception areas in order to alleviate the pressure on the billets, thus taking themselves outside of the scheme, but who now wished either to return home or find more suitable housing within the reception areas. It was not the Government's intention to exclude people who had used their own initiative, therefore they were eligible to take part in the official scheme if they informed the relevant regional offices that they wished to do so. Unaccompanied children created other problems. The local authorities in the evacuated areas informed their counterparts in the reception areas of children who should remain in their areas because of lack of accommodation, or even room, in their homes. It was necessary that these children should be reunited with their families as soon as possible and in order to do this there was thought to be no alternative but to regard the whole family unit as 'inadequately housed'. This would then give the authorities just cause to rehouse the family using the same powers as indicated previously. In many cases this was to be a last resort. Having received details of unaccompanied children awaiting return to their homes the local officers re-visited the proposed accommodation to verify that it was unsuitable for their return. If there was no room, the family were actively encouraged to make alternative arrangements of their own but, at the same time, their names were added to the housing list. As soon as suitable accommodation had been found the reception area was to be informed and the child sent home. If under exceptional circumstances the family had moved out of the original evacuated area, the local authority in the new area were to be responsible for the re-housing.

This scheme sounds idealistic and in reality it was. There was a tremendous housing shortage, especially in previous target areas, and the early re-housing of evacuated families was impossible. The Government and local authorities realised the situation but the scheme did demonstrate that they were making a start. They were concerned to ensure that billeting allowances should remain available until families were either re-housed or children were able to rejoin their parents, while at the same time encouraging as many people as possible to make their own arrangements. The Government tried to help those who simply did not have enough basic equipment to ensure that all the family could be accommodated. Some families, especially those who had been away for a long period, were supplied with beds and bedding, and with basic furniture, on loan or purchased from local authorities. This provision, implemented in December 1944 remained in effect until the 30th June 1947.

There were also some psychological and sociological problems which faced families after years of separation. Therefore, as well as providing the necessary physical help the Ministry of Health advised local authorities in the previously evacuated areas to instigate follow-up visits to ensure that any problems or re-familiarisation with family and neighbourhood could be overcome swiftly. Some of these problems were caused simply by lack of physical space or the fact that the children had grown up significantly during their absence. This was particularly true of those who had been evacuated overseas and who had not seen their families for six years or more. Barbara Shawcroft found relationships with her family so difficult and life in 'austerity drab' Britain so depressing that within weeks of her repatriation from New England she had decided to return to the USA and become an American citizen.[13] Quotes from evacuees returning from Australia indicate the same emotional stress felt by Barbara, which, in the following example was brought about by simple non-recognition:-

> *'Barbara Helical stood on Leeds station. There was a heavy mist swirling and everyone had gone. I'd passed this couple about three times. They didn't know it was their daughter, and I didn't know it was my parents. I felt so lonely, as if I was the only person left in the world....'* [14]

The possible problems faced by returning evacuees are unquantifiable. There were so many different individual experiences, both in the reception areas and in the home situation post-war, that it is only possible to view the ensuing problems in general terms or to look at a vast number of individual case studies which, in isolation, would not necessarily have any bearing on the experience on another evacuee. One only has to interview ex-evacuees to realise that this is the case. Even child psychologists researching into the effects of evacuation immediately after the war disagreed and contradicted each other's findings. How can one equate the experiences of a child who had returned from an excellent billet to a poor home background with a child who had been perhaps abused or ill-treated in the reception area. What about those children who were returning home to parents who found it difficult to come to terms with the loss of their independence. There was also the problem of adolescents reverting to childish behaviour and seeking attention from their parents and just wanting some love and care. The varied experiences are vast.

Another survey of evacuees still remaining in the scheme was taken in March 1946 to cover the period from July 1945. The number had dropped to 38,000, primarily mothers and children, 26,000, and families living in family groups, 3,000.[15] The fact that they were now living in temporary accommodation did not necessarily distinguish them from any other person in the same situation across the country therefore, gradually, the label of evacuee was 'removed' and they became increasingly the responsibility of the local authority within the reception areas.

But one category of evacuees is never mentioned in the text books and rarely mentioned in other media. What happened to those unaccompanied children who were unable to return to their original homes? What about those who, while in the reception areas, were orphaned?

When the 'official' evacuation scheme ended on 31st March 1946 there were 5,200 unaccompanied children left in the reception areas. These were either in billets with foster parents, residential nurseries or hostels.[16] Although this was below the estimated figure of 10,000 it still represented a significant social welfare problem for the authorities. Although, if seen in relation to the total number involved in the whole evacuation scheme one could argue, like Titmuss that these numbers were in fact insignificant and could have been a lot worse.[17] The make up of this group needs to be examined in context before any blame for their being overlooked can be apportioned to any authority or social group. For the majority, they remained in the reception areas because of the housing problems which still existed in the former target areas. Others had been orphaned and a very few, only 29 out of a total of 9,000 in July 1945 had been deserted by their parents.[18] It needs to be remembered that under any other circumstances in peacetime some of these children would have become the responsibility of the poor law authorities. Other institutions such as Dr. Barnardo's Homes, the National Children's Home and Orphanage took in children. According to Bob Holman there was an increase in the interest of adoption in the 1930s but the basic provision was in the area of residential care. The evacuation scheme, perhaps inadvertently, had taken over the responsibility for the social welfare and child care of some evacuee children who normally would have been taken from their home environment. There had been 32,700 children in poor law institutions in 1938-9.[19]

Endnotes

1   J.B.Priestley. Postscripts. Heinemann. London.1940

2   Duchy of Cornwall Archive. Duchy Office. St. Marys Isles of Scilly.

3   See Appendix 11.

4   Ministry of Health Circular. 185/44

5   Devon Record Office. ref.30584/19

6   31st March 1945 in England and Wales there were 175,000 mothers with children billeted in private houses, 68,000 in requisitioned houses, 109,000 unaccompanied children in billets, 23,000 in hostels, camps and residential nurseries, 36,000 old people, 3000 invalids, 1200 blind and 19,000 other adults. Titmuss. op.cit. p433.

7   ibid. p431

8   ibid. p433

9   ibid. p434

10   Ministry of Health Circular. No.69/45

11   ibid.

12   Ministry of Health Circular 2845

13   Interview with Barbara Shawcroft. op.cit

14   E.Stokes. Innocents Abroad. op.cit. p197

15   Titmuss op.cit. p435

16   ibid. p437

17   ibid.

18   ibid. p437 footnote.

19   ibid.

Were the Evacuation Schemes as Successful as School Text Books and Other Media Would Have Us Believe?

'....The whole experience marked me for life. Until fairly recent years I suffered bad bouts of homesickness if I was away from home for any time.....I am angry that the whole scheme was so ill thought out and put into operation. They were messing about with children's lives, for God's sake. How dare they give it so little thought.'[1]

The evacuation scheme of September 1939 was not as successful in its original aim as it should have been because of three major factors:-

Firstly, there was a certain element of panic in the original instigation of measures before there had been any evidence of a bombing campaign being waged against the country. This was to some extent influenced by the over estimation of potential bomb damage and resulting casualties.

In 1937, the Imperial Defence Committee calculated the cost of compensation rates for expected casualties in any future war where the main thrust of the attack would be from the air. Working on the assumption that there would be 1,800,000 casualties, 600,000 in the first two months, the cost would be £120,000,000 and for the first two years between 1 million and 2,800,000 hospital beds would be needed, depending on the length of stay. They continued in this statistical vein and worked out that 20 million square feet of timber would be needed for coffins each month at a cost of £300,000, a figure so unacceptable that they were resigned to using lime pits and mass graves.[2] Revised costing resulted in the stockpiling of thousands of collapsible papier-mâché and cardboard coffins. The committee concluded that the cost of damage would work out at £35,000 per bomb and 5% of all British property, valued at £550,000,000 would be destroyed in the first three weeks of the war. Finally, in 1938, they stated that 3,500 tons of high explosive would fall on London in the first 24 hours and then 700 tons every day after that for the first fortnight.[3]

Titmuss intimated that, if useful for nothing else, these figures do show why war-time emergency services put their energies overwhelmingly into aiding the effects of death, destruction or crippling hurt, and had little consideration for the less obvious and possibly greater side of effects on humanity such as confusion, anxiety, dislocation and distress.

There was also some belief that schools would make easy targets and provide a morale sapping coup for the enemy should they hit any. In 1938, civil servants started collecting information and press cuttings about the bombing of a school in Getalfe, in Madrid, in October 1936 when 70 children were killed. They were concerned as to what the effect on civilian life would be should a similar result occur.[4] In the event, any such situation had the opposite effect and strengthened people's resolve to secure a victory. Such a raid did take place on the 20th January 1943 when fighter bombers from Jabo Staffel Jagdgesschader 26 carried out a daylight raid on London and a diversionary attack on Maidstone. The main force dropped bombs on the Sandhurst Road School in Catford south-east London, killing 38 pupils aged 5-12 and 6 teachers. The photographs taken at the time showing bodies of children covered in tarpaulin were not released until 1983, although the raid was widely reported in the press and a great deal of anti-German propaganda resulted from the raid which some believed was intentional. Instead of having a negative effect on morale, this particular raid seemed to increase the bitterness and hatred towards the Germans. Although there had been other hit and run raids which had resulted in the deaths of children, for example 31 had been killed in Petworth in September 1942, the media coverage in Britain and abroad, maintaining that the school had been hit deliberately, continued to increase the propaganda effect. The idea that this school had been a designated target may have arisen from a misinterpretation of an interview with one of the pilots of the raid in a broadcast on German radio on 21st January and reported in the British press on the 22nd. A phrase 'we dropped our bombs where they were to be dropped' was considered to be an admission that the school had been bombed deliberately. However, if one looks at the transcript of the broadcast other targets are mentioned but the school is not, although it could of course be intimated in the last phrase! It really depends on how you want to read it, an excellent example of interpreting or misinterpreting information for propaganda purposes.[5]

Secondly, Britain wanted to maintain peace, or be seen to be doing so, in the period before 1939. Thus most of the Government and local organisation was carried out in secret with the result that, in many cases, neither side knew what the other was doing or planning. In July 1934 Stanley Baldwin stated:-

> *'We feel with regard to the protection of the civil population that our plans have been carried as far as possible without the wider publicity that has hitherto been deemed to be in the public interest. The next stage involves communications with local authorities, with public utilities and so forth, and with all those on whom responsibilities for action would fall in the emergency contemplated, and before long, steps will be taken to communicate the necessary instructions to the public generally'.[6]*

Any pre-planning could be seen as anticipating war and panic could have ensued. In 1931, the first committee dealing with evacuation saw it as a problem not of getting people away from London but as a way of preventing a disorderly and panic-induced exodus. So paranoid were they about panic flight that in 1931 it was suggested by the Sub-Committee on Evacuation that the Police Force should be increased and a cordon should be put around London. Also, between December 1937 and the Munich Crisis in September 1938, there were a number of discussions between the Army and the civilian authorities, notably the Commissioner of Police, for the use of 17,000 troops. On 29th April 1939 orders from the War Office to Commanders in Chief explained in some detail the role the army would play in preventing panic and restoring civilian order.[7] These, together with an extra 20,000 reserve constables, would prevent panic at tube stations and mainline stations.[8] These concerns about panic had been strengthened by the reaction of some members of the public during the Munich crisis in September 1938 when 150,000 people moved into Wales. There was a mass exodus of cars leaving London and panic buying in the shops. It has to be said that in this instance Government secrecy about what was going on certainly did not help the situation and the hasty digging of one million feet of trenches in London and the distribution of 38 million gas-masks did little to allay the fears of the population. The Government did not mention anything publicly about any evacuation scheme until 29th September, by which time the crisis was over, although there is evidence to suggest that some schools took the initiative to make their own arrangements.[9] On 26th September 1938 there was a meeting of parents with pupils at the Becontree Infants School, Dagenham, where they were told what evacuation would entail should war be declared. Teachers were instructed to keep their rucksacks packed with essential items and their gas masks at school in case the order for evacuation was given.[10]

It was a fact that during the planning stages more attention was given to the evacuation than to the reception, a situation which inevitably heightened the frustration of those people trying to organise the social service infrastructure within the reception areas. Ineffectual communications between central, local and district government also added to the confusion, especially with regard to the billeting of evacuees which, in many cases, became the responsibility of small Rural District Councils which, until the outbreak of war, had spent most of their time discussing road sweeping, planning applications and very localised issues. These were usually chaired by a local dignitary or solicitor with limited experience of anything beyond their immediate community and they were ill-prepared for taking a responsible part in a national scheme. The Minutes of such councils can give an interesting insight into their priorities. The following is taken from the East Retford Rural District Council, in Nottinghamshire,[11] and is a reply to a memo sent by the Ministry of Health to all Rural District Councils asking for help with the reception of evacuees:-

> *'The Parish Council wish me to acknowledge the receipt of your letter but regrets it cannot help because the Rector has left'.*

Presumably the war needed to be delayed until they could find another incumbent![12]

As late as the 23rd August 1939 the Billeting Officer in Edeyrnion wrote to the Clerk at Bala Urban District Council asking:-

> *'I wonder whether you would be kind enough to let me have a copy of your scheme 'Evacuation'. I know you have made a very thorough job of it and it would help me greatly and give me a good idea as to what ought to be done'.[13]*

Under the circumstances it is perhaps surprising that more mistakes were not made. However, some errors, not necessarily the fault of the local and district councils, were made with potentially devastating results. The following list from the Berkshire County Council Minutes, September 1939, indicates the great differences between the numbers of evacuees expected and those which actually arrived. It also demonstrates that even the local councils who were well advanced and organised in their planning had to respond on an ad hoc basis when the scheme was actually implemented. One can just imagine the panic measures which had to be enforced in order to house all the evacuees who eventually turned up. Especially the Billeting Officer in Hungerford, who probably thought he was going to have an easy time! When confronted with such evidence of bureaucratic confusion one can sympathise with the billeting officer in 'Living with Strangers' who, when interrupted during dinner, says ' Who'd be a billeting Officer?'[14]

It is no wonder that many evacuees returned immediately to London or found the reception areas unwelcoming. From such a simple occurrence myths about unwelcoming hosts can be created and remain in the memory.

NUMBER OF EXPECTED EVACUEES AND ACTUAL NUMBERS ARRIVING IN BERKSHIRE SEPTEMBER 1939		
Region	**Numbers Received**	**Numbers Expected**
EAST BERKSHIRE		
Maidenhead Borough	4,040	3,958
Cookham Rural District	2,160	1,408
Wokingham Borough	1,800	1,004
Wokingham Rural District	6,498	3,056
Easthampstead Rural District	5,000	1,687
Windsor Borough	4,000	2,004
Windsor Rural District	3,200	1,726
Total	**26,698**	**14,843**
SOUTH BERKSHIRE		
Bradfield Rural District	3,200	1,436
Newbury Borough	2,400	1,310
Newbury Rural District	2,424	483
Hungerford Rural District	800	Nil
Total	**8,824**	**3,229**
NORTH BERKSHIRE		
Abingdon Borough	1,400	381
Abingdon Rural District	2,600	1,341
Faringdon Rural District	2,400	1,234
Wallingford Borough	500	557
Wallingford Rural District	1,900	1,346
Wantage Urban District	480	279
Wantage Rural District	1,920	705
Total	**11,200**	**5,843**
GRAND TOTAL	**46,772**	**23,915**

Source [15]

This vagueness in communication resulted in both central and local Government being able to accuse the other of ineptitude. Central Government seemed intent on issuing memos and circulars to the reception areas with little thought for the implementation of the recommendations contained in them . For example the Board of Education had thought that local authorities had been warned of the possibility of evacuees having head-lice and that they could overcome the problem by giving the children steam baths..[16] They had successfully shifted the responsibilities to the local authorities without, seemingly, any comeback. Central Government adopted a complacent attitude which was to make the success of evacuation questionable from a very early stage. After receiving evidence of the problems inherent in the evacuation 'rehearsals' which had taken place in some areas in September 1938, Ben Smith MP wrote to the Board of Education in December of the same year stating that:-

> '...there would be enough ill-clad and poorly shod children to hinder the successful operation of any evacuation scheme'.[17]

In reply Earl de la Warr, President of the Board of Education, denied that this would happen...and let the matter rest.[18]

One could suggest that the evacuation in 1938 was far more significant than a mere rehearsal. During the Munich Crisis the London County Council drew up a very basic plan to move 637,000 children from London and other plans were instigated in cities such as Birmingham. The LCC actually evacuated 1,200 nursery school children and 3,100 children whom they labelled as 'physically defective'.[19] All these were brought back from the reception areas immediately after the conclusion of the Munich conference. What this mini-evacuation demonstrated was that improvised schemes introduced by the local authorities on an ad hoc basis would be detrimental to the success of any scheme, which is what the planners had been saying from as early as 1933. Titmuss highlights a few examples.[20] Children were to be evacuated from the East End of London to Essex at the same time as Essex County Council were evacuating children to other areas. After King's School, Canterbury were to be moved to Scotland, children from London were to take over their school. Such occurrences continued into the war. Detailed investigations into the unwitting testimony continued in the propaganda film 'Living with Strangers' shows that the people in the film had been moved out of London to Essex. The evacuees are shown getting off a bus with a destination board saying 'Chingford'.[21]

Samuel Hoare, in a censure debate in the House of Commons on 3rd November 1938 defended the Government's actions against those MPs who criticised them for not having an overall evacuation policy when the country was near to war by stating:-

> *'...On the broad question of evacuation I claim that the plans were laid on sound foundation, and further that if we had been compelled to bring them into operation, they would have worked satisfactorily'.*[22]

This may have been true but it should be noted that the correspondence to Local Authorities indicating the number of evacuees to expect together with a memo 'Instructions to Billeting Officers', were not sent out until the last week of September 1938 and after these had been processed by the Clerks of the Council were not distributed to the Parish and Rural District Councils until the 30th September, after the Munich crisis was over. This was true in Dorset. A letter in the correspondence file of the County Council dated 30th September 1938, indicates that the County was to expect 30,000 children from Croydon and these were to be billeted in rural areas. The tone of the letter indicates the rapidity of the implementation and also the fact that they were somewhat unprepared. For instance, Billeting Officers had yet to be appointed, although it has to be said that they did have transport arrangements in place for those coming from London in the first wave.[23] Plans had been instigated in other areas. In September 1938 Ellis Davis, WVS Organiser for Caernarfon and Anglesey reported to the Penmaenmawr Urban District Council:-

'In the event of hostilities on Monday next about 500 children with their teachers, with day rations, 1 blanket and gas mask will arrive. The children of local schools are to be given a holiday, and those from further away will occupy the rooms temporarily. They will lie on straw in schools and at the expiration of three days arrangements are to be made for billeting'.[24]

These examples are an indication that the Munich evacuation in 1938 was not as ad hoc as some historians have previously been led to believe. A document in the Dorset Record Office, again dated 30th September 1938, lists the stations of arrival, the name of the reception schools, the evacuated schools and the estimated number of evacuees expected at each venue. It had obviously been well-planned and required the co-operation of a number of parties.

AIR RAID PRECAUTION: DISPOSITION OF SECONDARY SCHOOL CHILDREN FROM CROYDON				
	Railhead	Dorsetshire Secondary School	Croydon School	Estimated No. of Croydon Children
First Railway Zone	1. Semley Jn. Shaftesbury	Shaftesbury Grammar	Tennison Boys	150
	2. Gillingham	Gillingham Grammar School. (Mixed)	St. Michael's	200
	3. Sherborne	Sherborne Fosters (boys)	Selhurst Boys	400
		Sherborne Lord Digby's (girls) Also public schools	Selhurst Girls	400
	4. Lyme Regis	Lyme Regis Grammar	Heath Clark	350
Second Railway Zone	1. Poole	Poole Grammar (Boys)	St. Joseph's College	350
	2. Swanage	Swanage Grammar (Mixed)	Ruskin	350
	3. Dorchester	Dorchester High School (Girls)	Girls High School	750
	4. Weymouth	Weymouth Grammar (Mixed)	Old Palace	350
		Weymouth Technical (Boys)	Stanley Technical	250
Third Railway Zone	1. Blandford	Blandford Grammar (Mixed)	Lady Eldridge	250

Source [25]

(Ref. DC/SYR/E3)

From C.P.Bruton. Clerk of the County Council of Dorset.

To the Clerks of the Borough, Urban and Rural District Councils in the County of Dorset.

30 September. 1938

Dear Sir,

I am informed by the Home Office that they have authorised the evacuation of 30,000 children from the Borough of Croydon to Dorsetshire and I am requested, in consultation with the Clerks to the Rural and Urban Districts in the County, to make arrangements as soon as possible for the accommodation of this number of refugees. I shall therefore be glad if you will let me have the names and addresses of persons to be appointed as billeting officers, which should be about 1 officer for every 100 refugees, for your area when I will issue to them a form of authority to act.

I enclose a copy of instructions to billeting officers for your information and assistance and will also forward a copy to each billeting officer with his authority.

I also enclose a list of the Croydon Secondary and Elementary school children which you would be expected to accommodate in your area and shall be glad if you would instruct the billeting officers to make provisional arrangements for billets immediately pending the receipt of official authority.[26]

These evacuees were to be allocated without any previous detailed accommodation survey therefore had the scheme been implemented there would have been severe problems.

AIR RAID PRECAUTIONS COUNTY OF DORSET: SCHEDULE OF ACCOMMODATION FOR REFUGEES			
	ACCOMMODATION		
AREA	TOTAL	ALLOCATED (CROYDON)	BALANCE
Boroughs			
Blandford	2,325	1,250	1,075
Bridport	3,500	-	3,500
Dorchester	4,600	3,750	850
Lyme Regis	2,000	2,000	-
Poole	7,300	5,700	1,600
Shaftesbury	875	850	25
Wareham	1,070	-	1,070
Weymouth	20,000	10,600	9,400
Urban Districts			
Portland	No figures yet available		
Sherbourne	1,370	1,300	70
Swanage	5,995	5,850	145
Wimborne	5,471	-	5,471
Rural Districts			
Beaminster	3,079	-	3,079
Blandford	3,498	-	3,498
Bridport	4,221	-	4,221
Dorchester	6,037	-	6,037
Shaftesbury	5,391	200 (Gillingham)	5,191
Sherbourne	2,693	-	2,693
Sturminster	4,613	-	4,613
Wareham	7,013	-	7,013
Wimbourne	5,995	-	5,995
TOTAL	**97,046**	**31,500**	**65,546**

DISPOSITION OF SECONDARY AND ELEMENTARY SCHOOL CHILDREN FROM CROYDON			
TOWN	**SECONDARY**	**ELEMENTARY**	**TOTAL**
Poole	350	5350	5700
Weymouth	600	10,000	10,600
Blandford	250	1000	1250
Dorchester	750	3000	3750
Gillingham	200	-	200
Swanage	350	5500	5850
Lyme Regis	350	1650	2000
Shaftesbury	150	700	850
Sherbourne	800	500	1300
TOTAL	**3800**	**27,700**	**31,500**

Source [27]

What is significant is that the information sent out to Billeting Officers did contain a great many of the details which would be reissued in 1939.

Thirdly, there was a certain amount of ignorance on the part of the planners and administrators of the incredible social impact that the scheme would have, both in the evacuated and reception areas.

The vast majority of evacuees and hosts alike were not prepared in any way for the culture shock that awaited them. It is true that evidence of poorly clad and under-nourished children, although not all were in this state, was a shock to many of the people in the reception areas but instead of seeing this as an opportunity to help the 'less fortunate' many tended to blame the parents for lacking care or were concerned about the effects such children would have on local health provision. Numerous letters were sent to local newspapers expressing concern about the topic. The following is just one example:-

> '*Sir,*
>
> *May I plead through your columns that the Medical Officers of Health for the County and the Borough will pay the closest attention to the health of the evacuees in our county. I am seriously concerned that these evacuees from London may lower our bill of health. In the first place it is obvious that in some cases our visitor's standard of hygiene is far removed from our standard, possibly through environment....the facts are disturbing.*
>
> *Signed Anxious Parent'.* [28]

It is important to remember that many parents of evacuees were not told how long their children would be away for and so only sent them with clothing to last for a few days. In fact they were encouraged to do so in order to cut down on children's luggage. Also, pay-day for many of the working classes at this time was Friday which, for some, coincided with the first day of evacuation, therefore household funds would be at their lowest, and although this cannot be used as evidence to account for the plight of the majority of evacuees it is nonetheless a consideration. One could argue that parents, realising that evacuation could have been a possibility at the outbreak of war, should have been better organised but, as the Government had effectively maintained the secrecy surrounding evacuation many parents were actually given short notice and were not in a position to react favourably to the situation.[29] Many children experienced the embarrassing complaint of Enuresis which, like other psycho-neurotic symptoms, is considered to be an expression of mental protest. Bed-wetting by a number of evacuees during the first few weeks of the war, estimated at anywhere between 1%-33% of evacuees, depending on reports by local reception committees, was caused by an acute sense of insecurity. The evidence of head lice and bed wetting is not indicative of domestic child abuse, although many Government officials and volunteers, usually from the middle-classes, resorted to this explanation when confronted with the problems and with ill-disciplined evacuees. In fact a lot of research had been carried out by the London County Council in 1919 and again in 1934 about the incidence of enuresis in residential and camp schools,[30] and a report entitled 'Our Towns' produced in 1943 by the Women's Group on Public Welfare identified widespread incidence in 'public schools, poor law homes, charitable institutions, approved schools, holiday camps, Ministry of Labour training centres and shipping companies.'[31] This phenomenon of enuresis was not restricted to young evacuees. An interesting comparison can be found in an article in 'The Lancet' where the three authors state:-

> 'In a proportion of the soldiers evacuated from Dunkirk in 1940, enuresis was noted as a response to feelings of stress and insecurity'.[32]

The Ministry of Health had actually recognised there could be a possible problem with the enuresis and in May 1939 ordered rubber underlays for an estimated 60% of those evacuees under 5 years of age. By the beginning of the war few had been delivered to the reception areas and no account had been taken of older children who might suffer from the complaint.[33]

What is often overlooked is the fact that some evacuees were affected by the bed-wetting of a third party. Lyn Mendlson (née Blacker) describes how she and her brother had to share a bed with a persistent bed-wetter:-

> 'When we returned to London I was able to sleep in a dry bed again. Most nights our bed at Kettering was wet because Tony, the other evacuee who slept with us, had a weak bladder and couldn't help wetting it, so we all had to sleep in soggy sheets and blankets. The wetness always made me feel cold'.[34]

As well as bed-wetting, the other serious complaint from the reception areas was the number of evacuees who many officials and hosts in the reception areas considered to be verminous. The summer of 1939 had been a very hot one in which head lice would have thrived and as evacuation took place at the end of the long holiday many had not been checked by the School Medical Service for some time. This is an important fact when one considers how many of the evacuees from the poorer areas of the cities relied on this Service for all their medical needs. It is also a known fact that head lice can be transferred from people in close proximity and as many of the evacuees were crammed into railway carriages it is obvious that many of them could have picked up the infestation during the journey to the reception areas. What was unfortunate, and possibly one of the reasons for the outcry in some areas, was that the Minister of Health had assured the House of Commons in March 1939 when outlining the evacuation scheme that:-

> *'Any householder who raises a question as to the cleanliness of the children may be assured that schoolchildren are subject to regular medical inspection, that there is no greater danger of dirt or infection from these children than from any other representative group in the country, and that the best possible arrangements will be made for their medical supervision'.*[35]

In May 1939 H.W. Lowe announced to an evacuee planning conference in Caernarfon that:-

> *'...the people of Liverpool would go to Caernarvonshire in good order and the children, in properly organised parties in the charge of their teachers, would be clean and free from infectious diseases'.*[36]

Unfortunately, this was not to be the case and there were serious problems between hosts and evacuees over their state of well-being on arrival. As early as 1938 the Senior Medical Officer in Liverpool found that the number of children in the city's schools found to be verminous was 24,130, or 20.8% of the total school population. This was the highest in the country.[37]

It would seem from accounts and complaints in the North Wales reception areas that little had been done between the time of the report and the evacuation of Liverpool children to control the situation. Some authorities did ask for assurances regarding the general health of expected evacuees. In May 1939, the Ruthin Borough Council attempted to find out from the Liverpool evacuation authorities what steps they were taking with regard to the immunisation of children being sent to Ruthin. The Medical Officer stated that there was:-

> *'...danger of serious disturbances of the epidemiological balances of the districts into which these town dwellers are introduced arising from the differences between the immunity values of town and country populations'.*[38]

But, as Titmuss stated this fear, whatever its scientific basis in the light of contemporary knowledge of immunity never reached the point of materially influencing official policy.[39] The question of immunising Liverpool evacuees continued to be an issue during the early part of the war. Although some progress was made the problem of funding the scheme made this slow. Immunisation could only be carried out if the money was available and if parents gave their consent. In March 1941 Liverpool agreed to pay 3/6 for every evacuee immunised if parental consent was forthcoming.[40]

Although only a small percentage of evacuees were considered to be in a 'deplorable state' adverse publicity and a plethora of complaints created the impression that this was the whole story.

As early in the scheme as 6th September 1939 the Clerk of Buckley Urban District Council in Flintshire wrote to the County Council and Welsh Board of Health:-

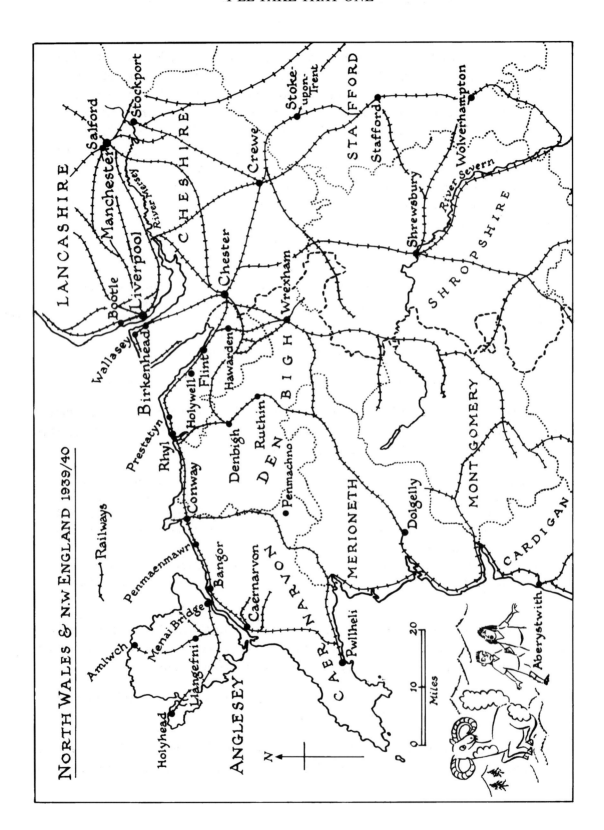

North Wales & N.W. England 1939/40

'I regret to inform you that serious difficulties have arisen in connection with some of the evacuees who have come to this Urban District from the County Borough of Birkenhead. They arrived here on Friday and Saturday last. Several occupiers of Buckley houses have called at my office to complain of the verminous condition of the children and that the children are suffering from skin diseases. In addition many of the children are apparently, according to the report, filthy and they are not observing the ordinary decencies in the houses where they are billeted. Regarding adult women, more than one complaint has come that they are not merely offensive in their behaviour but also that they are guilty of excessive drinking. In addition, a certain number of women are as filthy as the children who have come with them'.[41]

The Clerk of the Rural District Council revealed he was:-

'...daily receiving complaints of their (evacuees) verminous condition. Several householders complain that they have already had to burn their bedding and the unanimous opinion in the district is that it is time to call a halt to the evacuation scheme'.[42]

The WVS organiser in Llanrwst reported on 4th September 1939 that:-

'Unless steps are taken to remove these people I am afraid that we shall have rioting here'.[43]

In the October issue of the Welsh Nationalist the correspondent used the opportunity to reinforce their party's concern about the general effect the evacuation English mothers and children would have, and had already had on the population of Wales.

'Welsh people will never forget the English evacuees. Some of the diseases they brought with them are well-known....diphtheria, whooping cough, measles, TB, chicken pox. Congenital syphilis is not so well-known in Wales, neither are bugs and body lice. One wonders whether the English Government will compensate the families of Llyn for the destruction of bedding and furniture. One cannot but pity the evacuees but we are left in frank amazement at the inhumanness of a Government which allows such a condition of affairs to exist in its country, while preparing a war of many years in order to teach the German people about the inestimable benefits of English civilisation'.[44]

In Anglesey some schools were used as Cleansing Stations. In March 1940 the Merionethshire Medical Officer 'inspected every mother and infant from Liverpool and found the large majority being unfit for admission to billets mostly because of a verminous condition'.[45]

This could account for the traumatic physical experiences that Lillian Evans and her classmates went through when arriving at their billets 'clean'.

The problem of apportioning blame on their visitors was not confined to Wales. In one particular village in North Oxfordshire it was the local nurse who blamed the incidence of head lice on evacuees! When this nurse went on her rounds checking hair and heads of all the school children she stated that:-

> *'...if any of the village children were found to be verminous it would be due to London children'.*[46]

One evacuee recalls that the first thing that happened to him and his siblings was a 'hair inspection by a nurse wielding a comb dripping in disinfectant.' [47]

Scabies was also a problem, but one that was around in the reception areas before evacuation took place. The scabies mite is small and burrows beneath the skin therefore the sufferer could not have been segregated from fellow passengers on the trains and other transport had they picked up the complaint before leaving for the reception areas. Close personal contact with infected others would led to the contraction of the disease which thrived in the warm atmosphere which would have been found in overcrowded train carriages. Circular 2517 issued on the 14th November 1941 and known as the Scabies Order, increased the power of Local Authorities to combat the spread of the disease. A report from the Holywell Rural District Council stated that:-

> *'The treatment of scabies is, from the point of view of this department unsatisfactory in that many children sometimes within a few days of discharge, break out again and have to be sent back again to the sick bay for further treatment. Some children have been sent back several times and a report in one case was sent to the Ministry Inspector'.*[48]

One particular council, Cricklade and Wootten Bassett RDC, expressed concern in March 1940 about the cleanliness of evacuees in general but specifically adolescent girls:-

> *'The Council appreciate what is being done with regard to medical examination and improvement in the health of children, but something more is needed, i.e. education in how to be clean, particularly girls of over 13 years of age, who in many instances appear to have no knowledge of nature and how to be clean. This was a cause of a number of soiled beds and of considerable annoyance'.*[49]

In Circular Ev.10 issued to parents in the Portsmouth area in 1940 instructions were given about cleanliness, a rather patronising hint that not all parents knew how to keep their children clean:-

```
What must a parent do in preparation for evacuation?......

Make sure the child is CLEAN and ready to go at any time......

After evacuation had taken place last September complaints were made by
Householders in the Receiving Areas that some children were not clean.
You will wish to be sure that this cannot be said about your own child
and do everything possible to make sure that he goes away with clean
clothes, clean hair, clean body. Children from the cleanest homes have
sometimes had the misfortune to get lice in the head which they pick up
from other children.......'
```
[50]

Similarly, the Liverpool Public Health Authority issued a leaflet in February 1940 entitled 'Advice to Householders on the Care of Children's Hair' and the WVS printed one called 'The Cleansing and Care of Children's Heads...Be Thorough'.

It should also be remembered that the problems of head lice was not confined to evacuees nor indeed children. During April 1942 a number of letters were sent to 'The Times' complaining about the prevalence of head lice especially among women workers living in close proximity in industrial areas and women refugees living in hostels. Many remedies were suggested such as:-

> *The Department of Entomology in the London School of Hygiene and Tropical Medicine has evolved a simple and effective means of delousing by the rubbing with the fingers into the roots of the hair a suitably medicated cream, and not washing the hair for eight to nine days so as to allow time for the lice to be killed'.*[51]

This correspondent also suggested that the 'Permanent Wave' fashion be prohibited because it was a waste of time and electricity and did nothing to alleviate the problem of head lice.[52]

Another correspondent writing a few days later, supported the use of the 'Perm' and cited the example of the many high-ranking officers in the Women's Services who had their hair 'permed' regularly.[53]

The letters also give an interesting indication of how some people thought that head lice could lead to an outbreak of Typhus.

> *'It is imperative that the louse be got rid of when there is a danger of typhus reaching this country'.*[54]

There is absolutely no evidence whatsoever that head lice was, or ever could be, a source of Typhoid.[55]

Any such suggestion would seem to be rather irresponsible and inflammatory but one concerned correspondent suggests that evidence of a link was supported by both the Ministries of Labour and Health. If this statement had been made public it is no wonder that many people were concerned that lice should be eradicated, but one has to say that there is no evidence that the Ministries were involved in spreading such misinformation.

However, in the light of other evidence cited earlier, it is interesting to note that none of the letters refers to head lice as a symptom of poverty. Also, although many authorities were quick to lay the blame for bringing various diseases into the reception areas on the evacuees, little mention is ever made of the risk some of the latter were exposed to in the choice of hosts. There was serious concern in Wales about the high incidence of Tuberculosis. A report by the Anti-Tuberculosis service in Wales and Monmouth expressed concern and in the light of this the Ministry of Health sent a letter to the Deudraeth Rural District Council on the 28th August 1939 notifying them that the Housing Inspector would make an early visit to ascertain the nature and extent of the problem.

Before this visit could take place Deudraeth took in 800 evacuee children and no account was taken of the high incidence of TB.[56]

There are no general records of how the hosts dealt with the problems they faced when dealing with their evacuees although accounts from some evacuees would suggest that some were rather draconian.[57]

Although local authorities reacted to overcome some of the physical ailments such as delousing, the extra burdens of finding new clothes and cleaning became the responsibilities of the hosts,[58] and this was partly responsible for the resentment shown by some who felt they had been misinformed as to their role and responsibilities. The problem of bed-wetting and body and head lice, although still apparent in the later evacuations in 1940 and again in the 'doodle-bug' raids of 1944, never reached the same level of recrimination as it had in 1939. This was due to a combination of three factors:-

Firstly, after 1939 the Government abandoned the principle of mass-evacuation which meant that it was easier to conduct medical checks on evacuees. One needs to remember that although the initial evacuation scheme had been worked out in the summer of 1939, when it came to putting it into practice there was no time for each individual child to be medically examined and so some children suffering from various complaints and illnesses were taken into the reception areas through nothing more than bureaucratic oversights. When faced with this criticism of inaction, the Government's defence had been to state that to search for lice while bombs were falling would not have been possible. However, as early as 10th March 1939, the Board of Education and Ministry of Health had concluded that all routine medical inspections of schoolchildren in all areas would have to be suspended in the event of war.[59] A memo. from Sir George Chrystal to Sir Maurice Holmes the Permanent Secretary at the Ministry of Health dated 10th March 1939 admitted that medical checks would be impossible and other routine medicals would have to be abandoned.

```
'It is quite impossible to arrange for the inspection of 1.5 million
children so that it could be said that the children were handed over to
the reception areas certified as healthy. At least one of the three
routine medical inspections normally carried out during a child's
school career would be dispensed with altogether'.[60]
```

But, in some areas, it could have been possible to have included a medical examination in the evacuation practices which had taken place in August 1939. Also, checks could have been carried out by the reception authorities at the time of arrival. Although again this happened in some areas others were too understaffed to carry them out effectively, if at all. The later evacuation schemes, carried out in perhaps a more relaxed way, enabled the administrators to introduce a scheme of medical screening. In March 1940 the Ministry of Health sent out a general letter to local newspapers stating:-

'It is an unfortunate fact that the lamentable condition of some of the children who were received in clean and bright country houses has caused many rural householders to dread a repetition of the scheme. As a matter of fact we now have the assurance of the minister that the examination of children will take place prior to their leaving London and also on arrival in the reception areas before the billeting officer allocates them to different homes'.[61]

There were problems because according to a newspaper article on 4th April 1940, there were conflicting reports. Although the Minister of Health had given this assurance, the evacuating authorities told the local authority in Dorchester, Dorset, that they would only have time to check those children who had been registered for evacuation. This proportion would be very small as in the event of an air raid, parents would wish their children to be evacuated whether they were registered or not.[62]

However, after May 1940, children were all examined and their details entered onto cards in a coded form. These codes, a series of symbols, were transferred to the labels worn by the children so that they could be easily identified on arrival in the reception areas as requiring special help.[63] From evidence of the time, it is noticeable that the number of pupils suffering from specific conditions and complaints was in fact quite low, which tends to refute the myth that all pupils from the evacuated areas were suffering from something.[64]

Studies carried out at the time by teachers, members of His Majesty's Inspectorate, social workers, and schools medical officers emphasised the remarkable ability of most children in the target areas to maintain an emotional equilibrium as long as they were able to remain with their parents or relatives who were generally cheerful in their outlook and were not too depressed by the war situation.[65]

A school medical officer reported:-

'I have had the opportunity to see several hundred children during the last month. On several occasions I saw them and watched them while bombs were falling in the neighbourhood and air raids were overhead and asked them questions relating to the war, sirens etc...Children have adapted themselves to present condition of life surprisingly well...Even children who were bombed out of their homes did not seem to suffer in any way...There is no question of shock'.[66]

This was supported by work done by Anna Freud in Hampstead. She found that evacuation and the break up of family units did induce an emotional response where the family stability was lacking. This was heightened when the evacuees were under stress during air raids.[67]

Secondly, during the evacuation of 1940, a number of hostels had been established to house evacuees and any others suffering from enuresis so that they could be removed from potentially unsympathetic householders. It has to be said that in some areas staff in these hostels were just as unsympathetic. A survey of hostels carried out by Liverpool University in 1939-40 found that:-

'...there was widespread misconceptions regarding enuresis for a visit to one such institute gave the feeling that we still live in the Middle Ages. In this clinic the children were treated like little criminals and threat and punishment were the means of teaching them cleaner habits. The results can easily be imagined; no progress was made at all'.[68]

Despite the initial misgivings of teachers about the billeting of children in hostels, the belief, in January 1939, that there was insufficient time to build a network of camps and hostels in rural areas and the Government's reticence to spend money at a time when the country was re-arming, they did agree, in February 1939, to build a limited number.[69] Plans were submitted by a joint inter-departmental committee which recommended the construction of 100 although this figure was halved by the Treasury. In May 1939, the Camps Act gave the contract to two non-profit making bodies, the National Camps Corporation Ltd., to cover England and Wales, and the Scottish Special Housing Association. The sum of £1.2 million was provided for the building of 50 camps which would each house 300 people. They were to be finished by March 1940 and have three uses:-

- School Camps, housing complete evacuated schools.

- Camps for those children deemed difficult to billet.

- Holiday camps in peacetime.

Early in 1939 the Ministry of Health had requested the sum of £405,000 to cover the estimated cost of adapting existing premises as hostels and maternity homes and for providing extra toilets at rural railway stations and in city dispersal centres. The Treasury questioned the need for such expenditure and by August only £22,500 had been sanctioned.[70]

The toilets provided for evacuees on the stations comprised of wooden seats on top of galvanised buckets inside a canvas construction with the back and the roof covered but the front open to view. One of the reasons why so many children were in a bad state when they reached their destinations on the outward journeys was that the vast majority travelled in third class carriages with no corridors and no toilets. At every station where the trains stopped the Women's Voluntary Service the Women's Institute and other bodies provided them with free drinks and in consequence the children had nowhere to relieve themselves.[71] Some of the boys resorted to urinating from the windows[72] but many, including the girls, for basic physical reasons, simply wet themselves because they either did not have time to use the station toilets during a stopover or, as some evacuees have said in interviews, refused to suffer the indignity of using toilets which were open to view.

'We may have been busting to go but we were not using those with everyone gawking at us'. One evacuee described the outcome of such a situation rather poetically...'One small boy in our compartment wet himself and it ran in a little stream along the floor, changing direction as the train went around bends or braked'.[73]

It is no wonder that when they reached their destination and were lined up to be chosen, some of the children would not have looked very suitable for fostering! There is little evidence of the same sort of problems occurring on the return journeys in 1945, although the circumstances under which the physical travelling took place were similar and drinks, again provided by the Voluntary Services, were readily available.

As late as the 31st August 1939, no hostels had been completed in the reception areas nor had any of the proposed camps. Equipment allocated for these establishments had either been sent to the wrong place or had not been ordered.[74] This created a problem for some reception authorities who needed to find accommodation for those children who were difficult to billet, usually because of health or behavioural problems. Some such placements were available early in 1940 in Buckinghamshire as this entry from a school log-book would indicate.

> '18th April 1940. Paul Goldstein was removed today to a school for Difficult Children at Bourne End. This has been approved of by the Billeting Officer since the boy has been difficult in four billets'.[75]

An earlier entry in the same log-book shows that Paul had been admitted to the Sick bay for Children at Aylesbury for observation because of his 'nerves' which might suggest that these might have been the cause of his actions rather than just plain misbehaviour.[76]

In other areas the Government ordered that makeshift hostels, where available, were to be opened and as early as 12th September, they authorised the payment of compensation to those householders who had had damage caused by evacuees.[77] This order was reinforced in October when specific compensation guidelines were issued.[78] The Treasury did not give full approval for the hostel scheme until May 1940 as it was cheaper to keep evacuees in home billets rather than provide full board, lodging and social welfare on a 24 hour basis. It was as a result of unease in the reception areas that the Government made plans to give more active encouragement to local authorities to construct, or adapt existing buildings, for use as hostels. These were to be made available in the reception areas for those unaccompanied children who, on arrival, were thought to require special help. The Government estimated that this would amount to 5% of the evacuee population.[79] Thirty-one camps to house 11,000 evacuees were under construction by mid-1940 at an estimated cost of £900,000. One of them had been planned in advance of the war by West Ham Council who, because of the areas close proximity to the London docks and therefore a prime target for any enemy bombing, had purchased 38 acres of land in Pixie's Hill in Boxmoor near Hemel Hempstead. They erected a camp school which consisted of five dormitories, a school house, an assembly hall, a dining room with kitchen and even a small hospital. It was designed to take 200 boys aged 11-13 from various schools in the West Ham area together with teachers, catering staff and a resident nursing sister. This school opened in July 1940 under the headship of Mr Moon who had toured the schools explaining to both boys and parents about the school and its merits.[80]

By July 1941 there were 660 hostels in England and Wales housing 10,000 children.[81] By January 1942, 30 special hostels had been established for children of secondary school age.[82] These hostels were also to be used as 'Clearing houses' for 'normal children' who had to be removed from their billets because of illness or any other reasonable cause. However, they were to return to their billets as soon as possible after the emergency so that places in the hostels could be freed for newcomers. In this way it was hoped that temporary relief could be given to a large number of householders, while if children remained for prolonged periods the effect would have been to simply relieve a small number of householders of an obligation they perhaps ought to have shared with neighbours or other organisations.

Brian Maystone recalls his time in the Lismore Hostel in Woking which at the time was run by an ex-jockey and his wife. These were helped by assistant wardens, one of whom was dismissed for 'having a small boy in bed with him'. The hostel was a large house in its own grounds. The boys were housed in two large dormitories and three smaller ones, these were on the first floor. On the ground floor was the warden's office, the front room, the games room and the dining room. There was also the servants wing which contained the kitchen and showers. The boys spent their time playing sports, making model aircraft out of balsa wood and building crystal sets. They were taken to swim at the local open-air pool which could be extremely cold. Brian is not sure what type of hostel it was but remembers that the Warden would often be at the Magistrates Court pleading for one of the boys. He remembers one of them climbing up the drainpipe of the hostel entering the storeroom window and stealing blankets which he then posted home![83]

In a circular entitled 'Notes for Billeting Officers' produced in 1940, they were instructed to say, in answer to the question:-

> *'Why can't all evacuated children be housed in Hostels and Camps?' that ...'it was all a question of arithmetic. Over 400,000 children were already in the reception areas and plans were in hand to send another 500,000 should more attacks take place'.*[84]

However, there were problems with organisations competing for the same accommodation. Whole factories and Government departments had also been evacuated and some owners did not want their buildings used as hostels at all, especially by evacuees, and preferred instead to allow their use as convalescence homes for servicemen. This was not only a local issue. The following example, quoted by Titmuss, is an indication of the infighting between individual Government departments.

> *'One MP with three mansions and at least six servants voluntarily offered his houses for the reception of evacuees at a time when the military seemed about to take possession. When the danger was past, attempts were made by the military to recover the premises and eject the evacuated children. The Ministry of Health resisted these attempts'.*[85]

Some areas found the billeting of extra evacuees to be particularly problematic. In response to the government Circular 1968 15th February 1940 requesting that reception areas take in more evacuees the Rural District Councils of Cricklade and Wootton Bassett and Marlborough and Ramsey and the Warminster Urban District Council all complained independently that there were too many service personnel in their areas to take any more. In fact the Warminster Council hinted that they would request that one of the three large schools billeted in their area should be removed because of pressure of finding accommodation for servicemen. They also pointed out that they were concerned about the pressure placed on the Public Health services in the area. The Council at Marlborough laid the blame for an outbreak of Spotted Fever, Scarlet Fever and an epidemic of Measles on the influx of so many new people. They also had a public health problem which resulted in the military having to bury their rubbish and waste water from the cook houses. Wootten Bassett already housed 500 soldiers and a new airfield was under construction at nearby Lyneham.[86] The same problems arose in September of the same year when Circular 2140 was sent out again requesting more billets to be made available, many more letters were sent to the Wiltshire County Council from various Urban District, Borough and Rural District councils complaining that there was just no space left because areas of Wiltshire had become an armed camp. Calne and Chippenham RDC wrote on 30th September 1940 that:-

1.   *Unofficial evacuees are flowing into this area at the rate of 50 a day.*

2.   *We already have 1500 persons billeted under the evacuation scheme.*

3.   *Our allocation under Plan VI.B is 500 unaccompanied children.*

4.   *In response to the urgent appeal of the Ministry of Health we offered to accept not more than 100 mothers and children. The Ministry advised us that they were sending a party of 82 and actually 140 arrived on Sunday last.*

5.   *There are four large Aerodromes, two RAF Training Camps, and one large Ammunition Dump in the area of this Council and large numbers of the personnel attached to these places are billeted in our area and I estimate that there has been an increase of approximately 5000 persons in this area since the outbreak of war'.*[87]

Pewsey RDC....30th September 1940

About 1200 women and children have come into this area during the past 3 weeks and 900 of these are from London. We are dealing with them as fast as we can but the work of issuing billeting notices is in arrear.

In addition to this the Military Authorities have requisitioned all empty houses, village halls etc. and have many soldiers and Airmen in private billets.

During today the Air Ministry has taken 57 of my billets and filled them with airmen!' [88]

Borough of Devizes 30 September 1940

'.....I informed the Ministry of Health it would be impossible for us to take further Mothers and Children....As you are aware Devizes is the Depot Town of the Wiltshire Regiment and in addition

we have Camps around the Town and wives and relatives of soldiers are arriving daily to take up accommodation....As far as I can ascertain any available house which might be used for billeting has been requisitioned by the military Authorities'.[89]

Borough of Wilton 30th September 1940.

'...The Ministry do not seem to appreciate, although it has been impressed on them, not only by me but also I understand by the War Office, that we now have in Wilton a very large Army establishment and a great portion of the Staff, both Military and Clerical are living in the town. Therefore billets are limited'.[900]

Borough of Marlborough 28th September 1940

'.....Since the arrival of evacuees from Bexhill we are continually being asked to provide accommodation for stragglers from London. The provision of this has entailed the use of all Condemned Houses and the point has been reached when no further accommodation is available.

At the moment we have four mothers and babies in the Rest Room waiting for billets'.[91]

Even after taking possession of such premises the local authorities were faced with the problem of furnishing them during a period of extreme hardship. It was estimated that for a residential home housing 40 children over 4,000 items of equipment were needed.[92] They also had to pay for the upkeep. There was a great deal of discussion at the Dorchester Rural District Council in June 1942 who received a report from the Billeting Committee about the cost of running a hostel for evacuated families at 'The Hollies', Buckland Newton, which housed seven mothers and twenty children. It was reported that the revenue received from the families living at the hostel was not sufficient to cover the cost of basic maintenance. The Council had already asked the Ministry of Health for permission to make up any financial shortfall from the 'Evacuation Account' but they were denied permission and told that the deficit had to be made up from local rates. The Council recommended that:-

'...the Ministry should be informed that they were no longer prepared to accept any financial responsibility and, unless the Ministry allowed them to charge for the costs of past and future maintenance, the Council would close the Hostel down and de-requisition the premises. By doing the latter the property would revert back to the original owner and no further compensation would have to be paid'.

Although there were a few dissenting voices who felt that having spent a great deal of money getting the building into good order they should not be too hasty in agreeing to close it down. The discussion went on at some length until it was decided to do nothing about the recommendation and pass the matter back to the Billeting Committee for further thought![93] What this does illustrate however, is how much financial burden was placed on the reception areas and it can be seen as another reason why some local rate payers were not keen to have evacuees. Problems such as these could only have heightened tension between the evacuees and the hosts.

Thirdly, having learned from the experience of the first evacuation, both the reception areas and the Ministry of Health knew what to expect and the distribution of rubber sheeting for the protection of beds was better organised. Also the Ministry of Health agreed, somewhat reluctantly, to authorise extra payments to hosts to cover the costs of extra bedding where any evacuee was suffering from enuresis.[94] This scheme turned out to be costly. According to Titmuss, in one Welsh village a host was paid 3s 6d extra allowance for one week in October 1940. The other villagers got to know about this and a total of £350 was paid out to the village by the end of the financial year March 1942, despite a reduction in the number of evacuees.[95]

Much has been said in books and in the media about the poor state of evacuees reaching the reception areas[96] but it must also be remembered that there was a great deal of rural poverty which, in a number of cases, was a contributory factor in the decision of some evacuees to return home. Although, in a report entitled 'Our Towns: A Close Up' published by the OUP in 1943 members of the Women's Group on Public Welfare stated that:-

> '...although poverty and low incomes were also found in the country such areas did not suffer the special town conditions of overcrowding, lack of open space, smoke and noise'.[97]

Even the BBC ignored the fact when it reported that evacuation had 'brought home to the British public and Government alike the disturbing widespread poverty throughout much of Britain'.[98] Presumably this referred to both rural and urban poor. At the outbreak of war 3,432 parishes in England and Wales had no piped water and 5,186 had no sewage systems. It was estimated that 30% of the population living in rural houses were not connected to a water main.[99] A survey conducted by the Women's Institute in 1944 found that in 21 counties 50% of the villages schools investigated had earth or bucket toilets. In many schools in Wales using this form of sanitation, no toilet paper was available and in one school in Wantage the situation was so bad that playtime had to be staggered in order to allow children, including evacuees, access to the toilets.[100]

Also, contrary to popular belief, the health of city children did not suddenly improve because they were now breathing fresh air and eating 'natural' food. Some teachers did in fact report that children's height and weight were improving but when the Government tried to substantiate the claims in order to keep the children in the reception areas, they could not prove it because there were so many variables to consider. These included the type of food available to them, the general care taken by the hosts, and simple things such as whether or not the evacuees were living on a farm with daily fresh milk.

The patronising values of many people in the reception areas did little to break down the social barriers between city and country, if anything they reinforced them. One can see that to view evacuation as the key to initiating universal social awareness and change, as some contemporary politicians did, and many people today still do, is not necessarily valid. What it did do however, was to make more people aware of the need for social policies which would alleviate some of the plight of the poor but not, as text books would have us believe, that which existed purely in the inner cities, but also among the rural poor.

Without the evacuation scheme one could argue that this basic awareness would have taken longer to come into the wider public domain and some of the social welfare services would have been established long after their original dates of inception.

Establishing Social Welfare

Where does the media and text books and other material leave us with Evacuation? According to the majority of school text books the children were sent away, some returned and were caught up in the bombing and, in some books, some children were re-evacuated. There is little more than a cursory reference to Overseas Evacuation and the Second and Third Government schemes, and usually nothing at all about the problems faced in 1945 when evacuees came home. To all intents and purposes Evacuation was just another simple event which took place during the war.

Authors and editors should illustrate the significance of the Evacuation process in the wider social history of the time, especially in the development of the Social Services, services which have been significant in the lives of pupils in today's classrooms. This is certainly one area which was a positive development amidst some of the administrative problems of the evacuation scheme and should not be dealt with lightly. The care of those in society who required help had its foundation in the Elizabethan Poor Law Act of 1597 and the Relief Act of 1601. The former contained little that had not been tried before. In 1563 the need for a compulsory poor-rate had been recognised and in 1572 the method of collection of dues had been introduced. 'Houses of Correction' were introduced under the Act of 1576 and reinforced the apprenticeship of paupers which was implemented in 1536.

In 1834 the Poor Law Amendment Act introduced social welfare practices which were to have an effect for the next one hundred years. By introducing Workhouses for the 'able-bodied' destitute who required help, the Act created a social stigma of social failure which was to affect many of the needy up to the end of World War Two.

In 1939 the Workhouses, or Public Assistance Institutions, as they were then called, still contained 100,000 people.[101] Some MPs, including the Christian socialist George Lansbury, wanted the Poor Law abolished but Parliamentary lobbying only resulted in the responsibility for the administration and implementation of the Poor Law being taken from the Guardians and placed with the Public Assistance Committees of the local authorities, which in turn were under the overall control of the Ministry of Health.

During 1939 and 1940 little had been done to improve the social welfare of unaccompanied evacuees and those who went as families. But it needs to be borne in mind that, despite the seeming lack of social care in general, the social service provision was worse in the rural areas than in the major cities. However, if social welfare was to be improved it would have been expensive and the local authorities were disinclined to spend their money and, it has to be said, where they were willing to do so, they were restricted by Government legislation until a plethora of Government circulars were sent out from Central Government from October 1940 which removed many of the restrictions imposed on local spending. However, the contents of the Circulars, encouraging local authorities to introduce feeding centres, nurseries and hostels created a great deal of administrative work. It was very difficult to put some of the schemes into practice because many of the major building projects came at a time when materials were in short supply.[102]

Many Women's groups took responsibility for investigating the social welfare provision in the early 1940s. One in particular, the Women's Group on Public Welfare, made an important and significant contribution to the whole debate and influenced even the most conservative of middle and upper classes. This group concerned themselves primarily with the social problems highlighted in the evacuation scheme. It established a committee of eight women who called witnesses, including health visitors, social workers and members of local authorities. In 1943 the group published a report entitled 'Our Towns: A Close Up'. published by OUP in 1943 which highlighted the deplorable home conditions of many of the poor in the city areas which resulted in high infant and child mortality rates. They estimated that between 22-30% of children were in dire poverty.[103] This report is significant because for the first time the blame for such conditions was not apportioned to the town councils controlling the areas from where the evacuees had come, but on the national situation. The evacuees and those in what we would refer to today as the poverty trap, were not an underclass which could be ignored.

Having reached their conclusions the committee suggested social reforms which at the time were considered radical and which in some cases have still not been implemented today. Some of the recommendations included:-

1. Nursery Education for all children.
2. Education.
   No classes with over 30 pupils.
   Secondary Education to be available to all.
   School Leaving Age to be raised to 16.
   Committed teachers with the time off for courses every 7 years.
   No bar for married women teachers.
3. Good Housekeeping. To be promoted as key to a good family life.
   Landlords to provide bathrooms and inside toilets.
4. Better health provision for all.
5. Measures to be taken against poverty to include:
   Payment of child allowances.
   Abolition of low wages
   Food price control

It is also worth noticing that one or two suggestions hint at the conservative and upper-class make-up of the committee, for instance it makes the assumption that working class girls needed an education which was best suited to train them for being mothers.[104]

Though some of the social measures had been suggested pre-war, according to Macnicol, evacuation itself had little specific effect and he suggests that it is difficult to find evidence that brought absolute fundamental ideological shifts, notably in Whitehall.[105] However, evacuation was in fact the catalyst which helped bring the social service plans into reality. Without evacuation and its attendant problems the school meals service, nursery provision and other measures would probably not have been introduced as quickly as they were. In the same way that aircraft and weapon technology grew out of necessity so to did the social welfare schemes. One needs to consider that those evacuees who had been evacuated to homes better than their own saw how the 'other half lived' and wanted the same for themselves. Many were no longer prepared to put up with life in below standard housing in areas of economic decline and were resolved, as Holman states, to 'vote for the politicians who would make their demands a reality'.[106]

> *'We could take a book or comics but there was no room for teddy bears or dolls, so they had to be left at home. I remember being quite upset about that and in the years which followed, when I had to cope with prolonged home-sickness, my teddy bear would have been a great help. By the time I finally returned home he had gone, but I was then too old to want a teddy bear!'*

> *(James Roffey. Letter to the author. 9 June 1998)*

Endnotes

1   Freda Costa (née Risely) cited in <u>No Time to Wave Goodbye</u>. Ben Wicks. Bloomsbury.1989 p207.

2   Titmuss op.cit. p13

3   ibid. p15

4   Memo. SRO.ED.24/1. cited in <u>War and Social Change</u>. ed. Harold L.Smith. Manchester University Press. 1986. p11

5   The Blitz. After the Battle. Vol 3.p 214. See Appendix 9.

6   House of Commons Debates. 30 July 1934. vol 292.cols.2335-6

7   Titmuss op.cit. p19

8   ibid.

9   ibid. p31

10   Letter to the author from Win Lewis and Sylvia Elliott. April 1998.

11   This council no longer exists.

12   James Roffey. op.cit. Personal Archive.

13   Penllyn RDC File. Evac. Arrangements. 1939. Letter 23 August 1939. Dolgellau R.O.

14   <u>Living With Strangers</u>. MoI Film. 1941. op.cit.

15   Berkshire County Council. Minutes. September 1939.

16   PRO.ED.10/245

17   Ben Smith to Earl de la Warr. 21 December 1938. PRO.ED 50/204.

18   ibid. Earl de la Warr to Ben Smith. 13 January 1939.

19   Titmuss op.cit. p29

20   ibid.

21   <u>Living With Strangers</u>. op.cit.

22   House of Commons Debates. vol.340 col.446

23   Dorset County Council. Correspondence File. Letter dated 30 September 1938.

24   Penmaenmawr.UDC. ARP Evac.File No1. Caernarfon RO. cited Wallis op.cit. p16

25   Dorset County Council. DC/SYR/E3

26   ibid.

27   ibid.

28   Bedfordshire Times and Standard. September 1939.

29   Titmuss. op.cit. p122

30   London County Council. Annual Report. 1915-19. Vol.III. p95 and LCC Memo 'Enuresis in Residential Schools. 28 November 1934 cited in Titmuss op.cit.p123.

31   Report. Our Towns. Women's Group on Public Welfare 1943. See also Appendix 8.

32   C. Anderson, M. Jeffrey & M.N.Pai. The Lancet 12 August 1944 ii.p218

33   Titmuss op.cit.p121

34   Lyn Mendlson. Letter to the author 29 January 1997.

35   House of Commons Debates. 2 March 1939 Vol 344 col 1524

36   North Wales Chronicle. 12 May 1939.

37   Our Towns a Close OUP. 1939-42. Women's Group on Public Welfare Oxford. 1943 p7.

38   Epidemiological Aspects of ARP Evac. Scheme. p174. cited Titmuss p15.

39   Titmuss. op.cit p15.

40   Denbigh Borough Council Letter book. May 1942 - March 1943. Ruthin RO. BD/A/412.

41   Flintshire County Council.Clerk Evac, Minutes. Letter from Llewellyn Jones to Welsh Board of Health. 6 September 1939 Flintshire R.O. FC/C/4/2/50.

42   ibid. Letter F. Grimley to J.Harvey Davies. 13 September 1939.

43   Denbighshire County Council File 8/9 Llanwrst UDC. Letter to clerk Llanwrst UDC from N.Jones and J.M. Parry Jones. WVS 4 September 1939. Ruthin R.O Z1348.

44   cited Wallis. op.cit. p87.

45   Menai Bridge UDC. File GES 39-40. Letter to Liverpool medical officer from Medical officer Menai Bridge 2 March 1940. Llangefri RO cited Wallis.p85.

46   Letter to Author from John William O'Connor. March 28 1998.

47   Letter to author from J.Roffey 9 June 1998.

48   Holywell RDC Council Minutes. No 36. April 1942-3. Meeting of Evacuation. Committee. 10 June 1942. Flint R.O. Cited Wallis.p120

49   WRO/F2/850/1-12.

50   ibid.

51   British Medical Association Journal. 11 April. 1942

52   Sir Leonard Hill to 'The Times' 15 April 1942. cited Livesey op.cit. p142

53   W.Neville to 'The Times' 24 April 1942 ibid. p143

54   Sir Leonard Hill. op.cit

55   Interview with Dr. Robin Borthwick. Theale Medical Centre. 9 January 1997.

56   Deudraeth RDC Minute Book. 1937-40. 28 August 1939. Dolgellau R.O. cited Wallis p49

57   See Yesterday's Children. L.Evans.

58   Titmuss. op.cit.p133

59   ibid. Footnote p145.

60   PRO HO/186/128/643/3.

61   North Berkshire and Oxfordshire Advertiser. March 1940.

62   Dorset County Council & Swanage Times. 4 April 1940.

63   Ministry of Health Circular 2027 & Board of Education Circular 1509. 21 May 1940.

64   J.Macnicol. The effect of the evacuation of schoolchildren on official attitudes to State intervention. in War and Social Change. ed. Harold L.Smith op.cit.p17

65   ibid.p5

66   Testimony by Dr. J.Gavronsky. Board of Education Memo. 'Nervous Strain in Children' 1941. PRO ED.50/206.

67   Macnicol op.cit. p5

68   Our wartime guests. Opportunity or Menace? University Press Liverpool 1940 p 20.

69   Titmuss op.cit. p36

70   ibid. p92

71   See film 'Westward Ho!' Ministry of Information 1940.

72   Oral testimony from a number of ex-evacuees.

73   J.Roffey. Letter to the author. 9 June 1998.

74   Titmuss op.cit. p111

75   E/LB/8/1 op.cit. 18 April 1940.

76   Oral testimony from a number of ex-evacuees.

77   Ministry of Health Circular 1871.12 September 1939.

78   Ministry of Health Circular 1897. 24 October 1939

79   Titmuss op.cit. p165

80   Taped interview with James Barclay. op.cit. November 1996.

81   Government Evacuation Scheme. Notes for Billeting Officers. 1940. Exeter Blitz Box 5. Devon Record Office.

82   Titmuss op.cit. p372

83   3 Brian Maystone. Letter to the author. February 1997.

84   Exeter Blitz Box. 5 op.cit.

85   Titmuss op.cit. p372

86   WRO/F2/850/1-12

87   Clerk. Calne and Chippenham RDC. 30 September 1940. WRO/F2/580/1-12

88   Clerk. Pewsey RDC. 30 September 1940. WRO op.cit.

89   Clerk. Borough of Devizes. 30 September 1940. WRO op.cit.

90   Clerk. Borough of Wilton. 30 September 1940. WRO op.cit.

91   Clerk. Borough of Marlborough. 30 September 1940. WRO op.cit.

92   Titmuss. op.cit. p372

93   Dorchester Rural District Council. Minutes. June 1942.

94   See Wiltshire News p6.

95   Titmuss op.cit. p125

96   Poverty in the cities was common place in the 1920s and 1930s and was not confined to specific geographical areas. Any district containing a majority of the working classes experienced at some time the three-phase 'poverty cycle' which had been identified by social researchers long before the 1914-18 war. These phases included :-
a. The ages between birth and 15.
b. In the first years of marriage and bringing up young children.
c. Old Age.
Social Welfare legislation in the early part of the century and immediately post-(Great)war had alleviated some of the problems but there were still some sectors of the community who existed below the poverty level. At this point people could experience anything from total destitution to a precarious existence where the economies involved in attaining the basics of life... housing, clothes, food and health provision was a continual struggle, and, according to Stevenson became 'life on the knife edge'. John Stevenson. British Society 1914-45. Penguin. 1990. p138 & 140-141.

97   Holman. The Evacuation. op.cit. p144.

98   Sian Nicholas 'The Echo of War'. Manchester University Press. 1996. p75

99   House of Commons Debates. 10 May 1944. vol.399 cols 1930-1 and Cmd. 6515. 1944.

100   Titmuss. op.cit. p178

101   Holman. The Evacuation. op.cit. p113

102   Titmuss. op.cit. p370

103   Holman op.cit. p144.

104   ibid. p 146

105   Macnicol. The Evacuation of Schoolchildren. op.cit. p27

106   Holman. op.cit. p147

An Evacuation Case Study

'The Billeting Officers have worked splendidly and ungrudgingly and through the Council I want to appeal to the Burgesses generally to give more support and help to them than some have yet done.'

William Farley-Rutter. January 1940

Introduction

Having discussed the problems related to many aspects of the Government Evacuation process it is worth highlighting the experience of the small town of Shaftesbury in Dorset, which, from 1939, became a reception area for evacuees.

By taking a specific example like this, one can see not only that the whole exercise was extremely complex but it was also far-reaching in social, logistical, economic and local political terms. It also highlights the pressure brought to bear by Central Government on the local areas and the shift of responsibility from the macro administrations to the micro.

Such a case-study also demonstrates how the scheme brought together various institutions and bodies within the community and created a great deal of tension and frustration. Above all it demonstrates that despite what the propaganda of the time would have us believe not everybody was working for the common good.

The information contained in this case study comes from the minutes of the Dorset County Council, the Shaftesbury Rural District Council and the Shaftesbury Town Council and the extensive notes and reports made by the Town Clerk of the Shaftesbury Town Council at the time, William Farley-Rutter. Other references relating to supportive evidence are indicated.

(Please note that the names and locations of some of the people mentioned were often transcribed in different ways by the secretary at the time. The author has made every effort to rectify these mistakes but apologises for any remaining inaccuracies.)

Shaftesbury, Dorset

As in other areas, the Government Evacuation scheme for dealing with evacuees threw upon the Local Authorities such as Shaftesbury, the duty of compiling a survey of the town with a view to ascertaining the amount of accommodation available for evacuees on the basis of one person per habitable room, including living rooms and kitchen. As in other areas this census was carried out with the assistance of certain volunteer workers. The Borough was divided into nine districts. The local authority was then asked to nominate certain persons from whom the Mayor might choose Billeting Officers and members to form an appeal tribunal against billeting. It was the duty of these Billeting Officers to billet evacuees, when received, on persons having the accommodation laid down by the Ministry of Health.

In Shaftesbury, the Appeal Tribunal who decided whether or not people should have evacuees, or whether evacuees could be moved etc. consisted of the following people:-

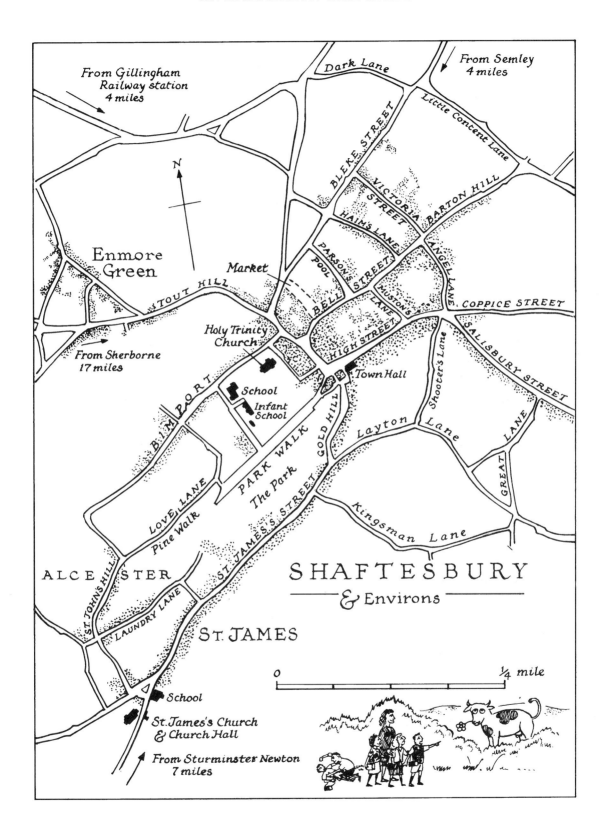

From Gillingham
Railway station
4 miles

From Semley
4 miles

Dark Lane

BLEKE STREET

Little Content Lane

N

VICTORIA STREET

BARTON HILL

Enmore
Green

HAIM'S LANE

ANGEL LANE

Market

PARSONS POOL

STOUT HILL

BELL STREET

MUSTONS LANE

COPPICE STREET

Holy Trinity
Church

HIGH STREET

From Sherborne
17 miles

SALISBURY STREET

Town Hall

Shooter's Lane

BIMPORT

School

Infant
School

Layton Lane

GREAT LANE

PARK WALK

GOLD HILL

The Park

LOVE LANE

Pine Walk

ST. JAMES'S STREET

Kingsman Lane

ALCE STER

SHAFTESBURY

ST. JOHN'S HILL

LAUNDRY LANE

& Environs

ST. JAMES

0   ¼ mile

School

St. James's Church
& Church Hall

From Sturminster Newton
7 miles

- Mrs J. A. Norton (Chair)

- Mr. G. E. Norton

- Rev. Obediah Davies

The appointed billeting officers were:-

- W. Farley-Rutter. Chief Billeting Officer.[1]

- Mrs J. B. Justin for Enmore Green.

- Miss Large for Brimport St.

- Miss Cockcroft for St. James St. (North Side)

- Mr. F. Mansfield. Bleke St., Grosvenor Rd. Etc.

- Miss Baker. Bells St., Angel Lane etc.

- Mrs Watts and Mr G. Durrant.
  Coppice St, Old Boundary Rd, Christy's Lane, St. Rumbold Rd.

- Miss C. D. Butler. St James St. (South Side). French Mill Lane.

There were two vacancies owing to Mrs Woolmer, who had to deal with Salisbury St., having resigned and Mr. F. R. Matthews who had died. With all the administrative infrastructure in place, the Town Clerk, W. Farley-Rutter, had been recalled from his holiday on 31st August 1939 to carry out the Government Evacuation Scheme over the following three days.

On the morning of 1st September he met all the Billeting Officers and other workers and explained the duties which would have to be carried out, how the billeting forms were to be completed, and generally explain other details relating to the scheme. The numbers he had been told to expect were 250 on the first day, 250 on the second day and 200 on the third. These figures had been released to him as early as 25th April 1939 and he had also known in April the predicted time of the trains' arrival in September.

Those who actually arrived on 1st September fell short of the expected number and only 117 detrained at Semley Station.

A Mrs Morris assisted by a number of women workers gave the newcomers a meal in the Guildhall on their arrival which, according to the press, was very much appreciated. After this the evacuees were taken in small groups through the Mayor's Parlour where a list was made and then on to the Council Chambers where the Billeting Officers and their assistants decided on their billets and made out the required billeting papers.

Semley Station

On their way out to the billets, Mr Durrant, who was in charge of the ration store, gave each person his or her food parcel which was to see them through the first two days in their billets. The supply of these rations had been arranged as early as 28th April 1939[2] and were the overall responsibility of the Food (Defence Plans) Department. The department had acquired the necessary stocks of emergency rations which were initially held centrally. They were then sent to the relevant detraining stations in the reception areas where the receiving Local Authority had to appoint an authorised representative to take general charge at each station and assume responsibility for distributing the rations. The amount of emergency rations sent to each area had been calculated in accordance with the number of people actually deposited at the stations. The original consignments were sent to the relevant Station Masters. In the case of Shaftesbury, these rations, comprising of Canned Meat, Corned Beef, Biscuits and Chocolate, were then moved to the Guildhall.

They were to last each evacuee a maximum of 48 hours and were allocated in a carrier bag on the following basis:-

> *'Child...1 can of meat, 2 cans of milk (1 sweet/1 unsweet), 2 packets or 1 pound of tea, a quarter of a pound or 2 x 2d Chocolate biscuits.*

> *Adults...exactly the same plus one extra can of meat'.*

The whole process was not exempt from the usual administration. When the rations were issued notice ER1 had to be handed to each adult. This ER1 stated:-

> The food in this bag is provided free of cost.
>
> It is an emergency ration for your consumption during the next 48 hours. After that interval, the retail food shops will, it is anticipated, have received sufficient supplies to meet the requirements of an additional population in the area you are to be billeted. You are asked to make as few purchases as possible during the first 48 hours.

At the end of the day Form ER2 had to be completed by the Distribution Officer, in this case Mr. Durrant.

> ER2
> Daily return or Emergency Rations Issued.
>
> 1. Name of Detraining Station.
>
> 2. Name of Reception Area.
>
> 3. Number of Evacuee persons to whom rations issued.
>
> 4. Signature of Officer i/c distribution.
>
> Date.....'

It is evident from other documents that any unissued or spare rations were sold. A letter from the Town Clerk of Chipping Norton to the Ministry of Food on 20th January 1940 provides an account of the food originally supplied under the Evacuation Scheme which had not been used and an indication that cheques totalling £16.15s were being forwarded to the Ministry.[3]

After these rations were issued, the evacuees were taken to their billets, some in cars loaned for the purpose. This in itself created problems over the question of insurance. In July 1939 the Clerk to the Shaftesbury Council had contacted the Alliance Insurance Company in Bournemouth to clarify the situation when the Council had organised an evacuation rehearsal. They advised that leading Insurance Companies regarded the use of private cars by Volunteers on behalf of any authority in connection with the preparation of hostilities as coming within the scope of their own insurance policies provided that the use of the cars was on a voluntary basis and no payments, other than allowances for running costs, were received. All the drivers were asked to do was to contact their own insurers and make an application to have their policies endorsed extending the indemnity to cover the Council's Public Liability.[4]

On the second day Shaftesbury received 246 evacuees and on the third day 66. The total number included:-

- Unaccompanied children 327
- Mothers 22
- Accompanied children 41
- Teachers and helpers. 39
- **Total** **429**

The success of this initial reception was very much due to the help of all the various officials and the staff of the population but it was apparent that although the total fell way below the numbers originally expected it would have been very difficult, if not impossible, to have found billets for many more than were actually received.

Although the demands made on the billeting officers and their assistants were the greatest on the three days of the reception it became clear that they would have a great deal of work to do in dealing with complaints and in altering billets from one house to another where circumstances made it necessary to relieve the pressures on some households.

For the first few weeks the Billeting Officer established an Evacuation Office at the Town hall where evacuees and hosts could attend by rota so that any requests for blankets or bedding could be received and investigated. The provision of blankets and other domestic supplies had given rise for concern at the very beginning of the Evacuation Scheme. On the 6th September 1939 the Chairman of the Evacuation Committee, Admiral W. de M. Egerton reported to the Dorchester Rural District Council that they had been asked to procure a certain amount of household items including blankets and kitchen utensils. The Ministry of Health had arranged for Dorchester to receive 2,000 blankets and 800 mattresses but only 150 blankets had arrived. He had telegraphed the London County Council on 1st September and suggested that all evacuees should each bring a blanket but they had replied that this was not possible.

The problem of blanket provision was particularly serious in the rural areas where agricultural labourers did not usually have a large supply of extra bedding and this was of particular concern in one small un-named village where the locals were expecting to receive nine mothers and babies. Beyond sending another strongly worded telegram to the Ministry the local Council could do little.[5]

Some blankets did eventually arrive in the Dorset area and advertisements like the one below appeared in the local newspapers but again the distribution was held up by people having to apply for them, even though it was already known that some individuals and whole areas required them urgently:-

BILLETING NOTICE
BLANKETS AND BEDDING

A further supply of blankets is now available and householders who have evacuees billeted upon them should send applications in writing to me stating:-

a. The number of blankets.

b. The number of camp beds needed to make up their requirements for the use of evacuees now in their homes.

A limited supply of waterproof sheeting is also ready for issue where needed for the younger children.

These blankets, beds and sheeting are Government property and will be delivered to the householder against his signature, within a few days of application.[6]

When blankets were provided they were not very good. According to an article in the Dorset County Chronicle and Swanage Times on 9th November dealing with social conditions in the Dorchester area the investigative reporter C. K. Young wrote:-

'It was with a disgusted gesture that Mr Groombridge, Deputy-Chief Evacuation Officer for Dorchester, threw down the blankets that the Government has provided for refugees whose foster parents have insufficient.

'Feel them.' He said. 'How much cold are they going to keep out? You would need six or eight to feel any difference at all.'

I felt the thin cotton stuff and prayed for a mild winter in Dorset'.[7]

In the initial stages the evacuees who presented the greatest difficulty for the Billeting Officers in the Shaftesbury area were the Mothers with children. Some of these cases were so difficult to deal with that in order to ease the situation the Town Clerk had to requisition an empty cottage at the foot of St. John's Hill and partially furnish it. It soon became evident to him that some of these women with their children were not really suitable for billeting in ordinary homes, although he gives no specific reasons for his concerns. Even where they were suitable it soon became apparent that it was extremely difficult for such women to be accommodated in other people's houses. One appeal in respect of such a case was made to the Billeting Tribunal but the action of the Billeting Officer was upheld.

Many of these women did not like the country conditions and they very soon started to drift back to London. With regard to the unaccompanied children they and their teachers had come from three London schools, the Roman Catholic English Martyrs School at Walworth, the Penrose Street School and the Archbishop Temple's Central School in Lambeth. It was not long before the teachers in the Shaftesbury school contacted the teachers from the evacuated schools and fixed up some arrangements for the education of their charges when the schools were reopened. The original arrangements provided for the normal scholars at Shaftesbury Senior School and the Penrose Street School to occupy the Senior School buildings during the morning whilst the same buildings were occupied by the Archbishop Temple School in the afternoons. Holy Trinity School was occupied by local children in the morning and English Martyrs in the afternoons. This was a satisfactory start but it made no provision for the education of local children in the afternoon or for the evacuated children in the morning. Fortunately, the weather was fine and eased the problems considerably as presumably the children not attending schools could at least be outside and not in the billets.

There was also the problem of school meals to consider. This was met partly by the headteacher of the Senior School providing a midday meal for the evacuee children attending that school. This worked well except that it deprived the local children attending there of the meal formerly provided for them. As these arrangements could not be regarded as permanently satisfactory the Town Clerk contacted the Rector of St. James' Church who was willing to place the Church hall at the disposal of the billeting officers for education purposes. He also contacted Mr. C. J. Stretch who agreed to provide the same officers with the Park hut if the military authorities were prepared to give up their intention of turning it into a military canteen. They agreed to the proposal because an alternative canteen was provided by the Revd. H. H. Coley and members of the Women's British Legion at the Guildhall.

The Town Clerk then arranged for an Inspector of the London Education Authority who was at Dorchester, to inspect the premises and contact the relevant head-teachers with regard to using the buildings as effectively as possible. As a result of his endeavours the St. John's Church Hall was used in conjunction with the Senior school and the Park Hut was used by Holy Trinity School in such a way that provision was for both local and evacuated children to attend school all day. There was still some confusion about the children who required school meals. It had been the intention of the London Education Authority to provide the equipment needed to enable a midday meal to be cooked at St. James' Church Hall but the equipment was delayed so initially the evacuated children who were having their meal at the Senior School now had to have their meal in their billets and this inevitably caused a great deal of annoyance on the part of many hosts, especially those who worked during the day. The provision of midday meals at St. James' was eventually organised from Tuesday 16th January 1940, when the equipment was put in place. Later, on 24th September 1942, a British restaurant was opened in the town and run by the WVS. Here, children under 15 could have a two course meal for 8d.

By November 1939 the number of evacuees remaining in the Shaftesbury area had fallen to 369. Most of the mothers and accompanied children had gone back to their homes. So too had those unaccompanied children who had reached school leaving age and those who returned at the request of their parents.

After the initial evacuation, the area did not receive any further requests until 1941 but the Government made it possible for women accompanied by children of school age and for elderly people to come out of the evacuated areas provided they could find persons willing to billet them in the reception areas. In consequence of this quite a number of persons, approximately 140, found their way into Shaftesbury and were given billeting notices. Some of these were accommodated in requisitioned properties, notably:-

- 83 St. James Street.

- Cottage in New Rd, Enmore Green.

- Cottage in Long Cross, Enmore Green.

- 'Martinscott' Angel Lane.

It soon became evident to all those concerned with the Shaftesbury evacuees that some after-care work would be needed, particularly in relation to clothing. Some of the children who had gone to the town had come from poor areas and some of their parents had become unemployed because of the general upheaval in London. To help alleviate the problem the Town Clerk established an after-care committee with a Mrs Tutin as the Chairwoman and Miss Dewey acting as Secretary. As far as possible they carried out their work in co-operation with the Headteachers. When cases of insufficient clothing and footwear were reported to the Committee, members contacted after-care workers in the relevant areas of London to ascertain the financial position of the parents. Where the parents were able to supply clothing all was well, but in a number of cases the parents were unable to do so. Some money had been raised locally and the Headteachers had access to some small funds. However, there was still a significant problem and in the second week of November 1939, an appeal was put in the Western Gazette asking for clothing of any description and monetary help. The office in the Town Hall, formerly used by the Borough Surveyor, was designated as the depot for the clothing and voluntary helpers were appointed to make up the clothes received into suitable garments for the evacuee children. It was pointed out to critics of the scheme that such clothes were only issued in really necessitous cases and only then after parents had done what they could to help. Foster parents were informed that when they felt there was a need for their charges to be issued with clothing they were to inform the relevant teachers. In no case were they to supply the clothing themselves and claim a refund for the cost retrospectively as any such payment would not be made.[8]

Other areas of after-care in the area concerned:-

- The provision of baths for the children. In some cases baths were not available in the billets so arrangements were made at the Senior School and the Public Assistance institution to provide baths and showers when required.

- The question of infection and contagious diseases. The Vine House Hospital at Sturminster Newton was made available by the Sturminster Rural District Council for minor cases and the Isolation Hospital at Blandford Forum for the more serious cases. In a letter dated 15th July 1940, the Minister of Health stated that where evacuees became sick and were nursed in the billets the host was to be granted an extra five shillings a week if a Doctor certified it. In

Shaftesbury, the Doctors instructed that evacuees were not to be nursed at home if a place was available at Vine House unless there was a very good reason why the evacuee should stay.

By the 9th November 1939, the Town Clerk could confidentially report to the Town Council that:-

1. The transport arrangements for the evacuees were well organised and implemented effectively.

2. The evacuation of mothers with young children had been a failure through no fault of the reception area.

3. The evacuation of unaccompanied school children had worked reasonably well.

4. Insufficient care had been taken in evacuated areas to see that evacuees unsuitable for ordinary billeting had been sent.

5. There had been a lack of assistance from the Ministry of Health and the London Education Authority in helping to solve the many, and sometimes difficult problems related to the evacuees.

Between November and the end of January 1940, there had been a drift of unaccompanied evacuees back to London, largely due to the action of parents wanting their children home, though, as in September, some of the children reached the school leaving age and had returned to find employment.

Despite the travel restriction and the attempts by the Government to persuade evacuees to stay, some children went home for Christmas. This created a certain amount of relief on both sides. In most cases, the children were able to stay with their families for seven to ten days and their absence gave a certain respite to the hosts who wanted their families with them for Christmas.

For those who were unable to return home the Shaftesbury Council organised a Christmas party in the town Hall on Friday 29th December from 3.30-7.30. The arrangements had been made and carried out by the Mayor, Deputy Mayor and the Billeting Officers, ably assisted by teachers and other interested persons willing to give their time and help. It was reported that the evacuees were given tea, a paper hat and a cracker in the Guildhall at 4pm and while the tables were being cleared the children remained in their areas and took part in community singing led by a Mr Cliff.

The tables were then removed and a number of party games were organised. After these the evacuees were taken upstairs to see the Christmas tree loaded with presents before a Father Christmas arrived to distribute a gift to each child. When the children eventually left they were each given an orange and a bag of sweets. The party was also attended by the Mayor of Southwark, Mr Gates, who had travelled down from London at the invitation of the Mayor of Shaftesbury. Mr

Gates participated in all the games and spoke to the children, many of whom he had known from his visits to the English Martyrs and Penrose Street schools while they had been in London.

The London County Council had provided £13 towards the cost of the party and the small shortfall was met from local funds. The total cost was £15 15s 6d. Similar Christmas events, again the responsibility of the Mayor, were repeated in 1941 for those evacuees remaining in the area at that time.

By January 1940 it is obvious from reports and comments made in various committees that the 'honeymoon' period was over and one can detect a distinct shift in attitude on the part of those actively participating in the Evacuation scheme. In his tri-monthly report, the Town Clerk expressed serious doubts about the ability to billet some children. He was concerned that most people were not aware of the problems involved and the great demands made on the time, temper and patience of billeting officers who were having to deal with problems of both a minor and serious nature on a daily basis.

The tone of his language gives one the impression that he had become frustrated by the many problems facing his team:-

> *'The fact that many evacuees were very unreasonable.*

> *Evacuated children were not always models of good behaviour. He agreed that it would be surprising if they were.*

> *Foster parents were liable to become ill like other people and then require billets to be found for their charges.*

> *Clothing problems when parents could not, and in some cases would not, provide suitable garments for their children.*

> *Mending of clothes and other items.*

> *The extra bedding required especially in houses where the evacuees suffered from enuresis. At a Council meeting on 7th April 1941, it was recommended that Pulham Rectory be taken over for the sole purpose of accommodating bed-wetters. It was to be administered by the Sturminster Rural District Council.*

> *The damage done to beds and bedding and other items of furniture which in some cases had been vandalised by evacuees'.*

The Town Clerk gave full vent to his feelings and it was obvious that he felt that not everybody was pulling their weight. This is evident in his report where he states:-

> *'The Billeting Officers have worked splendidly and ungrudgingly and through the Council I want to appeal to the Burgesses generally to give more support and help to them than some have yet done. There are some townspeople who have never yet received into their homes any evacuees and*

who are still unwilling to do so. Is this quite fair? It means some personal sacrifice, but surely we should all be willing to help out in view of the difficult times in which we live. The future must belong to the children and their welfare should be one of our chief concerns.

Another matter to which I must refer is the amount of work connected with Billeting which is thrown upon Council Staff. The ordinary work of the office is being retarded and put on one side to meet the urgent demands of billeting. This is unsatisfactory and I think the Council should know. I am not referring to the accountancy side of billeting which is being kept up to date, I refer to the many calls on time interviewing people endeavouring to find solutions to billeting problems'.

Despite his concerns the Billeting Officers continued to carry out their duties to the full. The Minutes of their meeting on Monday 12th February 1940 relating to transfer of billets provides an interesting insight into the type of problems faced by the Billeting Officers when trying to sort out new accommodation.

'It was reported that alternative billets were required for the following children owing to the circumstances stated:-

Lily Mercer (11), Sidney Mercer (10), Jean Mercer (6) billeted with Mrs Wright.

Mrs Wright has an illness requiring complete rest by Doctor's orders. It is possible on recovery that these children, or some of them, could return to the billet.

Jean Richards (7), Joyce Richards (5). Illness of the children, possibly infectious. (Skin trouble). After two periods in hospital the billet is not open to them. The children returned from Vine House and immediately the trouble recurred and the attention required is more than a householder can be expected to give.[9]

Reginald O'Harro (12). Insufficient accommodation for a lad of 12. The householder has relieved another host who was ill of three small children, girls, 11 and 9, and a boy of 5.

Earl C.Crisp (13) and Fred Brown (13). Householders are over 70 and wife nearly 70, also involved sister coming to reside.

Robert Townsend (11) and Edward Townsend (10). Householder has had one of these boys ill. Also her own child and has asked for one month's rest.

John Saunders (11). Householder will be moving within a comparatively short time and will not have room for the boy.

Colin Morton (14). Illness at Householder's home and also the lad is unruly.

Edward Smart (14). This boy, with a younger brother and sister sent home owing to illness and because his mother preferred he should go home to another billet. But she wants him to return and the London County Council have asked that he should as he should take the Oxford Examination in December 1940'.

With regard to children who had gone home and wished to return to Shaftesbury, the Billeting Officer suggested that this practice should not be encouraged unless a definite billet was open which would not, for any reason, be open to any children in the town requiring an alternative billet.

The resolution was passed to ask the Shaftesbury Rural District Council to take a small number of evacuees, especially in those villages which had been prepared for evacuation, but which had not yet received any.

> *'The Billeting Officers wish to put on record that they have done all that is possible with the first billets but without success and they consider that owing to the fact that many of the residents are elderly and infirm, the town very full of lodgers for whom the Labour exchange have requested accommodation, that it is legitimately impossible to find further billets and they consider that unless Shaftesbury Council can itself assist with the question of billets the Government should be asked to provide a hostel and remove some of the children to the Rural District, a camp or elsewhere. Despite their problems the committee decided not to resort to compulsory billeting'.*

The questions of hostels was raised again at the Council meeting on the 13th April 1941 when the Dorset County Council issued a report on the arrangements of sick bays and hostels and suggested that there should be some co-ordination across the county for sick, difficult and unbilletable (sic) children. Although the Shaftesbury Council agreed in principle, they did not wish to relinquish the responsibility of overseeing such hostels as it was felt that as a Local Authority they were more in touch with the work being done in sick bays and hostels rather than the County Council and they felt the existing arrangement was far more efficient. Also, they suggested that so far as hostels and temporary accommodation of billetable children for whom some reason no other billets were available, these facilities should definitely come under the responsibility of the local authority in which the evacuees were situated.

On 15th July 1940 the situation was made even worse by a request from the Ministry of Health to take an extra 200 evacuees in the Shaftesbury area. The Chief Billeting Officer replied that the shortage of billets was so acute that he would be unable to take any extra evacuees unless they resorted to compulsory powers. The County Council had called a conference of representatives from all Local Authorities in the County to discuss evacuation problems and it had been decided to appoint a co-ordinating officer to assist with the proper and fair distribution of evacuees throughout the area. When the Co-ordinating Officer visited Shaftesbury to discuss the situation, it was pointed out to him that the billeting officers regarded the town as being almost full to capacity although it might be possible to accommodate an extra 50 children should the need arise. The C.O. having appraised the situation, agreed that the town was full and it was felt by the local authority that they were unlikely to receive further evacuees. However, as the situation deteriorated in London during 1941, the County Council asked Shaftesbury on 2nd April 1941 to be prepared to take parties of evacuees not exceeding 250, at short notice. The Chief Billeting Officer wrote back to say that this number was impossible. But, shortly afterwards on the 11th April he was informed that he was to receive 50 mothers and children on Thursday 24th April.

As he was left with no option but to take them, it was decided immediately to take over the flat belonging to the Officer of the Works in Angel Lane, known as 'Mount Elsie', and also to requisition parts of No. 6 High Street which were not occupied. Together with billeting in private houses this was considered enough accommodation for the evacuees to be housed. Both requisitioned premises were in reasonable condition and furnished but they did require some work done on them to bring them up to standard. Instructions were issued that this work had to be started immediately and completed by 24th April. However, events in London overtook the planning and the arrival date of the party was brought forward to the 21st which put the billeting authorities under extreme pressure. Not only had the premises to be fitted with Black Out, gas stoves, electric light and cleaned throughout, there was also the question of furnishing. In addition to this accommodation, Mrs J. Bell of Castle Hill House offered to let the evacuees use certain rooms and a small amount of furniture within the house.

At a meeting of the Billeting Officers on 18th April they considered what persons should be warned of the likelihood of receiving evacuees. It was decided that the Chief Billeting Officer should write to a number of people and warn them that they would be required to billet one mother and one or two small children as from the afternoon of the 21st April. These notices were dispatched to the following people on the same day:-

Mr R.W. Borley. Barton Hill House.

Revd. W. Floyd. Wesley House.

Mr Milverton. High St.

Mrs Broadway. New Buildings. Enmore Green.

Miss Woodcock. Sarum House.

Mr Burden. Roslyn.

Mr.S.J.Young. Everest.

Capt. Wrighton

Mrs Thorne. Alcester Cottage.

Mr George Mitchell. 15 Bell Street.

Mr Kelson. Hawkesdene Farm.

Mrs Thickness. The Chantry.

Mr Baker. Little Content.

Mrs Green. Cliffe House.

Mrs Harvey. High St.

Misses Primivesi.

Mr Perret. 4 Ivy Cross.

Mr Hoddinott. Salisbury Rd.

Mrs.E.Dennis.

Mrs Jesset. Holdwell. Enmore Green.

Miss Love. New Buildings.

Mr Leonard Hardy 15 Bell St.

Mr. E.J.Short.

Mrs Bevan. Minerva House. Fort Hill.

It was thought by the committee and the Council that these billets and the other accommodation available would be sufficient to house all the new arrivals. However, the replies to the letter were as follows and indicate why some people were not able or prepared to have evacuees. There is no criticism aimed by the author at any of these householders as many of the excuses were very worthy. They are repeated here simply as an example of the logistical problems faced by the billeting officer in Shaftesbury, a problem which was replicated across other reception areas. For example the Chief Billeting Officer in Dorchester sent out 5,254 forms to householders in his area requesting they enrol in the evacuation scheme. He received 84 positive replies offering help.[10]

Mr Baker, Little Content, Mrs Thickness at the Chantry and Mr Hoddinott were all willing to receive one mother and one child. Mr Milverton, High St, stated that he had the accommodation but that his wife was away until the following Thursday and he could not very well take in one mother and one child until that date. Miss Love of New Buildings, Enmore Green, was persuaded to take one mother and one child.

However, with regards to others the following replies were received:-

Mr. R.W. Berley stated that he was ill in bed and that members of his family were at Barton Hill House so there were 8 persons resident and consequently there was no room.

The Revd. Floyd, Wesley House, stated that there was some accommodation in his house but that he had already promised it to certain aged persons in London and he was about to go up to London to make arrangements for them to come and join him in Shaftesbury.

Mrs Green, Cliffe House, wrote sending in a Doctor's Certificate with regard to her mother's health declaring that 'billeting would kill her mother' and so formerly refused to take any evacuees.

Miss Harvey, High St. went to see the C.B.O. and explained that she and her husband were both busy in their business and that they really had no accommodation for a mother and a child, but they would be prepared to receive one evacuee girl.

Mrs Bevan, Minerva House, Fort Hill, did not wish to take in evacuees at all but under the circumstances would make provision for one mother and one child.

The Misses Primivesi stated that one of them was ill and they had no maid. Also their brother spent each weekend with them and that it was quite impossible for them to make any provision for evacuees.

Miss Woodcock stated that an Officer his wife and one child were occupying three rooms in her house which made it impossible for her to have mothers and children.

Mr Perret, 4 Ivy Cross, wrote that he had certain members of his own family there and could not accommodate evacuees.

Mr Burden, Roslyn, went to see the Billeting Officer and said that he did not wish to have a mother and child but was willing to have one evacuee girl. He was told that he would be reported to the Chief Billeting Officer because he had the accommodation to take more.

Mr S.J.Young, Everest, stated that his son, who was serving in the Army, and his fiancee, were at home and that Mr Brown's furniture was occupying one room of the house so it was impossible to take any evacuees.

Mrs Dennis, Salisbury St. admitted that she had the accommodation but her health was in a bad state and she could not have any evacuees. She enclosed a Doctor's Certificate with her reply.

Captain Wrighton of St. Edmunds Chantry, wrote explaining that he had at that moment only one small room which was an attic and he did not consider that this was suitable for a woman and child. The local billeting Officer, Miss Laye, visited him and confirmed that this was the case.

Mrs Jesset of Holdwell, telephoned that her daughter, son-in-law and their child were arriving on Saturday and there would be no room.

Mrs Thorne, Alcester Cottage, visited the Billeting Officer and satisfied him that she already had certain evacuees and other persons living with her that made it impossible for her to accommodate more.

Mr Mitchell, 15 Bell St. also called and admitted that he and his wife were the only two in the house, but that 'all the coming and going had to go through the living room' (sic) and he could not possibly put up with evacuees particularly in view of the fact that he had to conduct all his business from his home.

Mr Hardy, Bell St. stated that some of his children had come home and he could not house any evacuees.

Mr Kelson, Hawkesdene Farm, stated that he only had a housekeeper. He also sent a certificate saying that he could not look after evacuees and explained that the house was only partially furnished and there was no accommodation in which an evacuated women could cook.

Mrs E.J.Short of Highfield explained that there were two ladies occupying three rooms in their house and who had been there since September 1940 and therefore there was no further accommodation.

One can only imagine the frustration of the William Farley-Rutter and his team and he voiced this at a full Council meeting on the 29th April 1941. With a little bit of persuasion the team was able to find 49 places for the new arrivals.

One Woman and One Child to:-

Mr Mercer, Mr Burden, Mr Hoddinott, Mr Baker, Mr and Mrs Norton and Mrs Bevan.

One Woman and Two Children plus one woman and one child to Miss Love.

Two women and six children at Mount Elsie. Angel Lane.

One woman and two children to Mrs Olivers, Long Cross and Mrs Wheeler, St. Rumbolds Rd. (This was a temporary arrangement)

Two women and five children to No.6 High St.

Two women and three children, initially billeted at No.6 High St. refused to go and were sent to Mrs Gray. 'Canbiensis'.

One woman and two children to the Old Soup Kitchen. Parsons Pool.

Two expectant women and one boy to Mrs Bells.

By the time the evacuees did arrive on the 21st April everything was in reasonable order. Mount Elsie was almost totally ready and furnished and some of No.6 High Street, but not all. The mothers and children were given a mid-day meal at the Park Hut and, in addition, as an emergency arrangement the old soup kitchen in Parsons Pool, which had been requisitioned as a rest centre in case of necessity, was fitted up so that it could be used.

The Women's Voluntary Service arranged cars to collect the evacuees and take them to their billets and also provided assistance at the Town Hall during their registration, and while the billeting officers sorted out any specific difficulties.

Problems arose very quickly especially where mothers and children were in private houses and many threatened to return to London. By this time the C.B.O. had gained a great deal of experience in dealing with such matters and was of the opinion that the only satisfactory solution so far as mothers with children were concerned lay in the taking of empty houses and placing families in them so they could manage their own affairs. On the 21st April it had been impossible to billet two women and four children so they were placed temporarily in the soup kitchen. However, on the following day the C.B.O visited 'Church View' in Aspberry Lane, which the Mayor had informed one of the billeting team remained unoccupied. This was subsequently requisitioned, along with the furnishings, for the use of evacuees. It was thought that it would be ideally suited for joint occupation by the families in the soup kitchen. At first they were willing to use it but there was an unavoidable delay in getting the place ready, listing the furniture and mending a leak in the water pipe. While all this was happening one of the women visited the billeting officer to explain that on no account could she live in the same house as the other women! Having taken possession of the building he had no-one to place in it and to complicate the situation further, the owner returned stating that he wanted to live there himself.

At the Council meeting on 29th April 1941, the Chief Billeting Officer pointed out that although the numbers officially billeted under the Government Scheme would appear to be 350.

By 13th April 1941 the evacuee numbers were as follows:-

- Adults Billeted:. 24
- Children Billeted: 119
- Persons in requisitioned houses: . . . . 28 Adult. 33 Children.
- Persons finding their own accommodation
  and obtaining allowances afterwards: . . . . Adults 80. Children 47.
- Total 331. With the comings and goings of evacuees this number increased to the 350.

It had to be pointed out that from the point of view of accommodation, members of the Council needed to remember that a good many people had come into Shaftesbury who had not been officially evacuated and also there were a significant number of nurses billeted in the town. He went on to outline the problems he faced when trying to overcome all the problems inherent in trying to accommodate extra people.

He stated that when he knew he had to house an extra 50 people he requisitioned Abbey Lodge, an empty property in Park Walk. However, at the same time, Mr Blades of the Assistance Board explained that he himself was living in lodgings in Shaftesbury as he could find no house in which to live. On the night of the 16th April his wife and two daughters, whom he had left in Weymouth, had the whole of their house blown down on top of them and they had come to the town seeking accommodation. He pointed out that there was a Ministry of Health Circular which stated that in such circumstances a house may be requisitioned subject to the appraisal of the situation and subsequent approval of the Regional Officer. He telephoned the Regional Officer in Reading who agreed to confirm the requisition of Abbey Lodge for Mr Blades and his family. The reason why he had proceeded to put them into Abbey Lodge was because he thought they were people who would respect the property and also the Abbey excavations in a way which might not be done by some of the evacuee women and children from London and in the meantime he felt he would be housing people who had been bombed out in his own County. However, he had received an abusive letter from a Mrs Claridge who owned the property when she received notification that the property was to be requisitioned.

The Chief Billeting Officer experienced a good deal of trouble in trying to furnish and equip requisitioned properties. Although the matter of furnishings was dealt with by the Ministry of Health Circular 2266 which stated that:-

```
'The local authority may, as the occasion arises, purchase locally from
existing stocks of equipment those items that are essential for the
business of daily living. If local stocks are adequate reference should
be made to the Regional Officer'.
```

On 6th April 1941, he received an updated version of the Circular from the Regional Office in Bristol informing him that regional stocks had been set up for certain articles. He was to inform the

Regional Office of the articles needed and the address they were to be sent to. However, at this time the overall responsibility for Shaftesbury switched from the South West Region in Bristol to the Southern Region HQ in Reading and this involved a certain amount of administrative difficulty which was unfortunate but unavoidable.

As he was finding difficulty obtaining the relevant equipment the C.B.O had written to the Reading Office on 24th March asking them to supply him with chairs, chests of drawers, tables etc. He received a reply on the 3rd April asking for the address of the property to be requisitioned, the accommodation available and a list of the articles required. This list was sent on the 16th April and included all the items needed for Mount Elsie, Angel Lane, No.6 High St, Abbey Lodge and a cottage in Coppice St, as well as those needed to augment the furniture in the Cottage, Enmore Green. He also asked for additional equipment such as jugs, bowls, teapots etc., for 20 housekeepings and also cutlery for 50 persons and additional blankets. He returned the list with an accompanying letter explaining that the items were urgently required for the arrival of mothers and children on the 24th April. When he learned that the new group of evacuees would be arriving on the 21st he telephoned Reading and asked if they could be sent immediately. He was informed that they did not have the items in stock and they would have to come from the manufacturer and this would take 14 days. He was also told that under the circumstances he could purchase some of the bare necessities locally, even if they were second-hand, and the cost would be covered by the Regional Office. He was to inform them of his purchases and they would be removed from his original list. This created problems because not even some of these essentials could be bought locally and it was fortunate that the Shaftesbury Rural District Council let him have some of the kitchen utensils and four chairs from their own surplus store. This does beg the question why did they not offer these items in the first place!?

The Billeting Officer considered that the Ministry should have allowed him to keep a permanent stock of equipment and furniture for use in the requisitioned buildings and he wrote to the Regional Office to this effect but received no reply. Despite the problems there was sufficient equipment to enable the women and children to make a reasonable start in their new accommodation.

A suggestion was made that the Council should approach the WVS to ask them whether they would inspect and supervise the requisitioned properties into which the evacuees had been placed. Although this had originally been the responsibility of the Billeting Officers it was felt that because the numbers were increasing the matter might be reconsidered. He was concerned not to do anything that would run counter to the work of the billeting officers, some of whom were in fact members of the WVS, but if the Billeting officers were in agreement then the WVS could take extra responsibility.

He was particularly pleased with the Crèche being run by the WVS at the Gold Hill Institute. He had been approached by the area representative of the WVS, Mrs A. Stewart, to see if it would be possible to establish a crèche for the assistance of women evacuees in the Borough who had small children. The idea was to help those in particular who lived in the surrounding area and who had to go into Shaftesbury to shop and take their young children with them. Having agreed to the idea, the situation required suitable premises. The C.B.O informed Mrs Stewart that the military had requisitioned Gold Hill Institute, formerly occupied by the Working Men's Club, and that the rooms remained empty. If the military could be persuaded to relinquish them then these premises would be ideal for use as the crèche. The military were willing to release the building for this purpose. The Regional Officer in Bristol had then been approached and with his consent the Institute had been equipped and the crèche started.

The crèche was open from 2-5pm on Thursdays and Saturdays for children and in conjunction with this, classes in 'cutting out', presumably for dress-making, and 'keep fit' were started for evacuee mothers. The whole venture, run entirely by the WVS proved to be a great success and was particularly useful as the numbers of evacuees in Shaftesbury increased.

The WVS also agreed to open a club for boys and girls between 13-17, later raised to 14-17. This started on the 16th October for a trial period. Only seven youths, all girls, turned up on the first night but by the end of the month it had become more popular with 35 attending with an almost 50-50 gender division. It was later recommended that members should be charged a penny for entrance and they were also to be made responsible for clearing up at the end of each session.

Although the WVS were useful in these matters not all members were pleased. On 29th April 1941, the Mayor opened a Council meeting by stating that he was dissatisfied with the way in which the Government Evacuation Scheme had been dealt with over the recent weeks leading up to the meeting and mentioned a number of instances, including a letter he had received from the WVS in Dorchester suggesting that their services were not being used in the Borough as much as they might have been. The Town Clerk replied that these claims were inaccurate but one wonders why the WVS in Dorchester were complaining to the Council in Shaftesbury!

- On the 14th July 1941 the Town Clerk made reference to the Shakespeare Committee report to the Minster of Health on the Welfare of Evacuees. This committee, under the chairmanship of Geoffrey Shakespeare had been established by the Ministry of Health on 15th November 1940 to provide the answers to two specific questions.

- What should be done to ease the burden in the reception areas?

- What provision should be made to persuade evacuees to remain in the reception areas?[11]

The report, completed in January 1941 made recommendations under 45 separate headings. Most of them dealt with the better application of a variety of services and the day to day needs of the evacuated mothers and children. A copy of the report entitled 'Report on the Conditions in Reception Areas' and Circular 2307 were sent to all reception areas on the 14th March 1941 together with a request for action.[12] This report is worth reading because, although there are some sweeping and stereotypical generalisations, some of which are insulting in their simplicity, e.g.

'The London woman is gregarious.....she is not overburdened by domesticity. She has a partiality for tinned foods and readily resorts to the fish and chip shop', (almost the same words which describe the evacuee mother in the film 'Living with Strangers'), it does recognise that there were difficulties between the hosts and the evacuees which were not always the fault of the latter. It also recognised that with all its inherent problems the scheme should have failed. Why it didn't was because many people set out to make it work.[13]

The Town Clerk indicated that the Dorset County Council had appointed a Welfare Officer, Miss Magee, to deal with the North Dorset area and a Social Worker, Miss Gray, was working in the Shaftesbury Borough and Shaftesbury Rural District areas. He informed the Council that Miss Magee had suggested that the time had come when a Welfare Committee for the Borough could be established to co-ordinate all the welfare work relating to evacuees as distinct from the billeting aspect. Although the Council agreed to the committee in principle and that it would serve a useful function, it was unwilling to introduce such a body until the billeting officers had given their opinions.

The problems of billeting continued late into the year and from the communications available one gets the impression that there was a growing tension between the County administration in Dorchester and the outlying town councils.

At the Shaftesbury Council meeting on 10th November 1941, the Town Clerk read a letter from the Dorset County Council dated 9th October 1941, intimating that Shaftesbury would be expected to find billets for up to 30 women and children at 48 hours' notice. He also reported that since receiving this letter, the Council had been asked on 20th October to take 30 evacuees, including 6 mothers and 13 children, but fortunately they had been reallocated temporarily. After the latest request, the Clerk reported that he had met with Mr Lewis and Miss Mackinnon from the Dorset County Council and had explained the problems Shaftesbury was having in accommodating evacuees, especially as the Billeting Officers had rejected the proposal of compulsory billeting.

After considerable discussion within the Shaftesbury Council, it had been resolved that 'the County Council be informed of the position within the town, notably that its rural population already contained 10% evacuees and that, under the circumstances, the Shaftesbury Council did not consider they could accommodate the evacuees in question.

Despite this resolution the Town Clerk informed the Council on the following day, 21st October 1941, that the County Council had told him that 19 mothers and children would be sent to Shaftesbury on the 22nd October and, as the Town Council were not willing to billet them, a representative from the County Council would be sent to allocate the evacuees to accommodation in the Shaftesbury area. The Town Council agreed to this and provided a list of names of persons thought to have accommodation for billeting purposes to the officer from the County Council. As well as a list of 10 names it was suggested that 'Ludiana' Brimport St., was empty and the Town Clerk was instructed to make an inspection and if it was indeed empty, to then requisition the property. Further instructions were given that failing everything else, some women and children might be billeted in the upstairs portion of the Men's Almshouses in Salisbury St.

A later, undated, entry in the Minutes states:-

> '...In view of the difficulty which has arisen through the County Council undertaking the billeting of certain evacuees recently in the Borough, we recommend the Council to ask for a conference between a representative of the Regional Office of the Minister of Health, and representatives of the Shaftesbury Council to discuss the whole position with a view to some satisfactory working arrangements being arrived at....'

On 16th December, the Town Clerk reported that:-

> '...there had been a meeting between the various representatives and they had learned that no further immediate problems need be expected for Dorset and that unless the Blitz conditions again occur it would be fairly unlikely that further parties of Mothers with children were still being sent out, but parties of unaccompanied children were still being despatched from London and some of these might arrive in Dorset and possibly Shaftesbury. It was also learned that the position of the south coast Dorset towns might be reviewed and made more use of as reception areas in the event of further Blitz conditions prevailing and that the resources of the county would have to be heavily taxed and the existing percentage of evacuees in Shaftesbury could not be regarded as the limit of capacity and under such conditions it might even be necessary to suspend the standard of one person per room'.

By 1942 there were signs that things were getting better and the pressures on the Council and individuals were gradually lifting. At a meeting of the Council on 14th January 1942, the Town Clerk reported that there were no longer any evacuees at the Alms houses but the buildings would be held in reserve. There were problems of overcrowding at 'Mount Elsie' where a Mrs Sargeant and her three children and Mrs Mosely and her three children had been joined by their husbands. However, this situation did not last long as all the Moselys returned to London on the 11th February.

Two upstairs rooms at Martin's Cottages were now empty as Mrs James had returned to London but it had been agreed that Mrs Cole, living downstairs, could take over the whole house for 15 shillings a week plus electricity.

The gradual change of responsibility can also be seen in the yearly accounts which indicate a gradual build up of expenditure until 1942 and then a decline. These figures are also interesting in that they show how little money was spent on the initial evacuation scheme in the Borough.

ACCOUNTS

Expenditure on Evacuation	Incoming	Outgoing
April 1939 - March 1940	£177.18.6	£177.18.6
April 1940 - March 1941	£578.12.9	£578.12.9.
April 1941 - March 1942	£1207.4.11	£1207.4.11
April 1942 - March 1943	No figures available.	
April 1943 - March 1944	£763.4.4	£763.4.4

By January 1944 one can see the first signs of de-requisition when Mrs Compton went back to London and No.2 Enmore Green was allocated to a farm labourer. However, for some reason this ruling was overturned at the council meeting on 3rd April 1944.

On the 10th May 1944 the Evacuee Hostel in Old Boundary Road was taken over by the British Red Cross who used it as accommodation for relatives visiting patients on the danger list at the Military Hospital. The Christmas party for evacuees took place as usual in December 1944. There were only two final entries in the Council Minutes dealing with evacuation. On 11th July 1945:-

> *'The Council will no doubt be aware that the bulk of evacuees, both adults and children, have now gone back to their former home towns, though it is true that there are still a number of evacuated families in the Borough. Throughout the Government Evacuation Scheme the Council has been indebted to the Shaftesbury Branch of the WVS for their services in all sorts of ways and in all sorts of directions'.*

(Interesting that there were no formal thanks for the work of Farley-Rutter or the Billeting Officers in Shaftesbury and surrounding villages.)

The final link between the Council and the Evacuation Scheme was broken on 9th January 1946 when it was announced:-

> *'...Tenders are invited for the sale of evacuation equipment. Blankets 16/10d new, 10/- second hand. 45/- cupboards'.*

William Farley-Rutter. Shaftesbury Town Clerk (1888 - 1991).

Endnotes

1   The success of the evacuation procedures and other aspects of Shaftesbury's ability to cope with the pressure of external factors, is owed in no small measure to the work of William Farley Rutter (1888-1991)who gave sterling service to the town, before, during and after the war in many capacities. He was the great grandson of a John Rutter who had settled in Shaftesbury c 1812 and established a printing business and Reading Room. In the 1830s he qualified as a Solicitor and campaigned vigorously against corruption in local and Parliamentary elections. The family had always been Quakers and William, also a solicitor, had spent the war as a member of the Friends Ambulance Service in France. He died in 1991 aged 103.

2   Food Defence.1839/38.

3   Chipping Norton Borough Council. Doc.28. 20th January 1940.

4   Letter to William Farley Rutter from the Alliance Assurance Co. 20th July 1939,

5   Dorset County Chronicle & Swanage Times. 7th September 1939.

6   Dorset Daily Echo. 28th October 1939.

7   Dorset County Chronicle and Swanage Times. 9th November 1939.

8   There were concerns about the state of attire of many Liverpool evacuees in North Wales. Many travelled with clothes which were unsuitable for the rugged countryside they found themselves in. The WVS organised a door to door collection and also make and mend groups to make sure that at least some of the children had suitable clothing. Wallis op cit. p130.

9   A similar report was made at a later date. 'The girls are still showing signs of the illness and they should not be billeted on a normal household'. As a consequence of this it was suggested in January 1941 that the London County Council should place the sisters in a suitable institution where they could receive both the necessary treatment and continue with their education.

10   Dorchester Rural District Council Minutes. 2nd April 1940.

11   Other members of the Committee were Miss A.C.Johnson. WVS. Mr H.Darlow. Town Clerk Bedford.Members of the Committee visited 17 counties in 4 regions over a period of 17 days.

12   Titmuss op. cit. p379.

13   See Appendix 17 for the rationale of the investigation and selected extracts from the report.

Conclusion

'You have no right to take part in this veterans' parade. You were not machined-gunned or bombed.' [1]

It is very difficult for anyone to get a totally balanced view of what happened during the Evacuations of 1939, 1940 and 1944 for five basic reasons. Together these reasons account for many of the unsubstantiated facts and myths of the period since 1945, and in some cases earlier, being perpetuated and the lack of new material appearing in modern school text books giving the true story.

Firstly, there is always the problem that the emotional factors inherent in this period of history will influence the objective and rational views of those people who lived through the experience. This is a serious issue and illustrated most poignantly by the late Enoch Powell in a speech he made to the Institute of Contemporary British History in July 1991 when he stated:-

> *'When I resigned my chair (Classics at the University of Sydney) in Australia in order to come home to enlist, had I been asked... 'What is the State whose uniform you wish to wear and in whose service you expect to perish?' I would have said 'The British Empire'....I also know that on my deathbed, I shall still be believing with one part of my brain that somewhere on every ocean of the world there is a great grey ship with three funnels and sixteen-inch guns which can blow out of the water any other navy which is likely to face it. I know it is not so. Indeed, I realised at a relatively early age that it is not so. But the factor, that emotional factor, will not die until I, the carrier of it, am dead'.[2]*

An additional factor in this emotional area is the jingoistic and biased reporting and writing which is still being published in modern reputable magazines with a wide circulation. For example, the following quote is not, as one might think, from a piece of immediate post-war propaganda, although one can be forgiven for thinking so. It was in fact written in the summer of 1994 by Roy Faiers as part of an article entitled 'This was their finest hour' for the magazine 'This England'. This is a good example of the unhistorical and biased accounting of the events of the British Home Front during World War Two written 55 years after the event, to which many of the public are still being subjected:-

> *'Rationing, blackouts, bombs, shortages of everything.....such a diet would soon have destroyed the spirit of the people in most countries, but to the surprise and niggling annoyance of the Nazi regime, little Britain kept its pecker up and kept hitting back. Instead of whining and bemoaning our lot, we whistled as we worked and kept our spirits up with a string of memorable songs, both humorous and sentimental. If anything, the only secret weapon we ever possessed was our crackpot sense of humour which saw the funny side of almost everything. It flourished everywhere....at the Front, at work, in the bus queue and even in the air-raid shelter. It became stronger under the most trying circumstances, and it was this as much as anything else which enabled us to 'keep on keeping on', and so led to the ultimate defeat of Hitler. Indeed, there are those who believe that the Germans lost the war because then, as now, they don't have much sense of the comic and ridiculous. They take themselves far too seriously'.*

Many of the people I have interviewed would totally disagree with the sentiment expressed in this article, but it is a fact that such expressions of patriotism do appeal to many of those who participated in the war. That such material can still reach the published page in 1994 is an indication that the editors of 'This England' knew that such sentiments would be readily acceptable to the magazine's readership.

It needs to be remembered that emotion and basic human nature were, and still are, a very powerful force and it was apparent throughout the war that both played a significant role in shaping the attitudes and prejudices of many people coping with the situations they faced on the Home Front. Many people in the 1940s based their prejudices and opinions purely on hearsay and rumour and it is partly as a result of this that the stereotypes have become part of the social history of the time and also of the present. But, can we justly accuse many of the hosts of having anti-evacuee feelings with a clear conscience? Are we a more tolerant nation now than our forebears in the 1940s? Can we honestly say that we would not react in the same way if our communities were invaded by hordes of children from the cities who, as we may have heard from the rumours going about, are ill-mannered, lice ridden and basically badly behaved? Such emotional responses were and still are, unquantifiable and we cannot answer the question until we find ourselves in a situation where our life style or status quo is seemingly threatened. As an indication of this the following examples are a demonstration of the fact that, despite the lapse of almost 60 years we have not really learned from the experience and mistakes made in the evacuation process. The basic instincts and suspicions of some people will always lead them to assume the worst of their fellow men, women and children and as a result some of the concerns and opinions expressed by the minority of people today regarding children from the cities, are exactly the same as those levelled at evacuees in 1939.

These three newspaper cuttings from the Henley Standard were written as dated and they concern the setting up of a rural study centre for the use of children from the East End of London in the closed down village school of Turville Heath. The argument has been going on for some years and the file of correspondence is large, many from people protesting about such children staying in the village.

> *'We feel strongly that the facilities offered by this small hamlet, with no shop or any other kind of distraction for the children are totally inadequate and will have a disastrous effect both on the village and on the groups of bored children to be lodged there'. 22nd May 1992*

> *'We are not against the children, but they are not going to be happy here with two-thirds of the population retired and not even a playground to use'. 29th May 1992*

> *'The plans have stirred up a hornet's nest in the village with some residents claiming that it will ruin the peace and quiet of the picturesque hamlet'. 12th July 1996*

If it was not for the dates, these same comments could have been made in August/September 1939. They have a distinct similarity to those concerns expressed by correspondents to the Windsor Times in 1940 and by the Welsh vicar who, in 1939, was upset by the 'spoilation of decent homes and furniture, the corruption of speech and the moral standards of the children'.[3]

If these anti-East End child, or just anti-child, prejudices are being debated today what hope have we in educating people to be more tolerant and learn from the lessons of the evacuation schemes. How can we accuse wartime hosts and evacuees of intolerance when there is evidence of it even today?

Secondly, the Evacuation scheme, planned in detail as late as 1938, was affected by the 'non-war' or 'keep it from the masses' lobbies. Even when planning was complete and the scheme implemented events contrived against its smooth running. As a significant example one only has to look at the expected and actual numbers of evacuees who arrived in Berkshire to realise that there was a breakdown in communications between central and local Government brought about by this need for secrecy. One can only have a certain amount of sympathy with billeting officers who, having thought the task of finding billets was over, were now given the task of housing vast numbers of extra bodies. Also having planned for one evacuation scheme the Government were confronted with the need to plan for three and it is interesting to note that the text books tend only to concentrate on the first of these. Little is ever said about the 'trickle' evacuation in 1940 and the evacuation brought about by the German use of the V1 and V2 rockets in 1944.

There was also the additional problem of the Official evacuation organised by the Government running parallel to Private evacuation where individuals and families took themselves into areas of safety and took over billets previously allocated to 'official' evacuees. Together these two separate and unrelated groups of people put a great deal of pressure onto the billeting authorities within the reception areas.

There are also two serious omissions from the majority of text books and those museums providing wartime 'experiences'. The first is the official (CORB) and unofficial Overseas evacuation which took place in 1939 and 1940. This is an extremely important area which is usually totally ignored by teachers, text books and most museums with the exception of the Imperial War Museum. Yet the children who were involved in this process were often affected more in sociological and psychological terms than their peers who were evacuated within the UK. The basic reason being that they left the country for an unknown period of time to live in a culture which to some extent must have seemed alien to them. Also having been sent out of the country for their formative years they returned, some not until 1947, to find themselves having to renew relationships with parents and siblings they no longer knew. It must be said that this was not a problem confined solely to those who went overseas, it was equally applicable to those who remained in Britain, and not only for those who had actually been evacuated. James Roffey recalls that his elder brother, who had not been evacuated, once said to him:-

> *'...when you came back from Sussex it was like having a stranger in the house, we didn't speak the same language and had little in common'.*

For James himself, he felt as if he was an outsider looking on:-

'...The family seemed to talk about things and people that I knew nothing about and they took little interest when I tried to talk abut Sussex'. [4]

The second omission is the return of the evacuees, both from areas in the UK and from abroad. According to text books and other media, evacuees were all sent away to various places of safety, but the details of their return is rarely dealt with. Little is ever said about this important stage of the proceedings. In fairness to teachers and authors, it is difficult to get information about this phase of evacuation as many school log books, newspapers and personal diaries written at the time do not mention it. One can only assume that teachers were too involved in planning their own return. Therefore one has to go to the Government documents in order to get the true picture. This is very time consuming and beyond the remit of many teachers, and presumably, from the evidence available, some text book authors as well. However, it is very important for people to realise that it was not easy to get all the evacuees back, basically because some of the teachers and billeting officers did not know where all their charges were and whether or not some of them had already returned home. It is also important for people to have some idea of the bureaucratic procedures involved in returning the evacuees and in some cases finding temporary accommodation for those who returned to damaged buildings.

Thirdly, the Government Evacuation Scheme involved many individuals who took on specific roles. This proliferation of roles was immense. Add to this the fact that they all had different experiences depending on where they were geographically located and one realises it is very difficult to find any semblance of a 'norm'. It is impossible to find a typical evacuee because their personal experiences would have been so different and this is very apparent when listening to the oral tapes and reading the written accounts. The other thing one needs to remember is that what was a 'good war' for one person would not necessarily have been so for another. It would have depended greatly on the individuals expectations and their previous lifestyles and, to some extent, it also depends on their experiences since. Many evacuees have stated that they have been affected by their war-time experiences much more since they retired from work. Many put this down to the simple fact of having more time to think about what happened to them as children.

We see too much written about the poor evacuees from the cities but the experience was just as difficult for those from middle-class backgrounds who were sent into the homes of the rural poor. With such a variety of individual experience to contend with, there is a tendency by authors and editors to take the simple anecdotal reporting as being typical, especially when these anecdotes are attributed to somebody famous or where the source is easily accessible. When these examples are used nothing is said about selective memory, personal interpretations of events or even personal choice about what one would, or would not have written down in letters and diaries, or what photographs were or were not taken. None of these concerns are ever taken into consideration and yet they should be. This is why there is rarely any in-depth reporting or analysis in text books about the trauma of evacuees in 'difficult' billets, the sexual and physical abuse of some evacuees and the problems of returning home.

Fourthly, there is a problem of accessing the evidence available for use by historians studying this period. Most textbook material takes a specific perspective and too often this is from an anti-evacuee stance which perpetuates the myths of the poor ill-kempt, misbehaved child from the inner cities, although there are exceptions. Why is this so? Basically the modern day texts rely heavily on previously published text books and it is obvious that little research has been done using the documentary evidence now available at the Public Record Office and the individual County Record Offices. This, as already stated, is primarily because the authors, editors and the teachers do not have time to do the research. A lot of school material is also based on selected oral evidence which only gives one side of the story, or can be edited to do so. In evacuation, one often only gets the 'good' side of the story or the host's opinion because few children at the time had the courage to complain about their billets and any problems they were having. Even if they did, how many people would have taken their complaints seriously as both billeting officers and their teachers were often seen as authoritarian figures? Some were actively encouraged not to complain. Many oral accounts from ex-evacuees suggest that as children they had been told by their parents not to question those in authority. It is significant perhaps that while many evacuees have described how they suffered both physical and sexual abuse, in my own extensive research I have come across only one item of primary written evidence which describes an evacuee being sexually abused and this is in the teacher's personal journal. He makes no mention of it whatsoever in the official school log book.

Fifthly, there is a problem with the nature of the evidence. Not only was there a reticence on the part of the evacuees to complain about their circumstance, official reports and material for public consumption were also affected by the situation and so propaganda became inevitable. Realistically, one could not see a film which told the true facts about Britain's situation, or that of the enemy in 1939 or immediately post-Dunkirk, simply because morale would have suffered. Also, as there was already a middle and upper class fear of the negative response of the working classes to the war situation, especially in the early years of the war, those in authority were unlikely to permit the telling of the true story. It is also apparent that knowledge of certain events which took place within only a few miles of each other could be very localised and one side of the town or city may not have been aware of precisely what had taken place on the other. Ironically, this imposed secrecy and censorship created misinformation and specific details became distorted and rumours were started. Even in the 1990s these myths and prejudices abound. At a wartime parade and reunion in Weymouth in July 1998 an ex-evacuee was persistently verbally attacked by a member of the Women's Land Army who stated that the evacuees had no right to march in the parade because they had not been bombed or machine-gunned.[5] That such ignorance from fellow veterans should still exist today may cause some concern. But should it come as a surprise? We know that there is a great deal of evidence to show that the wartime experience of many evacuees was just as traumatic as others affected by the war. Many were bombed and machine-gunned. The problem is that such evidence is not reaching the general public and what we often see today is a reiteration of some of this self-same propaganda and misinformation. Media programmes and schools broadcasts in the 1990s use extracts from wartime Ministry of Information, Ministry of

Health or Pathe News films which, by their very nature were propaganda because of the situation and time in which they were made. They really ought to carry a 'Health Warning'. Rarely is the suitability and reliability of these films and/or still press photographs ever questioned. If this is the only diet available to the member of the WLA it is no wonder that she has no idea about the real extent of the evacuees' involvement in the war.

The combination of these factors militate against the possibility of getting the true facts into the public domain. If research into Evacuation and related areas, however it is done and whoever it is done by, is not taken seriously or just simply ignored, then the bounds of historical knowledge and understanding in such a potentially contentious area are unlikely to be pushed back and the true facts of evacuation will not appear for a long time to come. The trauma of separation, insecurity, abuse in all its forms, suffered by evacuees is too important an area to be handled in a cursory manner and those in control of school text books and the media have a responsibility to put forward the real story. Although this is happening on a small scale there is still a long way to go.

Endnotes

1   Member of the Women's Land Army to ex-evacuee taking part in a World War 2 Veterans' parade in Weymouth. July. 1998

2   Enoch Powell from a speech to the Institute of British Contempoary Historians. July 1991

3   Crosby. op.cit. p35

4   James Roffey. <u>Big Boys Don't Cry</u>. unpub manuscript. p164.

5   Correspondent to 'The Evacuee'. August 1998.

Appendices and Bibliography

'My own personal memories of evacuation can be likened only to one small snowflake fluttering down to earth in an arctic blizzard....to land....melt....and be forgotten'.

Mary Nickerson (née Caw) evacuated to Wofferton, nr. Ludlow. 1939. Letter to author. 1997.

This book has been an attempt to make sure that these memories are not forgotten.

Appendix 1

End this Anomaly in Evacuee Payments

Sir, I want to call the attention of your wide awake paper to the plight of a class of children who are getting a raw deal in the evacuation scheme.

In the hundreds of community feeding centres which are springing up all over the country with up to 90% of Government grant, children who are evacuated with their parents are given free meals if they cannot afford to pay. These children also get free milk in schools on the same basis.

Why then the strange anomaly in Government orders which expressly excludes the child evacuated without a parent from free meals and free milk?

The unaccompanied child, often lonely and in many cases unwanted in its new home, is made inevitably more unpopular and unwelcome by bringing with it a Government allowance as low as 8s 6d, 10s 6d for a single child. Parents remain responsible for clothing this war waif, but everything else it needs is supposed to be found out of the 8s 6d per week. Moreover, the Government claims that 3s of this sum is a lodging allowance to put the child on a par with the accompanied child for whom 3s is drawn. We are thus left with the astonishing Government attitude that a child who is supposed to be fed on as little as 5s 6d per week must not receive free meals and school milk however poor it may be.

The Government order says it is assumed that the householder who takes in such a child can afford to provide it with midday meals and milk. Why? The assumption in many cases is false and the 8s 6d child is a burden to many homes.

The child's food, washing and wear and tear of bedding and furniture cannot be met out of such a mean allowance in these days.

And this is the child who must not get a free meal at the community centre although a child next door who may have a mother to see to its welfare can be fed for nothing if there is poverty.

Surely all the government evacuated children should be entitled to free midday meals at a time when it is declared policy to augment the rations of the poorer people by community feeding. At least if some of the poor are entitled to free food, all should be. Free meals and milk would bring that miserly 8s 6d to a more reasonable figure.

It is well known to billeting officers that evacuees tend to congregate in poor homes. Many well-to-do people are able to evade their obligations, others deliberately make the evacuees so uncomfortable that they leave. I can quote cases of both.

The evacuated child is therefore often in a home where it is difficult to make ends meet before he came. And such a child, with no one to stand up for him, is supposed to be fed on 5s 6d a week.

Frank Lloyd.
165 Russell Court. WC1 and 48, Spetisbury. Dorset.

Appendix 2

Evacuation Seen Through the Eyes of Two Teachers

It is unusual to find recent accounts from teachers who accompanied evacuees to the reception areas as many of them have long since passed away.

The following letter was sent to the author in April 1998 by two teachers, Win Lewis and Sylvia Elliott, drawing upon their own diary entries written in the 1930s and during the war. Extracts from the letter have been used at specific points within the text but if one examines the content of the entire letter, it provides eye-witness testimony which supports much of what has been stated in the book and demonstrates that although everybody's experience was an individual one there were definite similarities. It is interesting to note the way in which they were treated and the problems they had simply doing their job.

The text is copied verbatim:-

'We began our teaching careers on Monday 22nd August 1938 at Beacontree Infants School, Dagenham, under Ilford Education Authority. On September 26th (1938) there was a meeting for parents to explain the evacuation scheme which would be put into operation should war be declared. All staff were told to have rucksacks containing essentials, and gas-masks, at school in case of sudden evacuation. Rather an un-nerving start for us, but at least it showed that contingency plans were well advanced.

Chamberlain returned from Munich, war was averted and we were able to take our rucksacks home.

On August 25th 1939, all Ilford teaching staff were ordered to return from holiday and report for duty. On Saturday August 26th we went to hear the final plans for evacuation. Term began on Monday August 28th. Cards were issued to each child giving their name, date of birth and school number.

On Friday September 1st instructions were received. We were to escort the children to Goodmayes Station by 3.30pm. As always, the children rose to the occasion. Carrying their luggage and gas masks they walked about three-quarters of a mile across the park to Goodmayes Station. Although only 5-7 years old there were no tears, to them it was an adventure. The platform was packed with other parties assembling. After false alarms a train arrived for us, no luxury train....no toilets! The train stopped at Ipswich and some misguided person called out 'toilets'...half the train emptied...only to hear another call 'everybody on board'! Like lambs and used to obedience, they all climbed back on board.

Next stop Saxmundham. No welcoming reception! We all trailed up to the local school, carrying our luggage, where a zinc bath of water sat in the middle of the playground. There were two or three enamel mugs, but there was no great rush! By 7.30pm with the mosquitoes biting, the numbers for each village had been sorted and our party put on a bus to Aldeburgh. At the Jubilee Hall the children were sorted into family groups, and each child was given a carrier bag containing condensed milk, chocolate, corned beef etc., and off they went with their escorts. By then it was 10pm and the billeting officer realised there were no billets for the teachers. 'Send for the Town Crier', said someone, and off he went with his bell calling out 'Anyone take in a teacher?' The people responded and by 11.30am a kind lady took three of us into her home.

We had all been instructed to report to the Esplanade Hotel which was to be our meeting place. The children played on the beach and we organised games on the promenade.

The peace of Aldeburgh was soon shattered when on September 10th the 'Magdapur' was sunk just offshore. History in the making for the children. They saw 82 Lascars come ashore in the lifeboat covered in oil and clasping their gas masks.

As things settled down, the children got used to their billets and school time got organised.

More Infants teachers were needed in Leiston, so we were both 'lent' to the evacuees at Leiston which meant a change of billet. Hearing of this, the owner of the Esplanade Hotel offered us the use of his beautiful house at Aldringham, 5 acres of land and only two of us to use it. So began our love of Suffolk.

At Leiston school, for one session each day, we had the use of one small room which we and our evacuees shared with a Dagenham headmistress, nerve racking for us as young teachers. We had no apparatus, no guidance as to what to do or teach, but the children were lovely and oh boy, did they know their tables! We gradually acquired a small collection of reading books, paper pencils and crayons etc. No high-faluting syllabus, or structured curriculum, but the children learned to read and write and calculate with enjoyment, always happy and singing.

The rest of the school day we had to play in the park, or walk the children round the lanes and go to the woods.

Christmas came and went. We teachers had our holiday staggered.

As the winter weather worsened with six foot drifts of snow, it was impossible to take the children out walking, so we were allowed to use the Scout Hut. That was heated by a stove which belched out thick black smoke so that we could hardly see the children. We never did master the art of stoking.

As the children drifted back home, some teachers were recalled, so the age range of our group increased from 5 - 7 to 5 - 11 years old.

Added to the problems of school, we had our own personal problems. We had to walk to and from school, three miles each way through the snow. The mill that pumped water to our house froze and for six weeks we had to draw water from a well 200 yards away.

After the dreadful winter, spring arrived and it was a sheer delight. The children were able to walk in the woods among the primroses and violets ...it was a different world.

Too soon this happy state was to end. On May 10th the Germans walked into Belgium and Holland. On May 13th we were recalled from our Whitsun holiday as it had been decided that the East coast was not a safe place for evacuees. On Sunday June 2nd the local people waved us 'Goodbye' and off we went with our charges into the unknown. We left Leiston station at 10am. The children were marvellous as we travelled all day across England finally arriving at Stratford-upon-Avon station in the late afternoon. Some 'high-ups' were there to meet us. The leaders of the various school parties tried to keep their groups intact, but when stressing the point they were told that 'beggars can't be choosers'. What a welcome! Tired and hungry the children got into a coach to take us to Earlswood, between Birmingham and Coventry. Our driver didn't know the locality, and we were roaming the leafy lanes of Warwickshire for some considerable time. However, all things come to an end, and when all the children were settled we reached our billet at 10.30 p.m...rather a long day. No families were split.

June 3rd 1940: School began.

Our evacuees joined the classes of the local Infant and Junior School and we teachers had to teach 5 - 11 year olds. As the school and the church were two miles from any habitation, all the children took sandwiches for dinner, and the staff took it in turns to boil the kettle on the open fire and make hot drinks for them.

After two weeks our hosts had to provide accommodation for their own family who wanted to get away from Birmingham. The Billeting Officer sent us to Moat Farm. It was truly moated, and also truly smelly! No running water! When we arrived with our luggage we found that our new hosts had given us their bedroom while they slept on the landing outside our door. They were not early risers, so for the next week each morning we could hear the school bell ringing, see the children going down the road, but we were still trapped in our bedroom! A very difficult situation, so back we went to the Billeting Officer. He sent us to a big house where we were paraded round the garden whilst the Lord of the Manor viewed us from a window to see if we were fit to stay in the servants' quarters. We said 'No thank you', and went back to the billeting officer.

This time we were sent to a two bedroom bungalow where we were made very welcome. We had a bedroom and a lounge and use of the kitchen. Just when things seemed to be settling down we went home for the weekend, and came back to find an invasion....Birmingham had been blitzed, and our hosts had taken in a whole family, Mother, Father, two married daughters, and their children. Our bed had been moved into the lounge and lined up beside the grand piano, but we coped.

Once again as more children went home, teachers were re-allocated and one of us had to go to Hockley Heath School. That took children up to the age of fourteen. So with no experience of teaching fourteen year olds it was a case of being thrown in at the deep end. It also meant a four mile cycle ride to school. Life went on fairly normally, with blitzes on Birmingham and Coventry.

The summer came and went and so did autumn, and by Christmas, we were both back at Ilford, searching for accommodation.

Devils for punishment, in June 1944 when the doodlebug raids began and the trickle evacuation scheme was organised, off we went again with our rucksacks. We reported to the Town Hall, and were allocated a group of children. One of us landed in North Wales, the other in Brighouse. As this was only escort duty, having settled our evacuees we both arrived back home the next day within half an hour of one another.

Although there has been much criticism of the evacuation we still feel it was a job well done and the organisation required to move so many children on one day was a Herculean task. Had air raids started straight away many children would have been saved because of the careful planning in advance.

As Evacuated teachers our experience was widened and we became more confident and more self-reliant. We didn't need counselling in those days despite our worries about families back home in London. Suffolk had cast its spell on us. We came back when we retired and have been here twenty years...still devotees of the Suffolk countryside and loving it.'

Sylvia Elliott and Win Lewis.

Appendix 3

Text of Princess Elizabeth and Princess Margaret's Broadcast to Evacuees. BBC Radio, 13th October, 1940.

'In wishing you all 'Good evening' I feel that I am speaking to friends and companions who have shared with my sister and myself many a happy Children's Hour.

Thousands of you in this country have had to leave your homes and be separated from your fathers and mothers. My sister, Margaret Rose, and I feel so much for you, as we know from experience what it means to be away from those we love most of all. To you, living in new surroundings, we send a message of true sympathy, and at the same time we would like to thank the kind people who have welcomed you to their homes in the country.

All of us children who are still at home think continually of our friends and relations who have gone overseas, who have travelled thousands of miles to find a wartime home and a kindly welcome in Canada, Australia, New Zealand, South Africa and the United States of America.

My sister and I feel we know quite a lot about these countries. Our father and mother have so often talked to us of their visits to different parts of the world. So it is not difficult for us to picture the sort of life you are all leading, and to think of all the new sights you must be seeing and the adventures you must be having.

But I am sure that you too are often thinking about the Old Country. I know you won't forget us; it is just because we are not forgetting you that I want, on behalf of all the children at home, to send you our love and best wishes, to you and to your kind hosts as well.

Before I finish, I can truthfully say to you all that we children at home are full of cheerfulness and courage. We are trying to do all we can to help our gallant sailors, soldiers and air-men and we are trying too, to bear our own share of the danger and sadness of war. We know, everyone of us, that in the end all will be well; for God will care for us and give us victory and peace. And when peace comes, remember it will be for us, the children of today, to make the world of tomorrow a better and happier place.

My sister is here by my side and we are both going to say goodnight to you.

Come on Margaret.

Goodnight

Goodnight to you all.'

Appendix 4

Mr Walter Elliott's Broadcast on the 6th January 1939. 'Transfer of Population in Time of War'

There are many big tasks we want to forward in the coming year. We want to press on with housing, with health, to make sure that in the schools, in the homes, in the factories, in the shops, in the countryside, the possibilities which our times open out, for a happier life for all, are secured. But there are possibilities of emergency ahead, as well as possibilities of peace.

One of the biggest problems is, undoubtedly, what is called evacuation, that is to say many people would leave, many people ought to leave, crowded or dangerous areas in time of war. Who are they to be? Where are they to go?

Well, first, I do not want you to think that the policy is to *empty* our big cities. Nothing of the sort. Most people will and should stay where they are, carrying on with their ordinary duties; for most of us, in fact, are engaged on work of real service to our country. There will, however, be many who should go to places where they will be relatively safer.

Of these, children must come first. There are many children in Great Britain, eight million of them. Many of them, of course, are in places of relative safety. But there are a million of these children in London alone. Without doubt there would be, in time of trouble, and even when trouble was feared, a widespread rush to get children away from dangerous areas. Unless that is organised beforehand there will not only be widespread distress amongst the families in exposed areas, there will be enormous disorganisation in areas into which people might flock. Take shops in these areas, for instance. they would be sold out of supplies in twenty-four hours if nothing was done.

To organise this, it is clear that we have to look for homes for the children mainly in houses where people already *are*. Empty houses and camps will be used as far as possible; but the mere numbers make it impossible to rely on these alone. We cannot always rely on summer weather. We may have wintry weather like tonight. In the recent storms many camps where children *were*, had to be cleared into surrounding houses.

What will the method be? Schools will be moved as units, with their teachers who will continue with their education. These school children will need both board and lodging. But when children have their mother or some one else to look after them the householder will be asked to provide lodging only. But it is not only the householder; we have all got a part to play.

The Local Authorities will arrange for reception.

The Government will provide transport, will put money in the householder's purse, and will see that there is food in the shops, at reasonable prices, for that purse to buy. *Detailed* arrangements for these matters are well advanced.

I know that money does not settle everything. So the Government and the Local Authorities are doing their best to make allowances for the thousand and one individual differences. We have to see not only that the houses for instance are suitable for the children, but that the children are suitable for the homes. We want this to be a matter of real human relationship and affection, a willing host and a willing guest. The whole nation will have to feel itself as one if such a crisis really comes. And remember, no one can say 'My house will never be destroyed'. It may be for any of us to ask, as well as to give, this national hospitality.

Is anything going to be done about it immediately?

Yes. That is why I am talking to you tonight. Amongst other things, Mr. Colville and I are asking the Local Authorities in England, Scotland and Wales to make a survey of housing accommodation by the end of next month.

What do we want to know? We want information about the number of rooms and the people already in the house. We want to estimate how many people could be properly accommodated, for we don't want either the guests or the hosts to be overcrowded. We also want to know about existing responsibilities of the household, whether, for example, the householder is aged or infirm, or out all day, or perhaps himself or herself expecting relatives. Whether a farmer, for instance, needs his spare rooms for extra workers; whether the householder needs extra bedding.

Obviously the more information we can get the better it will be for everybody.

So householders will shortly be visited and asked for this information. It will be confidential, collected for this emergency purpose alone, and will be used for no other purpose. I hope therefore, that every householder, whatever his or her personal circumstances, will give all possible help to the visitors.

Finally, this work differs from most of our work, the real tasks of which I spoke to you when I began. Here our great hope and prayer about this is that it may never be needed at all. But the foundations of our work must be sound if our life is to be happy; and one of the foundation stones of any nation is that it has thought of danger, faced danger, and decided on action so that in danger it may be secure.

Appendix 5

This is an example of a Detraining Schedule. These were sent to the reception areas before the war. This one deals with the movement of evacuees from London to Buckinghamshire. The figures in the second column under each of the headings are the amended numbers to be moved by train updated to 20th June 1939. Note the vast disparities in numbers expected and numbers received in some areas.

Detraining Stations	Total Capacity for Reception	Districts Allocated	Districts Served
BUCKINGHAMSHIRE L.N.E.R.			
Aylesbury 4,400 Metro or L.N.E.R	10,000	1,600	Aylesbury Borough
Amersham 7,400/6,000 Metro or L.N.E.R	10,400	6,000	Amersham R.D Chesham R.D.
High Wycombe 7,000/6,600 G.W.R or L.N.E.R	7,000	6,600	Chepping Wycombe
Beaconsfield 1,600/1,200 G.W.R or L.N.E.R	1,600	1,200	Beaconsfield U.D
Princes Risborough 6,000/4,800 G.W.R & L.N.E.R	6,000	4,800	Wycombe R.D
Total	**35,000**	**22,800**	
BUCKINGHAMSHIRE G.W.R.			
Slough G.W.R 5,000/3000	5,000	3,000	Slough Borough
Windsor & Eton	8,800		Eton U.D, 800 Eton R.D, 8,000
Maidenhead Berks. G.W.R	1,600		Marlow, 1,600
Total	**15,400**	**13,600**	
BUCKINGHAMSHIRE L.M.S.			
Bletchley L.M.S 2,000/2,466	4,500	1,096 1,370	Bletchley U.D Winslow R.D, 2,500
Wolverton L.M.S	9,200	3,895 950 2,385	Wolverton U.D, 5,000 Newport Pagnell U.D, 1,200 Newport Pagnell R.D, 3,000
Total		**7,230**	
Leighton Buzzard	2,200	600	Linslade U.D, 600
L.M.S (Beds.) Excluding Nos. For Beds, 1,600/1,460		1,460	Wing R.D
Total	**15,900**	**11,756**	
NORTHAMPTONSHIRE L.N.E.R.			
Brackley. L.N.E.R 1,000/580	2,800	580 1,100	Buckingham Borough Buckingham R.D, 1,600/1,000
GRAND TOTAL	**69,100**	**49,836**	

(Source. Bucks Record Office. AR 177/81, no.356.)

Appendix 6

The following notice was printed in all London newspapers during August 1939:-

EVACUATION

A message to all Londoners concerned from Herbert Morrison M.P.

His Majesty's Government has now decided on the evacuation of the priority classes from London and the other areas regarded as vulnerable in case of air raids. In this great task of organisation the London County Council has played, and will continue to play, its full part. We all hope that sanity will prevail, that war will not come. Precautions are however, necessary. We must be prepared.

Now a word of appeal and advice to those concerned:-

To the Children.

With your teachers and friendly helpers you are going to the country, where the Government considers you will be safer than in London if war should come. London children are cheerful. I want you to be cheerful and friendly on your journey and when you get to the other end. It is a big task to move you all; so please do all you can to help make things run smoothly. Above all, be kind to each other. Help each other in any little difficulties that may arise.

To the Parents.

I know you will have your anxieties at this trying time. I understand your feeling. You will be cheered, however, by the knowledge that it is better for the children to be out of London as things are. More-over you are, I know, assured that the great organisation of the London County Councils' teaching staff will do all that is humanly possible to make the journey a success. Please help your children to go away in a cheerful mood. See that they bring with them all that their teachers asked them to bring and no more.

Arrangements at the other end are in the hands of other authorities. We are grateful to them for their work and we know they will have done all they can to ensure success.

About Difficulties and Snags.

However good the organisation some difficulties and snags are bound to arise. If and when they do I beg you all to take them as easily as you can. Don't get 'nervy', above all don't get on the nerves of those who are organising the evacuation. Take your troubles as lightly and cheerfully as you can. Remember, there are others, actively engaged in the service of our country, whose troubles may be much graver. As many of your fathers used to sing 'Pack up your troubles in your old kit bag and smile, smile, smile'. To all the evacuated and to those going with them...Good Luck. And a safe return to dear old London.

Herbert Morrison.
County Hall. London.

Appendix 7

Letter to All Householders in Shaftesbury, Dorset Relating to Government Survey. January 1939

Shaftesbury Rural District Council.

16th January 1939.

Dear Sir or Madam

GOVERNMENT EVACUATION SCHEME

The Council have been requested by the Government to co-operate in plans which are being made for the protection of civil life in the event of war.

Recent experience in other countries has shown that under the conditions of modern warfare the greatest loss of life is caused by bombardment from the air. This danger is most acute in crowded cities. It is to lessen this danger in case our own country were involved in war, that arrangements are being made now to enable children to leave the crowded cities and be received in homes elsewhere. This protection can only be given with the co-operation of those like ourselves who live in the less congested towns or villages. We shall all agree that it is necessary for all of us to help in this plan for saving human life.

We are aware that some arrangements were made last September as a matter of emergency which had perforce to be improvised, but we are sure that, in the light of the experience gained, we shall be able to improve on these. The plans for this, as for other branches of civil defence, must be made in time of peace. We hope that it will never be necessary to put them into operation, but we shall all be all the happier to know that the plans have been made and that if ever they do have to be put into operation, the work will be done in an ordered manner, and that all will know their parts.

The Government has asked each local authority in the country to find out what housing accommodation would be available in case of emergency, and what homes would be suitable for those children who would be given the means of leaving the great cities. It is particularly important to know in which houses homes could be provided for the children, where they could be lodged, boarded and cared for. Payment would be made by the Government at the following rate:-

For Unaccompanied School children lodged and boarded:

10s 6d per week where one child is taken.
8s 6d per week per child where more than one child is taken.

For Children under School age accompanied by their mothers, or some other person who will be responsible for looking after them:

For lodging only:

5s per week for each adult.
3s per week per child

For lodging for a Teacher or Helper only:

5s per week.

School children would be moved school by school, accompanied by their teachers, and arrangements would be made for the children to attend school in the districts to which they were taken.

A visitor, representing the local authority, will call upon you in the near future to find out how far you will be able to assist in this matter, and will produce to you a card showing that he or she is authorised to make these inquiries.

This note is sent to you now in order that you may be aware, in advance, of this enquiry, and why it is being made.

We give you an assurance that the information supplied by you will not be used for any other purpose than that which we have described, and that it will not involve you in any work or responsibility unless and until an emergency arises. We feel that we can rely on the people of the district to offer all the help they possibly can in this important branch of civil defence. It needs no words of ours to convey to you what that help will mean to children of the big cities.

Yours faithfully.

F.S.Miller.JP. Chairman of the Council

C.E.G.Vesey. Lt-Col. Chairman of the A.R.P. Committee.

Appendix 8

The following data relating to the welfare of evacuee children can be found in a report of June 1940. (PRO.ED 50/206. Cited in J. Macnicol. Evacuation of Schoolchildren.)

a. Out of 4 schools in the Shepherd's Bush area of London sending 670 pupils to Pontypridd, there were only one or two with nits.

b. Out of 300 children from Northwold Rd. Public Elementary School, in the East End in June 1940, only 8% were considered to be in need of special attention. 1 child had scabies, 5 had nits, 8 suffered with enuresis and 11 with other conditions.

c. Of 1, 211 children from the Stretford Schools in Manchester only 80 suffered from 'vermin or nits' and 14 from enuresis.

Appendix 9

Transcript of the broadcast made by Hauptmann Stuhman relating to the attack on Sandhurst Rd. School. 20th January 1943:-

"We have recently been harassing the English quite a lot on their southern coast. The low-level attack on London in daylight will probably remain for all our airmen an experience which they will remember for a long time. We reached our objectives and dropped our bombs where they were to be dropped. The British flak was active but bad, and the Spitfires which were in the air took no notice of us. While flying away we saw the barrage balloons slowly going up and used the moment to make a diving attack on them.

Interviewer: 'I understand you also attacked industrial buildings with machine-gun fire?'

Stuhman: 'Quite right. We shot, in London, two gas reservoirs into flames and at a railway station an engine was under fire. We also attacked some other things as well".

After the Battle. Vol 3 p214.

(Hauptmann Stuhman was later shot down near Charleroi in August 1943)

For a detailed account of the raid and its aftermath see 'After the Battle'. Vol 3 pp 204 - 214.

Appendix 10

Evacuees Remaining in Reception Areas in January 1940

	From Evac areas in England		From Evac areas in Scotland			
	Number Remaining	%	Number Remaining	%	Total Remaining	%
Unaccompanied Children	420,000	55	37,600	61	457,600	55
Mothers & Accompanied Children	56,000	13	8,900	9	64,900	12
Expectant Mothers	1,100	9	40	10	1,140	9
Blind Persons, Cripples & Special Cases	2,280	43	160	9	2,440	35
Teachers & Helpers	43,400	49	3,100	23	46,500	45
Total	522,780	40	49,800	28	572,580	39

Source. Problems of Social Policy. HMSO 1950 p172

Appendix 11

Return of Evacuees: Timetable.

Day	Adults & Accompanying Children	Unaccompanied Children
0	(2nd May 1945) Date of Circular informing local authorities that the return plans are to be operated.	
3	Complete delivery of notices	—
6	—	Complete delivery of notices to householders
10	Complete cards	—
11	Send completed cards to SRO	—
18	—	Complete cards
19	—	Send completed cards to SRO
20	Cards received back from SRO	—
22	SRO give first notice of trains	—
25	Complete delivery of notices	—
29	First trains run	—
35	—	Cards received back from SRO.
37	—	SRO gives notices of first trains
40	—	Complete delivery of notices
44	—	First trains run

Source: Devon Record Office. Exeter Box 5.

Appendix 12

Women's Organisations which became directly concerned with social poverty during the latter stages of the war and afterwards. This list does not include the Women's Institute and the Women's Voluntary Service which are mentioned in the text.

National Council of Women
13,000 'Educated' women. They spent a great deal of their time planning for post-war Britain.

National Union of Townswomen's Guild
This comprised of 554 branches containing between 10 and 20 members.

Soroptimist Clubs
3,500 professional women.

Women's Mutual Service Club
12,000 working class women.

Source: Holman. Pp142-3

Appendix 13

A précis of the recommendations for the development of education provision made by the Barnett House Study Group in the light of their research into a group of Evacuee children billeted in war-time Oxford.

1. Extension of the scope of education. Provision should be extended to include:-

   '...a lively environment in which, by pursuit of a variety of interests and activities, both boys and girls alike may bring to fruition the character and capacities with which they are severally endowed.'

2. Extension of Day-school activities: The scope of non-academic education in day schools should be extended.

3. Provision of Rooms for Private Reading and Study: They suggested that if children are to have a fair chance of developing their individual 'gifts and abilities' they must be provided with the opportunity for private study. As many pupils do not have access to this provision at home the school should provide it.

4. Residential Country terms for Urban Schools: Evacuation had created a greater awareness of life in the country and as an extension of this it was suggested that schools maintain a 'country department' which would be a residential facility where town children could spend at least three terms and provide the opportunity of studying all aspects of rural life.

Finally it was thought, surprisingly, that there should be more facilities for boarding education: 35 from 185 of London parents questioned by the group were in favour of some form of boarding provision. Although they did suggest that the sample was too small to reach any significant conclusion.

Source. Barnett House Study Group. A Study of War-time Oxford. OUP. Pp110-113

Appendix 14

In order to put the effect on a small school of a migrant evacuee population into perspective it is worth listing the schools where evacuees came from to join the two-roomed village school at Ashley Green in Buckinghamshire, the subject of the film 'Village School'. The information is taken from the school registers 1939 - 45 found in the Bucks. Record Office in Aylesbury.

Not all the pupils remained for a long time, in fact some only stayed for a few days and there is no indication as to which evacuees were privately evacuated or those which were sent under the Government Scheme.

1939
St. Thomas More's Roman Catholic School, London.
Crayford Council School, Kent.
St. Sepulchres, London EC1.
Central Street School, London EC1.

1940
Mile End Senior, London.
Mile End Central, London.
St. Lawrence School, Ramsgate.
Ellington Rd. School, Ramsgate.
All Souls School, London NW6.
Scarthoe School, Grimsby.
Methodist School, Canterbury.
Mount Pleasant School, London E5.
Detmold Rd School, London E5.
Downspark Grocers School.
Sigdon Road School.
North Hackney Central.
Wilberforce School, Paddington.
Coventry Road School, Nottingham.

1941
Ennersdale School, Lewisham.
Greenham School, Uxbridge.
Tottenham Road School, London N1.
Totworth School, Bristol.

1944
Culver School, Tottenham.
Headstone School, Pinner.
St. Joseph's Convent School, Sidcup.
Downhills School, London N15.
Haberdashers School, West Acton.
Chesterfield Road School, Enfield.
Chater School, Watford.

Appendix 15

School Attendance Statistics: December 1940-December 1941

(Average attendance pre-war. 87%)

Year/Month	Estimated No of Children of School Age in London	Number on Roll	Number on Half-time	% of Attendance
1st Nov 1939	70,000	—	—	—
31st Dec 1939	192,000	—	—	—
May 1940	240,000	—	—	—
July 1940	181,000	—	—	—
December 1940	80,400	44,400	—	—
January 1941	81,200	56,600	—	—
February 1941	89,200	75,125	2,246	—
March 1941	95,200	86,662	6,070	—
April 1941	103,300	94,445	7,228	—
May 1941	104,400	93,282	6,802	—
June 1941	105,500	98,470	4,070	—
July 1941	112,700	109,983	2,954	82.7
August 1941	120,400	117,355	2,212	76.6*
September 1941	128,500	125,145	2,546	79.9*
October 1941	135,800	132,858	1,866	83.5*
November 1941	141,100	138,793	1,192	83.1
December 1941	149,934	148,430	695	82.8

* These figures were affected by the number of children hop-picking in Kent.

School Attendance Statistics: 1942-1945

Year/Month	Number Of Schools	Estimated No. of Children of School Age in London	Number on Roll (4)	Under 5s on Roll	Number on Half-time	% of Attendance
March 1942	579	178,200	175,974	2,703	1,645	84.1
June 1942	630	202,800	200,915	4,315	1,741	85.1
September 1942	657	213,700	211,613	5,462	1,081	78.8
December 1942	674	222,500	220,887	5,523	454	82.8
June 1943	724	235,400	234,354	6,369	348	85.3
December 1943	741	243,100	241,419	8,858	39	77.9
February 1944*	—	245,000	—	—	—	—
June 1944	705	237,200	235,670	8,673	788	32.0
September 1944	661	128,994	127,273	4,116	174	79.8
October 1944*	—	136,500	—	—	—	—
December 1944*	668	173,178	172,418	5,227	347	84.7
March 1945	692	191,960	190,445	5,820	nil	82.1
May 1945*	—	213,500	—	—	—	—

* taken from statistics showing only estimated number of children of school age in London.

Source: Samways op.cit. p34.

Appendix 16

Letter from Clerk of the Bradford-on-Avon RDC,15th February 1941, Concerning Billeting of Expectant Evacuees.

Dear Dr. Tangye,

Government Evacuation Scheme.

I confirm my conversation with you on the telephone this morning, with regard to the difficulty which has unfortunately arisen in connection with the Billeting of Expectant Mothers.

The position is that my Billeting Officer found that one of the Expectant Mothers received in this district yesterday appeared, to use his own words, to be 'a lady of a very superior type', and he felt, in order to conscientiously carry out his duty, she should be billeted in a superior type of billet. He therefore billeted her in a fairly large house containing seven rooms, of which, he tells me, four are bedrooms. The Occupier was not at home, but the servant employed there informed the Billeting Officer that not more than three persons would be sleeping there that night, although friends were expected sometime. The Billeting Notice was duly served, and the Expectant Mother billeted, and I have been informed this morning that the Occupier last evening conveyed the Evacuee in her own car to Berryfield House, informed the Matron that the latter could not stay in the House, and she was, therefore, admitted to the Maternity Home, where she is now accommodated. My information with regard to this came from the Maternity Home, and I have had no communication whatsoever from the Occupier concerned, who still retains the Billeting Notice, so far as I am aware.

As you know, upon the facts shown above there would appear to have been an infringement of Defence Regulations on the part of the Occupier by reason of failure to comply with a Billeting Notice, but, apart from this, if the Occupier of a better-class type of house can be so easily relieved of the obligation to provide accommodation as required by a Billeting Notice, what will be the position of Occupiers of smaller houses who do not desire Evacuees and who may do the same thing? It seems to me that the present difficulties with regard to billeting will be increased, and that it will only be possible to Billet upon people who are willing to carry out their obligations, which will mean that certain sections of the community will be imposed upon, and that the authority of the Billeting Officers will count for nothing.

Unfortunately, there has been difficulty before in connection with Billeting Expectant Mothers upon this Occupier. Two expectant mothers were billeted at this house in January, and the next morning the lady who resides at this address called at this Office and to say the least, was far from courteous in her protest, that she should not be expected to co-operate in connection with the operation of the evacuation scheme. A few days later, this lady again called and stated that she had informed the Evacuees that they must leave the house each morning and stay out until the evening, and she was informed that, in my view, this arrangement was contrary to the requirements of the Billeting Notice. The evacuees later called to say that they had been forced to leave the house that morning at short notice, and without being given an opportunity to wash.

I gather that the Occupier contends that no notice was given of the intention to Billet, but, as you are aware, there is no legal necessity to give any notice, and in many cases it is not always practicable to do so. On many occasions I have arranged billets for expectant mothers, given notice of their time of arrival to the occupiers concerned, then at the last moment have found that the persons have not arrived. The results have been that the Occupiers to whom the notice has been given have been very resentful at being put to unnecessary trouble. In other cases Occupiers have deliberately left their homes and remained away during the period of Billeting, in an attempt to avoid having to provide accommodation. It is, therefore, difficult to know what to do for the best, and whatever is done does not meet with the wishes or views of everybody.

At the time of the complaint with regard to the billeting of the two expectant mothers in January, I gathered that one grievance was that certain large houses in the Parish of Westwood were not being used for the provision of accommodation for evacuees, but, as I pointed out, that was a matter for the Rural District Council.

I am sorry to trouble you with this matter, but I do feel that something should be done to prevent a repetition of action such as has now occurred, as, after all, the Occupier has a right of appeal to the Billeting Tribunal if she feels aggrieved, and if the matter is dealt with through the regular channels, no objection can be raised by anybody. On the hand, if the practice is allowed to continue, there is bound to be trouble as Billeting will be practically impossible, except in those cases where the co-operation of the Occupier can be secured. Any help or advice which you can, therefore, kindly give to me in connection with the settling of this unfortunate matter, will be very much appreciated.

Yours truly.

Robert Trace.

Appendix 17

Selected Extracts from the Report on Conditions in the Reception Areas - 14th March 1941.

THE NATURE OF THE PROBLEM.

5. In seeking to estimate the measure of success of this experiment it must frankly be admitted at the outset that evacuation on this large scale is neither a natural nor a popular process. In a country like ours, predominantly industrial, a wide gulf is fixed between the sentiments, habits and outlook of town and country. The London woman is gregarious. The busy multitudes, the crowded streets and shops, the cinemas and similar diversions for the background of her life. She is not overburdened by domesticity. She has a partiality for tinned foods and readily resorts to the fish and chip shop.

6. The life of the sister in the country parish or provincial town is more often centred in her home. She is more house proud and a better cook. Outside her home the social activities of the Churches and the Women's Institute occupy her leisure hours. The outlook of the London mother is hard for her to understand and she does not make allowance for habits so often due to bad housing conditions. These are broad generalisations to which there are many exceptions, especially in the larger towns, but we believe that many of the causes of friction in the scheme of evacuation are traceable to these differences of habit and outlook.

7. It cannot be expected that the invasion of the home of the housewife in the reception areas by the London mother will be achieved without friction. Even if friction be avoided, it is not a desirable process that the family life in London should be disrupted, that wives should be separated from their husbands or children from their parents. We desire to emphasise these fundamental facts which are sometimes forgotten. Furthermore, the evacuated mother so often arrives in a state of mental distress. She, too has her pride. For weeks she has borne the brunt of the night bombing with unconquerable spirit and under conditions that might well have impaired the strongest nerves. She feels the strangeness of her new surroundings. She is full of anxiety for her husband and her home. Time hangs heavily on her hands. If then an unfriendly atmosphere is suspected the urge to return becomes overwhelming. Evacuation on this large scale has no intrinsic merit; it can only be the lesser of the two evils, and justified by the necessity for the dispersal of population in wartime.

SUCCESS OF EXPERIMENT.

8. For all these reasons this great migration should have been doomed to failure. We were surprised to find that in the great majority of cases it is succeeding. The tremendous efforts made by the local authorities, by devoted members of the voluntary organisations and by the warm-hearted householders themselves, cannot be adequately realised without a personal visit to the reception areas. In many districts it has even become a matter of local pride to retain evacuees and it is

considered a reflection on the hospitality offered in the district if they return. The standard of achievement is not everywhere uniform and much still remains to be done, but by and large great progress is being made. The hard lessons learnt in the 1939 evacuation have not been forgotten. Nor is it generally realised what careful prevision has been shown by the Ministry of Health, both centrally and in the Regions, to ensure that all necessary powers are made available.

9. Broadly speaking, it can be stated that the most careful study of problems likely to arise has been continuously made and the procedure has been modified in the light of experience. The suggestions we make, therefore, are not of an iconoclastic or revolutionary nature but rather tend to emphasise certain features essential to the continued success of the scheme, so that the public conscience may be quickened and action taken immediately for the provision of further welfare arrangements and for the overhauling of machinery where this has proved deficient.

12. The work done by hostesses in looking after unaccompanied children is worthy of the highest praise and more recognition should be given to it. Very often the hostess is unable to join one of the uniformed or more spectacular war services because she is looking after children in her home.

RECEPTION OF MOTHERS AND CHILDREN

13. It is in the reception of mothers with their children that problems mainly arise. We heard many accounts of unjustifiable behaviour by London women. When traced to their source, most of these related to the earlier evacuation in September 1939, when the process was a novelty and less adequate arrangements had been made for their reception and welfare. But experience has now been gained. The sufferings of evacuees have created widespread feelings of sympathy and good will from housewives in the reception areas, which has evoked a better response in the conduct of London mothers themselves. Host and guest are making an effort to understand each other's point of view and there is a noticeable spirit of give and take. Where this is not forthcoming it is due perhaps in part to the too rosy picture of country life painted by canvassers in London in their efforts to induce mothers to leave their homes. Their disappointment on arrival leads to bad feeling and a display of ingratitude which is resented. But these we believe are now exceptional cases. It is abundantly clear from our investigations that where there is an atmosphere of friendliness and adequate welfare arrangements are made, London women are full of gratitude and are settling down with resignation but not with enthusiasm in their new surroundings.

Appendix 18

The Welsh Nationalist. February 1939. Memorandum on the Wartime Evacuation Policy of the Government.

The Welsh National Party Executive address the following criticisms and objections to the Government Department concerned with emergency plans for war time.

1. We affirm that Wales is a nation, separate in its language, habits and social tradition from England.

2. The Government evacuation plans completely and unjustifiably ignore this fundamental fact; the plans as published and the letter sent out to all Welsh householders propose to submerge all Welsh social traditions and the rural life of Welsh speaking Wales in the interest of only one nation, the English, and of merely English national security and military efficiency.

3. To treat Wales merely as an English reception area to the evident endangerment of all Welsh social tradition and social unity, is to show towards Wales a spirit of militaristic totalitarianism contrary to all principles of democracy and to the rights of small nations. The future of the Welsh child has as much right to protection as that of the English child and that entails the protection of his traditions and environment.

4. We hold that the emergency plans for war time evacuation ought to prepare for the internal re-arrangements of the population of England and Wales with full regard for the security and continuity of both nations, and for the survival of their separate traditions. We hold that this can be done without danger to the English civilian population and without destroying the separate nationhood of Wales.

5. We protest against the classification of the South Wales seaport towns and dense industrial districts as 'neutral areas'. The increased industrial activities there will make them important military objectives in case of war. We hold they should be classified as evacuation areas with first right to reception in the contiguous Welsh rural districts.

6. We suggest that responsible Government departments should forthwith get in touch with the large Welsh communities in all English evacuated areas; London and the South, Birmingham and the Midlands, Manchester and Liverpool and the Yorkshire towns. These Welsh communities are well organised in churches and are in touch with each other and have experience in organisation. They should arrange for these Welsh children to be moved in Sunday School units to Welsh speaking reception areas in Wales and should have first claim there.

7. We propose that Welsh reception areas should be classified for any further reception purposes than those named in Paras. 5 and 6 above into two divisions, namely (a) 70% Welsh speaking areas and (b) areas less than 70% Welsh speaking and that monoglot English school populations shall not be drafted into division (a) under any circumstances since to do so will destroy the continuity of Welsh Education, of Welsh religious life and Welsh rural and social traditions. It will overwhelm the religious organisation of Welsh rural life as well as its linguistic and cultural tradition.

8. Finally, in as much as all these evacuation plans are part and parcel of military preparation for the bombardment of civilians in congested areas of enemy countries, we urge that it is the Government's bounden duty to initiate international discussions for the confiscation of the bombing aeroplane as an instrument of war.

Signed. Saunders Lewis.

(Source. G.Wallis. A case study of Reception Area under the Government Evacuation Scheme 1939-45. unpub.thesis. 1979. Appendix 3)

Appendix 19

Timeline

1930

National and Local Government discussions regarding the general principle of evacuating specific groups of the civilian population to alleviate the expected chaos and possible panic caused by enemy bombing.

May 1938

The London County Council approved, in principle, of the evacuation of all schoolchildren within its jurisdiction in time of war.

July 1938

After detailed discussions the Anderson Committee reported that:
● Evacuation would not be compulsory.
● Billeting would be compulsory.
● Teachers would be responsible for supervising the movement of school-children into reception areas.
● Central Government would be responsible for all costs.
The Anderson Committee met a total of 25 times during which they called 57 witnesses and other representatives from 26 Government departments and private organisations.[1]

September 1938

During the Munich Crisis, the London County Council, in co-operation with neighbouring authorities evacuated some children of nursery school age, some disabled children and others with special needs. They returned after the agreement on the partitioning of Czechoslovakia was reached.

November 1938

Central Government began 'secret' preparations for the evacuation scheme. The overall responsibility was delegated to the Ministry of Health and the Board of Education.

1939

Priority for evacuation was given to:
● School children
● Younger children with mothers and guardians
● Pregnant women
The LCC co-ordinated the evacuation schemes for its own area plus eleven adjacent boroughs and districts in neighbouring counties. The LCC's 12 Education Officers acted as dispersal officers.

July 1939

Some people started to leave London voluntarily to find billets of their own or to stay with relatives in the perceived non-target areas. Some London schools were closed to become registration centres for the official scheme. Those who could afford to, sent their children to the USA and to parts of the Empire. In early 1939 Southern Rhodesia and Canada offered to take under 16s and over 60s. Australia offered to take orphans.

August 1939

By August less than 70% of those children in the LCC area eligible for evacuation had registered. It was estimated that only 35% of those eligible left in the first phase of the scheme.[2]

1-4 September 1939

More that 600,000 Londoners, including 393,700 unaccompanied school children, 257,000 Mothers with children, 5,600 expectant mothers and 2,440 disabled and 'special cases' left London.

November 1939

Schools began reopening in London but took in pupils from a wide catchment area.

January 1940

By this time an estimated 35% of London evacuees had returned home, especially to the East End. There was a gradual re-introduction on the school welfare services which had been suspended during the first weeks of the war.

Spring 1940

Saw the development of a plan for further large scale evacuation. This was to be carried out over a longer period of time than the first scheme and would take place only when the expected heavy bombing raids became serious. This scheme did not include Mothers with children.
Only 10% of eligible children in the LCC area registered.[3]

May-June 1940

160,000 children were evacuated from the LCC area.

June 1940

Recommendations made by the Children's Overseas Reception Board were accepted by the Government. When made public the details of the scheme generated a considerable response from people wanting to send their children abroad.

July 1940

'Trickle' evacuation. School children were removed from those areas considered to be the main targets for enemy bombing. Within the year more than 60,000 evacuees were moved. However, this created serious administrative problems just keeping up to date with the movement of individuals.
Total number of applicants wishing to go abroad reached 211,548.

July 16th 1940

Overseas evacuation technically, but not practically, suspended because of lack of Naval protection for convoys.

August 1st 1940

S.S. 'Volendam' was torpedoed. All survived as ship was towed back to Liverpool.

September-November 1940

Evacuation of homeless mothers and their children.

September 17th 1940

S.S.'City of Benares' was sunk with the loss of 77 evacuees and 170 adult escorts and crew. Government initiated evacuation abroad was suspended but private individuals could still make their own arrangements.

June-September 1944

Final phase of the evacuation schemes. 'Rivulet' was implemented when the V1s and V2s caused people to move out of London and other cities.

October 1944

Gradual return of evacuees from the reception areas. In London, the South East and other main target areas this return process was to be a slow one as many of the homes of evacuees had either been destroyed or were structurally unsound.

July 1945

By this time almost all the evacuees in the UK had returned home.

[1] Crosby. op.cit. p21

[2] Samways. op.cit. p5

[3] ibid.

Bibliography

<u>Absurd and the Brave.</u> Michael Fethney. Book Guild. Sussex

<u>Are we at War? Letters to the Times. 1939-45.</u> ed. Anthony Livesey 1989

<u>The Attacks on Plymouth.</u> G.D.Wasley. Devon Books. 1991

<u>August 1939. The last our weeks of peace in Europe.</u> Stephen Howarth. Hodder and Stoughton. 1989

<u>Backs to the Wall.</u> Leonard Mosley. Weidenfeld & Nicolson Ltd. 1971

<u>The Baedecker Blitz.</u> Niall Rothnie. Ian Allan. 1992

<u>The Battle for Britain. Citizenship and Ideology in the Second World War.</u> David Morgan and Mary Evans. Routledge. 1993

<u>BERKSHIRE COUNTY RECORDS OFFICE</u>. READING

- County Council Minutes. 1939 C/CL/CI/1/42

- County Council Minutes. 1940 C/CL/CI/1/43

- Bradfield C. of E. Primary School. Log Book. 1934-51 D/P 22/28/3

- Alfred Sutton Primary School. Log Book. 1934-62 89/SCH/37/1

- Purley (on Thames) Parish Council Minutes. 1939-41

'Big Boys Don't Cry'. James Roffey. unpub.manuscript. 1990

Blitz. The Civilian War. 1940-45. Waller and Vaughan-Rees. Optima. 1990

<u>The Blitz. Then and Now. Vols. 1-3</u> ed.W. Ramsey. pub. After the Battle. 1992.

<u>Britain and the Second World War.</u> Henry Pelling. Collins. 1970

The British Documentary Film Movement. 1926-46. Paul Swain. Cambridge University Press. 1989

<u>British Society. 1914-45</u>. J.Stevenson. Penguin 1990

<u>BUCKINGHAMSHIRE COUNTY RECORD OFFICE</u>. AYLESBURY

- Aston Clinton Evacuee School Diary. 1939-43

- Ashley Green C.of E. School Log-book. 1931-73

<u>Bundles from Britain</u>. Alistair Horne. Macmillan. 1993

<u>CABINET PAPERS</u> 1940-41 (Public Records Office)

- Minutes 21/389

- Minutes 23/79 31 July 1934

- Air Ministry 8/238

- PRO HO45/17636

    79/6 Folio 323

- PRO HO 186/128/643/3

- PRO.CAB 67/9 (41) 44
  - 81/82
- PRO.CAB 67/7/172
- PRO CAB. 67/7/170
- PRO CAB. 65/8/179
- PRO CAB. 65/7/174
- PRO CAB. 65/9/244
- PRO DO.131/29
- PRO DO.131/39
- PRO DO.35/259/B277/4
- PRO DO. 35/259/B305/8
- PRO DO.35/259/B305/4
- PRO DO.131/43
- Premier Papers 3/22/3 Folio 199
  - 3/314/2 Folio 64-5
  - 120/300
- PRO S.7248 [AIR 2/5238]
- AIR 20/1627
- War Cab.246.1940
  - 65/9
- PRO.ED 136/205 (13 Nov.39)
- PRO.ED 138/34
- GLRO EO/WAR/1/83
- PRO.ED 134/74
- PRO.ED 50/207 (26 Oct. 39)
- PRO.ED 136/125
- PRO ED 50/204
- Circular 2882 Ministry of Health (Evacuation)
- Circular 2539E Ministry of Health (Evacuation)
- Circular 2592/2592A/2592B Ministry of Health. Furniture Allocation
- Circular 2592C Ministry of Health. Furniture for Homeless
- Circular 2754 Ministry of Health. Utility Furniture
- Circular 1857/2273 Ministry of Health. Evacuation (Billeting)
- Circular 1640 Board of Education. 5.11.43. (Evacuation)
- Circular 185/44 Temporary Accommodation.
- Circular 185/44 Ministry of Health

- Circular 68/45 Ministry of Health
- Circular 2845 Ministry of Health
- Circular 69/45 Ministry of Health
- Circular 2027 Ministry of Health
- Circular 1871 Ministry of Health

CAERNARVONSHIRE RECORD OFFICE

- Amlwch RDC. Evacuation File.1939-41
- Evac. Group. Prince Rupert School. Liverpool. Log Book.1941.
- Evacuation File.
- Nant Conway RDC. Evacuation File.
- Nant Conway RDC. Evacuation 1939-45 Letters.
- Penmaenmawr. UDC. ARP Evacuation File No.1

Case Study of a Reception Area Under the Government Evacuation Scheme. 1939-1945. Gillian Wallis. unpublished MA thesis. University College of North Wales. 1979. Deposited in the Flintshire Record Office. Hawarden, North Wales.

Children's Wartime Diaries. Laurel Holliday. Piatkus.1995

The Children's War. Evacuation 1939 -45. Ruth Inglis. Fontana 1990

Civilians at War. Journals. 1938-46. George Beardmore. Oxford University Press. 1986

Coldwaltham. A Story of Three Hamlets. Sandra Saer. SMH Enterprises. 1987

DEVON RECORD OFFICE. EXETER

- Box 12. ARP Evacuation Nos. 117 - 135
- Ref. 39584/1 (9) WVS loans to enable mothers to purchase bedding or open up homes.
- Ref.441E (WVS) Arrival of Evacuees
- Form EV 60. Returns of unaccompanied children.
- Form EV 61. Returns of Evacuees & Homeless persons. March 1943.
- Ref. 30584/19 Return of Evacuees.

Diary of a Nightmare. Berlin 1942-1945. Ursula von Kardoff. Hart-Davis 1965

DOLGELLAU RECORD OFFICE

Dendraeth RDC. Minute Book. 1937-1940.

Penllyn RDC. File. Evacuation Arrangements. 1939

DORSET RECORD OFFICE. DORCHESTER

Beaminster DC/BE

- A1/1/10
- A1/1/11

Blandford DC/BFB

- Evacuation Scheme Register and Accommodation
- Civil Defence Papers.
- Council Minutes 1933 - 40 & 1940 - 45
- Civil Defence. Reception. Billeting and Schools

Bournemouth DC/BH Box 9 Acc.5157/3 Loc 5L 78 -86

Bridport DC/BTB

- Corporation Minutes 1906 - 45
- A.CC 1019/DC8 Contribution for Evac. 1941-5 Accounts
- A/1/1/8
- A/1/1/9

Dorchester DC/DOR

Minute Books.

- November 1936 - March 1940
- April 1940 - February 1943
- March 1943 - July 1945
- A/1/5/2
- A/1/5/3

Lyme Regis.

- Council Minutes 1934 - 1940
- Council Minutes 1940 - 1947

Shaftesbury DC/SYR

- Evacuation. 1930 - 45
- Correspondence. 1938 - 47. Evacuation. (2 boxes)
- Registers. Evacuation. 1939 - 45 (2 Files)
- Council Minutes. 1936 - 1940
- Council Minutes 1941 - 1944
- Council Minutes 1944 - 1946
- Evacuation (4 files) 1938 - 1942
- Parish War Books
- Register of Accommodation. c1939
- Register of requisitioned properties.

Sherborne. Committee Minutes. (4 Vols.)

Sturminster. Annual Minute Books 1939 - 46

Wareham. ARP Committee. 1938 - 1939

Weymouth DC/WYB

Wimborne.

- Committee Reports 1939 - 1947 (3 Vols.)
- Clerk. War Emergency Information.
- A/1/3/8
- A/1/3/9

East Anglia at War 1939-1945. Derek E. Johnson. Jarrold. 1994

The Echo of War. Home Front Propaganda and the Wartime BBC 1939-45. Sian Nicholas. Manchester University Press. 1996

Education and the Second World War. Studies on Schooling and Social Change. ed. Roy Lowe. Falmer Press 1992.

Education and the Social Order 1940-1990. Brian Simon. Lawrence and Wishart. 1991

Empty Cradles. Margaret Humphreys. Doubleday. 1994

England's Hour. An Autobiography 1939-41. Vera Brittain. Futura.1981

Evacuation. A Very British Revolution. Bob Holman. Lion 1995.

The Evacuee. Monthly magazine. Evacuee Reunion Asssociation.

Film and the Working Class. The Feature Film in British and American Society. Peter Stead. Routledge.1991

FLINTSHIRE RECORD OFFICE. (Hawarden)

- E/LB/11/5. St. Matthew's Infant School. Buckley.
- E/LB/11/12. Lane End School. Buckley.
- E/X/50/2 Prestatyn British Council School. 1891-1946
- E/X/50/5 Board of Education Returns. 1902 - 1940
- E/X/56/6 Board of Education Returns. 1898 - 1950
- FC/C/4/2/50 Evacuation Minutes.

The Fringes of Power. Downing Street Diaries. 1939-1955. John Colville. Hodder & Stoughton. 1985

Happy Evacuee. Mary Nickerson. unpublished account. 1996

Harold Nicolson. Diaries and Letters. 1930 - 1939. ed. Nigel Nicolson. Collins. 1966

Harold Nicolson. Diaries and Letters. 1939-1945. ed. Nigel Nicolson. Collins. 1967

'Here is to Valour' Elinor Mordaunt. pub. The Salvation Army. 1944

The Home Front. A.Marwick. Thames and Hudson. 1976

The Ideologies of Class. Social Relations in Britain 1880-1950. Ross McKibbin. Oxford University Press. 1991

The Impact of Civilian Evacuation in the Second World War. Travis L. Crosby. Croom Helm. 1986

Imperial Identities and Social Mobility: Class, Empire and the British Government. Overseas Evacuation of Children during the Second World War. Patricia Lin. unpublished PhD thesis. University of Berkeley. California. USA. 1994

International War Cry. Salvation Army Pub. week beginning:-

- 21.1.39
- 16.9.39

- 23.9.39
- 7.10.39
- 28.10.39
- 9.12.39
- 3.2.40
- 6.7.40

Innocents Abroad. The Story of Child Evacuees in Australia 1940 - 45. Edward Stokes. Allen and Unwin. 1994

Keep Smiling Through. Women in the Second World War. Caroline Lang. Cambridge Educational. 1989

Living Through the Blitz. Tom Harrisson. Penguin. 1978

London at War. 1939 - 1945. Philip Ziegler. Sinclair-Stevenson. 1995

London Children in Wartime Oxford. Barnett House Study Group. Oxford University Press. 1947

Mass-Observation Archive. Sussex University Library. Directives

- TC.Air Raids 9/B2
- TC.Transport 4/C
- Evacuation Box 1 File E

Mass Observation at the Movies ed. Jeffrey Richards & Dorothy Sheridan. Routledge & Kegan Paul. 1987

The Myth of the Blitz. Angus Calder. Jonathan Cape. 1991

1940: Myth or Reality. Clive Ponting. Hamish Hamilton. 1990

Nazi Germany at War. Martin Kitchen. Longman. 1995

'No time to wave Goodbye'. Ben Wicks. Bloomsbury. 1990

'Not like any other home'. Herbert White and the Children's Home and Mission. Bob Holman. Campaign Literature. 1994

'On the Way Home'. G.L.Carpenter. Salvation Army. 1944

The People's War. Angus Calder. Panther 1969

The People's War. Peter Lewis. Thames Methuen. 1986

The Plymouth Blitz. Frank Wintle. Bossiney Books 1981

Problems of Social Policy. Richard Titmuss. HMSO 1950

Realism and Tinsel. Cinema and Society in Britain 1939 - 49. Robert Murphy. Routledge. 1992

RUTHIN RECORD OFFICE.

- Denbighshire County Council. File 3/4.
- Denbigh Borough Council. Letter Book. May 1942 - March 1943. BD/A/412.
- Denbighshire County Council. File 8/9 OZ1348.
- Denbighshire County Council. File 36. Z1352.

Salvation Army: Actions and Attitudes in Wartime 1899-1945. A.S.Clifton 1988 (PhD unpublished)

A Social History of the Third Reich. Richard Grunberger. Penguin. 1971

Social Mobility and Class Structure in Modern Britain. 2nd Edition. John H. Goldthorpe. in collaboration with Catriona Llewellyn and Clive Payne. pub. Clarendon Press. 1987

Theatres of Memory. Raphael Samuel. Verson. 1994

Total War and Social Change. ed. Arthur Marwick. Macmillan. 1988

Under the Bombs. The German Home Front 1942-45. Earl R.Beck University Press of Kentucky. 1986

War Guest. Recollections of being evacuated to Canada in 1940. Patricia Cave. Adept Services Publishing. 1995

War and Social Change. British Society in the Second World War. ed. Harold L. Smith. Manchester University Press. 1986

Wartime Women. ed. Dorothy Sheridan. Mandarin. 1991

Wartime Bucks. 1939-1945. Bucks. Record Office. 1995

'What did you do in the War Auntie?' The BBC at War. Tom Hickman. BBC. 1995

WILTSHIRE RECORD OFFICE. TROWBRIDGE

WRO/F2/850/1-12. Wartime Correspondence Files. September 1938-March 1946.

Ministry of Health Circular 2140

Winston S. Churchill. Martin Gilbert. pub. Hutchinson

Biography

Vols.   V 1922 -1939 pub.1976

          VI 1939 - 1941 'Their Finest Hour' pub.1983

          VII 1941 - 1945 'The Road to Victory' pub.1986

Documents

Vols.   V 1929 - 1935 'The Wilderness Years' pub. 1981

          VI 1936 - 1939 'The Coming of War' pub. 1982

The Churchill War Papers.

Vol.1 September 1939 - May 1940. pub 1993

Vol.2 May 1940 - December 1940. pub 1994

The War Speeches Vol 3. compiled by Charles Eade. Purnell/Cassell (no date)

(Great) War Speeches. Sir Winston Churchill. Corgi 1978

The World We Left Behind. A chronicle of the year 1939. Robert Kee. Weidenfeld. 1993

Yesterdays Children. 1939 - 1945. Evacuees True Stories. A compilation. Lilian Evans. 1997. (Personal publication)

VIDEO TAPE.

Referenced in the text.

'Westward Ho!' Ministry of Information. 1940

'Living With Strangers' Ministry of Information. 1941

'Village School'. Ministry of Information. 1941

Imperial War Museum. Film Archive. These are available on a video entitled 'Keep the Wheels Turning'.

Others viewed.

The Heart of Britain. Humphrey Jennings. 1941

This film is centred on a visit to the industrial North and Midlands at the time of the Blitz and shows how life, war production and social culture was seemingly unaffected despite the attempts of the Luftwaffe.

Listen to Britain. Humphrey Jennings. 1942

This is a film with very little dialogue. Jennings used music and the sound of actual machinery and other natural features to provide the soundtrack for a film which was basically designed to show that Britain was unaffected by the war. It was produced by the Crown Film Unit.

A Diary for Timothy. Humphrey Jennings. 1946

This is a film which is both retrospective and futuristic. It provides details of what was happening on the day 'Timothy' was born, and looks to the future to see how his life may be different from his parents. It is full of social comment and stands alone as a film of its time.

How We Used To Live. 1936-53. Schools Broadcast. Yorkshire TV 1975.

This remains a popular school series of programmes taking various aspects of British History from the Abdication of Edward VIII to the Coronation of Elizabeth II. The films are only 20 minutes long and they combine acted sequences with contemporary archive film. However, as this film is often taken from Pathe News or propaganda films the wrong messages are being perpetuated. They are usually used with Years 5 and 6 in the Junior school and Year 7 in the Secondary school.

The Home Front. Britain at War. W.H. Smith video. 1992

This is an example of extracts from various sources being put together to provide a compilation of the events which took place in Britain in 1939-40. The selective editing has made it a 1990s propaganda film in its own right!

There are a number of examples of this type of composite film. Another in the series is 'Remembering the Blitz' released in 1993.

The Phoney War. 1989

This video, produced by Lamancha Trax, covers the period 1938 to 1940 and depicts Evacuation and the initial ARP procedures. Again it relies heavily on news bulletins and film propaganda material from the time and is therefore not a very objective account of the events.

'Goodbye Children'. BBC 1996

This was produced by Kevin Heathorn for BBC South-West as part of the 'Close-up' series. It includes visual and oral testimony from ex-evacuees who were evacuated to Devon and Cornwall.

FEATURE FILMS related to the topic.

'Gert and Daisy's Weekend'. 1940

This is a comedy starring Elsie and Doris Walters and a very young George Cole. It is full of stereotypical images of evacuees to the extent that the children were the obvious suspects when jewels were stolen during a weekend house party. It was also interesting to note that the film was set in a large country house, which gave the impression that this was the type of billet waiting for all evacuees!

'Hope and Glory' 1987

This semi-autobiographical film, directed by John Boorman was favourably reviewed by the critics. As a nostalgic depiction of life on the Home Front it is quite whimsical, but again it does leave one with the same stereotypical views. It does however show some of the anxiety involved in the decision about whether or not to evacuate the children overseas, but the scenes on the station where the mother pulls the child from the train is pure fiction.

Oral and Taped Accounts as a Result of Interviews and Correspondence with Ex-Evacuees, ARP Personnel and Teachers Involved in the Scheme

* Indicates where accounts have been taped.

+ Indicates written accounts.

Copies of these and other tapes, transcripts of letters and other correspondence can be found in the Bulmershe Court Library, University of Reading.

NAME	EVACUATED FROM	EVACUATED TO
* Joyce Amos.		
* Rosemary Barber (née Taylor). Shaftesbury.	Walworth 1.9.39	Manston 3.42
* Jim Bartley. Rainham Essex.		
* W.R. Bates. London.		
* Edna Bolton. Shaftesbury.		
+ Dorothy Brandom. Strood.	Peckham 5.40	Henley
+ Audrey Brien (née Carr) Stock.	East Ham 1.9.39	Warminster 45
+ Eric Broad.		
+ Dr. Muriel Broom.(née Parsons) Reading.	Hampstead 40.	Canada 5.44
+ David Brown. Winnersh. Berks.	Gosport	Upham, Bishops Waltham & West Meon.
+ Roy Brushett.		
+ Allan Buksh. Kettering.	Kentish Town 1.9.39	Kettering.
* Gladys Burchill. Chingford.	N. London 9.39	Old Stevenage
+ Gina Burrows. Chipping Norton.		
+ Harry Carmichael. Southend.		
+ J.M. Carter. Wilmington.		
+ Gillian Chamberlayne.(née Burt) Pinner.	London	Shipston-on-Stour
* Iris Charos. E. Sussex.	Clapham 9.39.	Eastbourne 12.39 then Holsworthy, Devon.
* Alan Charles. Chorleywood.		
+ Norman Clare. London.		
+ Joan Cresswell. Chichester.		
* Joyce Cundle. London SE1.	London 2.9.39	Sturminster Newton 4.42
+ R. Davison. London.		
+ P.G. Dent. (née Read) Enfield.	Enfield 9.39	Letchworth 5.40 then St.Keverne Cornwall
+ M. Downs. Barking.		
+ Sue Edginton.		
+ Audrey Elcock. Sheffield.		
+ Win Elliott and Sylvia Lewis. Halesworth. Suffolk.		
+ Lilian Evans. Liverpool.		
* Tony, Anne, Julia Falvey. Richmond.		
+ Joan Faulkner. Englefield Green.	Stepney 9.39	Virginia Water then Sunningdale

NAME	EVACUATED FROM	EVACUATED TO
* John Fenton. Reading.		
+ Dr. John Fox. London.		
* Stella Freeman.(née May) London.	Shepherd's Bush 1.9.39	Frome 12.39. Then Falkland. Bath. 8.43
+ Doreen Gates. (née Frisby) Camberwell.	Walworth 2.9.39	Sturminster Newton 4.43
+ Anton Galfrey. Bristol.		
+ Margaret Geer. Crowborough.	Woolwich 9.39	Warminster 45.
+ Joyce Goddard.(née Ireland) Halesworth. Suffolk.	Ilford 39.	Finnamore Camp School. Marlow.
+ Vernon Goodwin. London.		
* John Gould. Kent.	Ilford. 1.9.39.	Ipswich 40, Maesteg 42 then Kennylands Camp. 42-45.
* Edith Green. Newbury.	Walthamstow	Wellingborough. 9.39
+ Margaret Green. Gillingham. Kent.		
+ E.W.Grimmer. Dagenham.		
* Roy Guy. Surrey.	London 44.	Shadwell. Leeds 45
+ Margaret Hall.	Liverpool 3.9.39.	Melling
+ Margaret Harrod.(née Smith) Bristol.	Portsmouth 8.39	Sway. Hants.
* Joan Harsant.	Enfield.1.9.39	Welling Garden City 42.
* Judith Heron. Burton Joyce.		
+ A. Hindle. Stirlinghill.		
+ Mrs Hodgetts. London.	London.	Gloucestershire.
+ Colin Horlick. Tylers Green. Bucks.	Southall.	Radcliffe on Trent. 44
+ E.L. Hughes. South Harrow.		
+ Julie Hull. Sheffield.		
+ Jean Jackson. Cranfield. Beds.	St. Vincent de Paul Convent School	Leigh Halt nr. Tonbridge.
+ Stella Johnston. North Harrow.	Cricklewood 1.9.39	Kettering 1.8.40 then Hayle 10.40, then Camborne Cornwall 41.
* Laurie Keen.		Wales. 9.39 then Torquay.
+ G & M Kirk. Hanworth.		
* L. Knight. London SW15.	Wanstead.9.39	Kettering.40 then Redruth, Cornwall. 8.41
* George Knott. Wooton Bassett.		
+ M. Kojcinovic. Harrow.		
+ Jessica Lawson. London.		
+ S. Lenihan. Wood Green.	Hornsey 1.9.39	Cefneithin. Llanelli.
+ Sheila Malkin. Epsom.		
+ Joyce Marchant. Plaistow.		
+ Doris Marsh.(née Cramp) Sturminster Newton.	Walworth. 2.9.39.	Stalbridge. (Did not return. Stayed with family)
+ Ray Martell. London.		

NAME	EVACUATED FROM	EVACUATED TO
* Wilhemina Maxim. Loughton. Essex.	Ilford 39.	Evercreach Somerset 39 then Midsumer Norton. 40.
* Teresa Maynard.(née Stallion) SW11.	Walworth 2.9.39	Sturminster Newton 4.43
*Brian Maystone. Crawley.	Clapham. 8.39.	Pulborough then Lambeth to Pulborough then Clapham to Woking.
+ Ian McGreachan. Bromley.		
+ Lyn Mendlson. (née Blackler) Southgate.	Cricklewood 39	Kettering then Weston-Super-Mare.
* Alan Middleton. Caterham. Surrey.		
+ Robert Miller. OBE. West Wickham.	Bexley Heath.1.9.44	Pudsey. Yorks
* Shirley Monaco.		42-43 Merthyr Tydfill.
* Mary Nickerson. Holywell.	Portsmouth 9.39.	Tenbury Wells Glos. then Wimborne.
+ Terence Nunn. London. NW10.		
+ Audrey O'Brien. Stock. Essex.		
+ D.A. Offin. Carshalton.		
+ John O'Connor.		
+ Pat Packham. (née Hind) Witney. then Somerset, Nottingham, Rickmansworth.	Surbiton 39	Worthing until 6.40.
+ R.D. Parker. Hampton.		
+ Philip Picton. Patterdown.		
+ D.L. Rackham. Wimbledon.		
+ John Rawlins. Chipping Norton.		
+ Ken Relegous. Kilgetty.	London.1.9.39	Kings Lynne. 43.
* Marian Richardson. London SE3.		to Hamsswaite then Defynnog nr. Brecon.
+ Wilfred Richardson. Harlow.	Hartlepool 39.	Wingate Co. Durham 40.
+ Rene Ringwood.(née Alexander) Maidstone.	London 40.	Finstock. Oxon.
+ John Robbins.	Upminster 9.43	Wrexham 9.44.
+ Hazel Robbins.	Romford 6.44	Sheffield.10.44
* John Roffey. Dartford.	Camberwell. 1.9.39.	Pulborough 43.
+ James Roffey. Clayforth. Notts.	Camberwell 1.9.39.	Pulborough 43
+ Sylvia Rose.(née Eden) Gillingham. Dorset.	London 5.40	Sturminster Newton 7.42
+ Sheila Rowe.		
* Enid Self. (née Baker). Welling.	Orpington 44	Bridlington 8.44
* Ron Self. Welling.	Sidcup 1944	Manchester 1944
+ Constance Schwartz. (née Mabey) Hornchurch.	Brixton 40.	Hillingdon then Burnham on Sea 4 then St. Ives Cornwall. 43-44.
* Peter Shepherd. Slough.	E. Ham 9.39	Weston-Super-Mare (twice) then Nanty-Glo. until 41.
* Christophe Simonon. Nether Green.	Beckenham	W. Kensford Glos. 42.then St.Dominic's Convent. Cuttley. 45.

NAME	EVACUATED FROM	EVACUATED TO
* Victor Spink. Chertsey.	Wimbledon. 7.44	Keighley. Yorks. 5.45
* Maureen Starling (née Hedge). Hornchurch.	Barking 9.39.	Clevedon Somerset 12.39.
* Maureen Stephens. Harrow Middx.		
+ Peter Towse. London.		
+ Daisy May Tuck. (née Ball) London.	Walworth. 8.39.	Weymouth 7.44
* Dennis Turner. Kent.	Hampstead. 1.9.39	Berkhampstead. 12.44
+ T.J. Weldon. Exmouth.		
+ Nicholas Werner. Stamford Hill.		
+ Terry Weston (Mrs). London.		
+ Andrea White. Canvey.		
+ Kathleen White. (née Hull) Wroughton.	Leeds.	Stornaway 1.40
* Geoffrey Wilkinson. Hungerford.	London. 8.39	Uckfield Sussex then Torquay.
+ Jenny Wilson. Hemel Hempstead.		
* Keith Wilson. Bedford.	Acton 1.9.39	Newton Abbot. 8.40
+ Rose Wood. New Zealand.	SE London. 40.	Slough (few weeks) then Burton-on-Trent. 44.
+ Margaret Wood.	Stanmore.	Cape Town. South Africa.
+ Nicky Woods. Epsom.		

PLUS.

Dr. Robin Borthwick. Interviews regarding the health of evacuees.

* Mavis Cordery. Teacher in Reading during the war years who acted as a Billeting Officer.

+ Bill Finch. Teacher. Kennylands School. 1940-45

+ Nella Hughes-Smith. Kew. Host to evacuees.

+ Professor Barbara Shawcroft. U.C.Davis. San Francisco. California. Formerly an evacuee to the USA, 1940-44, under the sponsorship of the Ford Motor Co.

Mrs E.M. Young. Former teacher at Alfred Sutton Primary School. Wokingham Rd. Reading during the war years.

Index

About the Author

Dr. Martin Parsons is Director of the Secondary Post Graduate Certificate of Education course at the University of Reading.

Formerly a Senior Teacher at Theale Green Community School in West Berkshire, Martin moved to the University in 1990 to become Head of PGCE History and now lectures on both undergraduate and post-graduate courses.

Since 1992 he has been heavily involved in researching evacuation at the Micro level spending a great deal of time investigating a variety of sources within the former reception areas and relating his findings to the national situation. As a result his PhD thesis examined the perpetuation of the myths and images inherent in text book and media depiction of Evacuation and Air Raid Precautions.

Martin is a member of the Executive Committee of the Evacuee Reunion Association, has lectured and organised workshops on the topic at various Universities in the USA and Poland for students and teachers and has presented papers at a number of international conferences. In the UK he has given lectures to various groups and gave the Key-note address at the Imperial War Museum Evacuation Day. He has been listed in 'Who's Who in the World' for his work in this area.

He has recently completed a series of new text books and worksheets related to his research for Key Stage 2 pupils. These will be published by 'Wayland' in 1999. He is also collaborating with Homerton College Cambridge on their research project into Wartime Education and with colleagues in the Community Studies Department at the University of Reading who are researching into the effects of evacuation on babies. He has also established an Evacuation Archive at the University of Reading library on the Bulmershe Court campus.